T0301408

Overeducation in Europe

Overeducation in Europe

Current Issues in Theory and Policy

Edited by

Felix Büchel

Senior Research Scientist, Max Planck Institute for Human Development, Berlin, Germany

Andries de Grip

Head of the Division of Labour Market and Training, Research Centre for Education and the Labour Market, and Professor of Economics, Maastricht University, The Netherlands

Antje Mertens

Research Scientist, Max Planck Institute for Human Development, Berlin, Germany

Edward Elgar
Cheltenham, UK • Northampton, MA, USA

Published by
Edward Elgar Publishing Limited
Glensanda House
Montpellier Parade
Cheltenham
Glos GL50 1UA
UK

Edward Elgar Publishing, Inc.
136 West Street
Suite 202
Northampton
Massachusetts 01060
USA

A catalogue record for this book is available from the British Library

Library of Congress Cataloguing in Publication Data
International Conference "Overeducation in Europe: What Do We Know?" (2002 :
  Max Planck Institute for Human Development)
    Overeducation in Europe : current issues in theory and policy / edited by
  Felix Büchel, Andries de Grip, Antje Mertens.
        p. cm.
    "This volume presents selected and revised papers from the International
  Conference 'Overeducation in Europe: What Do We Know?' that took place at
  the Max Planck Institute for Human Development, Berlin (MPIB), on 22-23
  November 2002"–Pref.
    Includes index.
        1. Education, Higher–Economic aspects–Europe–Congresses. 2. College
  graduates–Employment–Europe–Congresses. 3. Labor supply–Europe–
  Congresses. I. Büchel, Felix. II. Grip, A. de. III. Mertens, Antje, 1967- IV. Title.

LC67.68.E85I58 2004
331.11'4235'094–dc22
                                                                    2003049489

ISBN 1 84376 361 3

Printed and bound in Great Britain by MPG Books Ltd, Bodmin, Cornwall

Contents

PART FOUR: SPECIAL GROUPS

Contributors

Alfonso Alba-Ramírez is Professor in the Department of Economics at the University Carlos III of Madrid. His research has dealt with a variety of labour market issues, including unemployment duration, skill mismatch, self-employment, temporary employment and women's labour force participation. His current interests include the operation of job placement services, the effects of unemployment protection on workers' careers, the relationship between overeducation and occupational mobility and the consequences of women's labour force participation for family formation. A full CV is available at http://www.eco.uc3m.es/personal/cv/alalba.html

Harminder Battu is a Senior Lecturer in the Department of Economics at the University of Aberdeen and a member of the Centre for European Labour Market Research (CELMR). His research interests include ethnic and gender differentials in residential mobility, overeducation in the labour market and the economics of identity. A full CV is available at http://www.abdn.ac.uk/~pec131/mywebsite1.htm

Maite Blázquez is a PhD student in the Department of Economics at the University Carlos III of Madrid. Her thesis project is focused on labour market topics. The theoretical part is related to matching models with heterogeneous agents, while the empirical analysis is focused on overeducation. Her current research interests include the analysis of school-to-work transitions and the relationship between skill mismatch and disability.

Felix Büchel is a Senior Research Scientist at the Max Planck Institute for Human Development in Berlin. His affiliations include an Adjunct Professorship of Economics at the Technical University of Berlin, an Honorary Professorship of Sociology at the Free University of Berlin, a Research Professorship with the German Socio-Economic Panel Study at the DIW Berlin and a Research Fellow status at the IZA Bonn. Büchel's current research interests include overeducation, occupational training, labour supply in a household context, educational institutions, income distribution and immigration. A full CV is available at http://www.mpib-berlin.mpg.de/en/mitarbeiter/cv/buechel.htm

Peter Dolton is the Sir David Dale Professor of Economics at the University of Newcastle-upon-Tyne, Senior Research Fellow at the Centre for Economic Performance at the London School of Economics and Research Fellow at the IZA Bonn. He is an associate editor of the Economics of Education Review and the Journal of the Royal Statistical Society. His current research interests are in the economics of education and the labour market and applied econometrics. He has written extensively on the market for teachers, active labour market policy and the problems of sample selection, discrimination and attrition.

Andries de Grip is Head of the Division of Labour Market and Training at the Research Centre for Education and the Labour Market (ROA) and Professor of Economics at the Faculty of Economics and Business Administration at the Maastricht University. His current research interests include various aspects of the relation between education, training and the labour market, in particular with regard to training and mobility, employability, skill mismatches, human resource management, labour market segmentation, atypical employment and upgrading and overeducation. A full CV is available at http://www.fdewb.unimaas.nl/roa/index.htm

Wim Groot is Professor of Health Economics at the Faculty of Health Sciences of Maastricht University and chairman of the Department of Health Organization, Policy and Economics at Maastricht University. He is also Director of an NWO Priority Program ('Prioriteitprogramma') on 'Schooling, Labor Market and Economic Development' at the Faculty of Economics of the University of Amsterdam. He was a visiting fellow at Stanford University (1992), Cornell University (1993), European University Institute, Florence (1995), University of California at Berkely (1995) and Monash University (1997). He has received research grants from NWO and the European Union (TSER, ACE/Phare).

Mombert Hoppe is a recent graduate in International Economic Studies at Maastricht University and holds a master's degree in economics. His interests lie in development economics and problems of European integration.

Uwe Jensen is Associate Professor of Statistics and Econometrics at the University of Kiel. His current research interests include microeconometrics, in particular efficiency measurement, overeducation, job satisfaction and individual earnings. A full CV is available at http://www.stat-econ.uni-kiel.de/jensen/jensen.htm

Markus Jochmann is a PhD student in the Department of Economics at the University of Konstanz and a member of the research group 'Heterogeneous Labor: Positive and Normative Aspects of the Skill Structure of Labor' at the University of Konstanz and the Centre for European Economic Research

(ZEW) in Mannheim. His research is in the field of Bayesian econometrics with applications to labour and health economics. A full CV can be found at http://econometrics.wiwi.uni-konstanz.de

Hannah Kiiver studied International Economics at Maastricht University and holds a master's degree in economics. She currently works at the Department of Economics of Maastricht University and at Merit (Maastricht Economic Research Institute on Innovation and Technology).

Henriëtte Maassen van den Brink is Professor of Economics at the Faculty of Economics and Econometrics at the University of Amsterdam. She is the co-ordinator of the research institute for Schooling, Labor market and Economic Development (SCHOLAR). She is member of the Central Planning Committee (CPB), The Hague, Crown-appointed member of the Onderwijsraad (Education Council), The Hague, and member of the board of the 'Max Goote' Knowledge Center, University of Amsterdam. Her research interests are in the areas of microeconomics, labour markets and human capital. A full CV is available at http://www.fee.uva.nl/scholar/mdw/hmvdb/

Michael Maier is a Research Fellow at the Centre for European Economic Research (ZEW) in Mannheim and member of the research group 'Heterogeneous Labor: Positive and Normative Aspects of the Skill Structure of Labor' at the University of Konstanz. He studied economics at the University of Mannheim, where he graduated in 2000. A full CV is available at http://www.zew.de/en/mitarbeiter

Antje Mertens is a Research Scientist at the Max Planck Institute for Human Development in Berlin and member of the Sonderforschungsbereich 'Quantification and Simulation of Economic Processes' at the Humboldt University in Berlin, Faculty of Economics. She received her doctor in Economics from the Humboldt University and holds an MA in International Economics from the University of Sussex. Her current research interests include the mobility of labour and the analysis of precarious employment contracts. A full CV is available at http://www.mpib-berlin.mpg.de/en/mitarbeiter/cv/mertens.html

Joan Muysken is Professor of Economics at the Faculty of Economics and Business Administration at the Maastricht University. He obtained his PhD degree at the University of Groningen. He was a Visiting Researcher at the University of Oslo, SUNY Buffalo (USA), the Catholic University of Louvain (Belgium) and the University of Newcastle (Australia). He is Director of CoFE-Europe. His research interests are (in general) wage formation, labour demand, matching problems, unemployment and endogenous growth. A full CV is available at http://www.fdewb.unimaas.nl/algec/staff

Friedhelm Pfeiffer is a Senior Lecturer at the University of Mannheim and a Senior Researcher at the Centre for European Economic Research (ZEW) in Mannheim. In 2002 he completed his post-doctoral habilitation thesis entitled 'Wage rigidity in a mixed system of wage formation.' His current research interests include the microeconomics and microeconometrics of education, entrepreneurship and wage formation. A full CV is available at http://www.zew.de/en/mitarbeiter

Winfried Pohlmeier is Professor of Economics and Econometrics at the University of Konstanz. He is associate editor of Empirical Economics, Research Associate at the Center of Finance and Econometrics (CoFE) and Research Professor at the Centre of European Economic Research (ZEW). Pohlmeier also serves as a coordinator of the EU Research and Training Network (RTN) 'Microstructure of Financial Markets in Europe.' His main areas of research are microeconometrics, labour economics and econometrics of ultra-high frequency data. More information on Pohlmeier's research activities is available at http://econometrics.wiwi.uni-konstanz.de

Mary Silles recently completed a DPhil in economics at the University of Oxford. She is presently a Visiting Lecturer at the University of Chicago. Her current research interests are in the economics of the labour market and applied microeconometrics. Her writings include papers on the economics of education, problems of sample selection and technological change.

Peter J. Sloane is Director of the Welsh Economy Labour Market Research and Evaluation Centre (WELMERC) located in the Department of Economics, University of Wales, Swansea. He is also Professor Emeritus of the University of Aberdeen, where he was also Vice Principal and Dean of the Faculty of Social Sciences and Law for six years. He is a Research Fellow of the IZA in Bonn, a founder member of the European Low Wage Employment Network (LoWER) and a Fellow of the Royal Society of Edinburgh. Current research interests include overeducation, job satisfaction, human capital spillovers, economics of education and economics of sport. A full CV is available at http://www.swan.ac.uk/welmerc

Thomas Zwick is a Senior Researcher at the Centre for European Economic Research (ZEW) in Mannheim. He received his doctorate from Maastricht University and holds a master's degree in economics from Regensburg University. His current research interests include microeconomic and microeconometric labour market research and personnel economics. A full CV is available at http://www.zew.de/en/mitarbeiter

Preface

This volume presents selected and revised papers from the International Conference 'Overeducation in Europe: What do we know?' that took place at the Max Planck Institute for Human Development, Berlin (MPIB), on 22–23 November 2002—the first that explicitly focused on overeducation.

The conference was jointly organised by the 'Education and Mismatch in the Labor Market' Project at the MPIB, represented by Felix Büchel and Antje Mertens and the Research Centre for Education and the Labour Market (ROA) at Maastricht University, represented by Andries de Grip. The programme of the conference reflected the state of art in the ongoing overeducation research.

We are most grateful to the MPIB that generously financed the conference and to Ilka Holzinger who carried out the local organising and managed the publication process. We also would like to express our gratitude to Doris Gampig and Christel Fraser from the MPIB Technical Media and Graphic Service for editing this volume. A final word of thanks goes to our external referees.

The Editors

Introduction

1. The Overeducated European?

Felix Büchel, Andries de Grip and Antje Mertens

The notion that a substantial number of workers are 'overeducated' challenges the relevance of more investments in the education of the European workforce. If many workers have a higher level of education than their job 'requires' the knowledge economy Europe seems to be a myopic view. Is the race between technology and education (Tinbergen, 1975) 'won' by education?

Although Freeman's *Overeducated American* (Freeman, 1976) started the analysis from a 'macro' point of view, the literature on overeducation usually merely focuses on the income effects at the individual level. Much more prominent in the macro-economic debate is the literature on skill-biased economic growth that shows that in the Western economies technological and organisational developments increase the demand for high-skilled labour (cf. Bresnahan, Brynjolfsson and Hitt, 2002; Machin and Van Reenen, 1998).

It should be noted that it is often difficult to distinguish between overeducation and an upgrading of the skills demanded in the job as in both cases higher-educated people obtain the jobs that were previously held by lower-skilled workers (Borghans and de Grip, 2000). In the case of overeducation this is due to an excess supply of high-skilled workers; in case of upgrading it is due to the increasing complexity of the jobs.

Borghans and de Grip (2000) show that, although it is common to state that an occupation requires a certain level of education, in most occupations there is a much looser relationship between productivity and a worker's educational background. On the other hand, in a perfect labour market the relationship between the wage and the level of education is equal for all occupations and varies only with the supply and demand developments in the labour market as a whole. This means that the notion of the 'required' skill level in a job actually refers to the match that is optimal given the relative productivity in the job of workers with different levels of education and the relative wage of low- and high-skilled workers in the labour market. In this sense overeducation is one of the adjustment mechanisms in the labour market in the case of an excess supply of high-skilled workers in their traditional educational domain.

3

Wieling and Borghans (2001) show that accepting a job at a level that is lower than a school leaver's level of education is indeed one of the most important adjustment mechanisms of the labour market. In the case of an excess supply of skilled workers far more graduates are employed in a job for which they are overeducated, than there are graduates that are unemployed. Dupuy and de Grip (2002) show that overeducation is also related to the strategic hiring policy of large firms. By hiring overeducated workers in a period when the supply of high-skilled workers is superfluous, large firms increase their opportunities to substitute high-skilled for low-skilled workers in times when high-skilled workers are scarce. Dupuy and de Grip show that these large elasticities of substitution between skilled and unskilled workers in large firms explain their higher labour productivity. Moreover, as Acemoglu (2002) showed an increase in the supply of high-skilled labour can speed up skill-biased technological change which increases the demand for high-skilled labour. He argues that particularly the acceleration in skill-biased technological change at the end of the 20th Century was a response to the rapid increase of the supply of high-skilled workers in the preceding decades.

The studies presented in this volume aim to further develop our understanding of the relevance of overeducation and the short-run and long-run effects of overeducation for workers who face overeducation. The various chapters of the book contribute to this understanding of overeducation in various ways. Moreover, the analyses refer to various European countries, especially Germany, the Netherlands and the UK. It is no coincidence that these are the countries with the most active communities of overeducation researchers. In addition, Alba-Ramírez and Blázquez use Spanish data drawn from the European Community Household Panel.

In Chapter 2 Sloane addresses several questions that the literature on overeducation raises and discusses the challenges of the existence of overeducation for human capital theory that assumes that a worker's productivity is not affected by the level of the job in which they are employed. In this sense the overeducation literature draws the attention to the relevance of the demand side of the labour market for the relation between a worker's human capital and productivity. Sloane also gives an overview of the different ways in which overeducation is measured, ranging from *objective measures* based on systematic job evaluation to *subjective measures* based on workers' self-assessment and the *empirical measure* that usually defines overeducation as having a level of overeducation one standard deviation above the mean level of education in the occupation.

Sloane also discusses the problem that the heterogeneity of workers with a particular level of education may be a serious cause of overestimating the *extent of overeducation*. This could be the case because 'overeducated' workers may simply be in this state because they have a low ability given their formal level of education or a different attitude toward work than other workers. Therefore, one could distinguish between *apparently* overeducated and *genuinely* overeducated workers (Chevalier, 2000). Carneiro and Heckman (2003) emphasised that the heterogeneity of workers with a particular level of education does not merely refer to differences in cognitive abilities, but may also refer to non-cognitive skills that are highly valued in the labour market as a person's motivation, persistence, reliability and self-discipline. It should be noted, however, that these differences might be not only the consequence but also cause of overeducation as mentioned in an early study on overeducation of Tsang and Levin (1985) who emphasised that 'workers with more education than their jobs require often exhibit counterproductive behavior in the workplace.'

Due to unobserved heterogeneity and a selection bias many studies in the prevailing literature probably also overestimate the negative effects of overeducation. This particularly holds for the effect of overeducation on workers' wages. If overeducated workers have a lower wage than those with the same level of education who are employed at a job level that matches their level of education this may simply be due to the fact that the overeducated workers have a lower ability, health problems or a different attitude toward work. In contrast to most previous studies on overeducation several studies in this volume control for unobserved heterogeneity and a possible selection bias.

The studies of Groot and Maassen van den Brink (Chapter 3) and Alba-Ramírez and Blázquez (Chapter 4) focus on the question whether overeducation at the individual level is a somewhat permanent problem or merely a temporary phenomenon at the start of workers' careers. Groot and Maassen van den Brink used Dutch longitudinal data and found that at least in the Netherlands only a small fraction of workers are long-term overeducated. The predominant way out of overeducation is found here to be job-to-job mobility. Internal mobility does not significantly contribute to switches out of overeducation. On the other hand, Alba-Ramírez and Blázquez, using Spanish data, found evidence supporting the hypothesis that overeducated workers whose formal training or education is very or quite closely related to their current job are more likely to be promoted within the same firm. This interpretation is consistent with the predictions of the occupational mobility theory.

These puzzling results suggest that empirical findings in overeducation research may vary across countries. Büchel and Mertens (in press) have, for example, shown for Germany that overeducated workers are not more likely to move to better positions over a five-year period. A strong state dependence in overeducated jobs has also been presented by Büchel and Pollmann-Schult (2002) who used a different German database and applied hazard rate techniques. Also, Dolton and Vignoles (2000) reported that overqualification can be a more permanent phenomenon in the UK graduate labour market. So it seems that—contrary to cross-country comparisons based on static designs such as the quantification of wage penalties caused by overeducation that yield rather consistent result patterns—overeducation dynamics show significant differences between countries. This may be due to strongly different institutional labour market settings across countries.

Three other studies focus on the effect of overeducation on workers' wages. In Chapter 5 Jochmann and Pohlmeier deal with the question whether overeducation really affects workers' wages or whether there is no causal effect. In their analysis they take care of the fact that overeducation is not randomly assigned to individual workers. Using cross-section data on the German working population they analyse the causal effect of overeducation on wages within a Bayesian framework based on the Markov chain Monte Carlo methods. Jochmann and Pohlmeier show that the negative effects of overeducation on workers' earnings are overestimated when selectivity effects are ignored. Their results indicate that if overeducated workers were placed in jobs where the job requirements were in accordance with their actual educational attainment they could not expect significant increases in earnings.

In Chapter 6 Muysken, Kiiver and Hoppe analyse the impact of education on wage differentials and wage growth in Germany. Tracking the development of wages over a long period from 1984 to 2000 they are able to show that returns to education, experience and also required skills are rather stable over time. Estimated returns to required skills clearly increase with the skill level. In accordance with the overeducation literature they find that there are advantages for certain job education combinations: For example, for a blue-collar worker the wage is highest in combination with an apprenticeship training. Indeed, the impact of skill levels in their wage equations reduces the variance of the residuals and, hence, unobserved heterogeneity. Comparing the results with similar analyses for the Netherlands and the US, the returns to experience are the same in all countries, while the premiums on required skills and education are much higher in the US.

In Chapter 7, Maier, Pfeiffer and Pohlmeier focus on another neglected problem in the overeducation literature, the possible endogeneity of the educational regressors in standard earnings functions. Education—and, therefore, also overeducation—can be understood as a choice variable and, therefore, usual coefficient estimates cannot be interpreted as causal effects. In order to assess this effect average treatment effect models are estimated. Based on German data they show that average treatment effects of an additional year of schooling and overschooling are indeed relatively similar, which differs from the evidence found in most conventional studies.

As mentioned above, Sloane discusses the various ways in which overeducation is measured in the literature on this subject. In Chapter 8 Jensen develops a most innovative way of measurement by estimating earnings frontiers. He proposes an income ratio measure based on potential incomes with stochastic earnings frontiers. Overeducation is measured by the ratio between potential and actual earnings. Based on this approach overeducation is associated with rather different personal characteristics than based on more traditional measurement techniques.

Finally, three studies focus on the way specific groups of workers suffer from overeducation. In Chapter 9 Muysken and Zwick deal with the labour market for licensed professions. Studying these professional markets is of particular interest as it raises the question whether overeducation is related to the barriers insiders in a professional labour market raise to restrict the inflow of new entrants into their profession. In their paper they set up a general labour market model with endogenous skill formation and qualification setting by members of the profession. The model clearly shows that members of such licensed professions may skim rents by increasing the qualification standards needed to perform the job. The new argument introduced here is that credentialism (which is defined as a rising qualification demand that is not matched by rising skill levels needed in production) is not performed by employers, but is based on the strategic behaviour of the members of the licensed profession. The model shows that in the wake of a positive demand shock that does not increase skill requirements, members of the licensed profession nevertheless increase qualification standards. In fact, this causes overqualification as the tasks could be performed by people with lower qualifications. The chapter by Muysken and Zwick, therefore, adds to the literature that has often attributed credentialism to the supply side (cf. Muysken and ter Weel, 2000).

In Chapter 10 Dolton and Silles analyse the extent to which university graduates in the UK suffer from overeducation in their early careers. Focusing on the overeducation of this group of workers is particularly interesting, since graduates who search for their first job are rather vulnerable for being overeducated. Moreover, the study of Dolton and Silles deals with the issues of the measurement of overeducation and the permanency of overeducation. With respect to the measurement of overeducation Dolton and Silles distinguish between educational requirements to enter a job and the education level needed to perform the job. Opposite to what they expected they find that the extent of overeducation is higher when the graduates are asked for the education level required to *actually perform the job* than when they are asked for the *minimum formal qualification level for entering the job*. This indicates that there is no evidence of credentialism in the sense that educational requirements to acqquire a job exceed the skills to perform the job. Dolton and Silles also deal with the selection bias in studies on the wage effects of overeducation. They show that OLS estimates of the earnings effect of being overeducated overestimate the negative effect of overeducation on earnings due to the endogeneity of overeducation and earnings determination.

Moreover, overeducation in the first job might not only just be a first step in a job search process, but might also be a more persistent characteristic of a graduate's career. In this way the study of Dolton and Silles is related to the studies of Groot and Maassen van den Brink (Chapter 3) and Alba-Ramírez and Blázquez (Chapter 4) that also focus on the permanency of overeducation. Dolton and Silles find that over half of the graduates were in overeducation initially, but this had fallen to about one in five university graduates not being employed in graduate level positions after spending some time in the labour force.

In the last Chapter Battu and Sloane deal with the question whether ethnical minorities who usually have a weak labour market position and may be affected by discriminatory selection procedures are particularly affected by skill mismatch. Based on data from England and Wales and utilising a modal measure of required education across sixty occupations they find, indeed, that different ethnic groups have varying levels of overeducation in excess of whites, whereas undereducation is lower. However, the group of ethnical minorities, as a whole, turn out to be most heterogenous with respect to the country of origin. This finding is consistent with other labour market analyses (cf. Büchel and Frick, in press). For example, language fluency increases the likelihood of mismatch, both in terms of over- and undereducation. Furthermore, a commendably aspect of the research design introduced by Battu and Sloane is the fact that they set a special focus on spatial diversity across local and regional labour markets. This important feature in explaining differences in skill mismatches is still underdeveloped in overeducation research (cf. Büchel and Battu, 2003; Büchel and van Ham, in press).

As indicated above the studies presented in this volume contribute, in various ways, to the agenda for further research indicated in the overview study of Sloane. Several studies show that overeducation is a less serious phenomenon than often thought since the incidence of overeducation is overestimated when no account is taken of the heterogeneity in the actual ability level or attitudes toward the employment of workers with a particular level of education. Moreover, it is shown that the negative effect of overeducation on workers' earnings is much smaller than indicated by studies that do not control for the endogeneity of overeducation and earnings determination.

The consequences of overeducation for the individual worker also seem to be less serious than often suggested, since for a large group of workers it is merely a temporary situation at the beginning of their labour market careers. This indicates that the high level of initial education of these workers compensates a lack of experience. However, on this point there are remarkable differences between various studies. It is not clear to what extent these differences are due to differences in methodology or measurement of the various studies or to differences between countries due to different labour market institutions, in as far as whether these institutions stimulate a severe selection in the labour market entrance jobs or not and the related stigmatisation of the workers who do not aquire a suitable job immediately.

The literature on overeducation also clearly indicates that overeducation is one of the most important routes of labour market adjustments in the case of an excess supply of high-skilled workers. In this sense, to some extent it is also a temporary phenomenon at the macro level, since on the one hand, excess supply of labour disappears in an economic boom and, on the other hand, a larger supply of high-skilled workers increases the demand for these workers because it accelerates the development of skill-complementary technologies (Acemoglu, 2002). Particularly the latter is highly relevant from a policy point of view, since it shows that the fact that part of the workforce is overeducated for their job is not an argument to restrict the inflow into higher education. There are many indications supporting the expectation that overeducation may facilitate the further development of the 'most competitive and dynamic knowledge-based economy in the world' that the European Union had formulated at the Lisbon European Council in March 2000 as it's major 'strategic goal for the next decade' (European Commission, 2002). If this is true, overeducation research deserves a more substantial interest that it has received up to now. This volume attempts to contribute to this aim.

REFERENCES

Acemoglu, D. (2002). Technical change, inequality, and the labor market. *Journal of Economic Literature*, **40**, 7–72.

Borghans, L., and de Grip, A. (2000). The debate in economics about skill utilization. In L. Borghans and A. de Grip (Eds.), *The overeducated worker? The economics of skill utilization* (pp. 3–23). Cheltenham: Edward Elgar.

Bresnahan, T.F., Brynjolfsson, E., and Hitt, L.M. (2002). Information technology, workplace organization and the demand for skilled labor: Firm level evidence. *Quarterly Journal of Economics*, **117**, 339–376.

Büchel, F., and Battu, H. (2003). The theory of differential overqualification: Does it work? *Scottish Journal of Political Economy*, **50** (1), 1–16.

Büchel, F., and Frick, J.R. (in press). Immigrants in the UK and in West Germany: Relative income position, income portfolio, and redistribution effects. *Journal of Population Economics*.

Büchel, F., and Mertens, A. (in press). Overeducation, undereducation, and the theory of career mobility. *Applied Economics*.

Büchel, F., and Pollmann-Schult, M. (2002). Overcoming a period of overeducated work: Does the quality of apprenticeship matter? *Applied Economics Quarterly—Konjunkturpolitik (Special Issue)*, **48** (3–4), 304–316.

Büchel, F., and van Ham, M. (in press). Overeducation, regional labour markets and spatial flexibility. *Journal of Urban Economics*.

Carneiro, P., and Heckman, J.J. (2003). *Human capital policy*. Cambridge, MA: National Bureau of Economic Research (Working Paper 9495).

Chevalier, A. (2000). *Graduate over-education in the UK*. London: London School of Economics, Centre for the Economics of Education (Discussion Paper 07).

Dolton, P., and Vignoles, A. (2000). Incidence and effects of overeducation in the UK graduate labour market. *Economics of Education Review,* **19**, 179–198.

Dupuy, A., and de Grip, A. (2002). *Do large firms have more opportunities to substitute between skill categories than small firms?* Aarhus, Denmark: Centre for Labour Market and Social Research (Working Paper 02–01).

European Commission. (2002). *Employment in Europe 2002: Recent trends and prospects*. Brussels: European Commission.

Freeman, R.B. (1976). *The overeducated American*. New York: Academic Press.

Machin, S., and Van Reenen, J. (1998). Technology and changes in skill structure: Evidence from seven OECD countries. *Quarterly Journal of Economics,* **113**, 245–279.

Muysken, J., and ter Weel, B. (2000). Overeducation and crowding out of low-skilled workers. In L. Borghans and A. de Grip (Eds.), *The overeducated worker? The economics of skill utilization* (pp. 109–132). Cheltenham: Edward Elgar.

Tinbergen, J. (1975). *Income distribution: Analysis and policies*. Amsterdam: North Holland.

Tsang, M.C., and Levin, H.M. (1985). The economics of overeducation. *Economics of Education Review,* **4**, 93–105.

Wieling, M., and Borghans, L. (2001). Discrepancies between supply and demand and adjustment processes in the labour market. *Labour,* **15**, 33–56.

2. Much ado About Nothing? What does the Overeducation Literature Really Tell us?

Peter J. Sloane

2.1 INTRODUCTION

There is now a substantial literature both in North America and Europe covering various aspects of imperfect job matching in relation to the educational attainments of workers and the educational requirements of jobs. We shall for shorthand purposes refer to this as the overeducation literature, but it has links with issues such as skill bumping, sheepskin effects[1] or more broadly with the literature on internal labour markets and labour market discrimination. Its coming of age is reflected in a special issue of the Economics of Education Review on Overschooling (Oosterbeek, 2000), two survey papers by Green, McIntosh and Vignoles (1999) and Hartog (2000), and an edited book (Borghans and de Grip, 2000a) as well as a substantial literature, much of which is summarised in Table 2A.1. Its significance rests on the fact that there has been a major expansion in the proportion of the population acquiring educational qualifications, particularly but not exclusively at degree level in many countries. Furthermore, the incidence of both over- and undereducation appears to be substantial with their incidence ranging between below 10 and above 40 per cent in Europe, though some differences reflect differences in measurement. In countries such as the UK, Germany and Portugal, studies have generally found overeducation to be more pronounced than undereducation, while in the Netherlands and Spain, some studies have found the reverse. Also in some cases there are gender differences.

Overeducation raises a series of questions which this paper will seek to address. First, are there any challenges to human capital theory, which in its crudest form suggests that the rate of return to education is not contingent on how or where the qualifications are utilised in the labour market? (Section 2). Second, what is it that we are measuring in terms of a perceived mismatch between educational qualifications and job requirements? If overeducated workers are of poor quality for their level of qualification, overeducation does not necessarily imply any inefficiency in the operation of the labour market (Section 3). Third, what is the impact of overeducation on the level of earnings in both the short-run and the long run? If there is a wage premium (cost), what form does this take and why are employers (employees) prepared to countenance it? Are earnings influenced by the distribution of workers with differing levels of education within particular establishments? (Section 4). Fourth, what is the impact on the provision of training by the employer? (Section 5). Fifth, does overeducation vary across regional locations? (Section 6). Sixth, what other questions are there relating to the dynamics of overeducation? For instance, to what extent does overeducation emerge as a consequence of overeducated workers moving into existing jobs or taking on new jobs and how does this impinge on the employability of previously matched workers? Does downward skill bumping continue throughout the skill distribution or is it restricted to certain skill levels? (Section 7). Seventh, how does overeducation impact on particular groups in the labour market as distinguished by their gender, age and ethnic origin? (Section 8). Finally, is overeducation a temporary or a permanent phenomenon and how does this relate to the operation of sheepskin effects? (Section 9).

2.2 CHALLENGES FOR HUMAN CAPITAL THEORY

The standard Mincer human capital model is sufficiently wellknown that there is little need to express it formally save to say that it uses both years of education and experience in quadratic form. This model has been remarkably useful in explaining various labour market outcomes. Yet, it is not often subject to formal econometric tests relating to the normality and the homoscedasticity of the disturbance term and specification error, which relates to the assumption of functional form. Nevertheless, such tests suggest, *inter alia*, that at least for British data educational dummies outperform years of education both in terms of the Ramsey reset test and explanatory power.[2] Potential problems arise from ability bias, the endogenous nature of schooling with respect to the optimal investment decision and measurement error. Furthermore, the long-run equilibrium specification of the human capital model omits the demand side of the labour market altogether.[3] As Hartog (1986) states:

> The model is compatible with perfect substitutability of labour by schooling levels within each and every job, as well as with ever perfect allocation; imperfect substitutability within jobs is circumvented by always assigning an individual to the job where his education has the proper value. Both assumptions are quite strong and seldom made explicit.

Yet, there is substantial evidence that precisely where a worker is employed has a significant effect on earnings. Thus, Bowles, Gintis and Osborne (2001) noted that apparently similar individuals receive quite different levels of earnings across the US. Correcting for race and sex as well as other personal characteristics including age, schooling experience and parental background between two-thirds and four-fifths of the variance in the log of hourly wages is unexplained. While transitory elements of pay and response error may explain some of this away, perhaps half of the variance in earnings is unexplained by the standard demographic variables. Studies by Wachtel and Betsey (1972), Dickens and Katz (1986), Krueger and Summers (1987) and Groshen (1991a, 1991b) found that a substantial part of the variance in wage earnings in the US can be explained by industrial structure. Krueger and Summers, for example, found that the pattern of inter-industry wage differentials across countries appears to follow a regular pattern with manufacturing industries tending to pay about 20 per cent more than service industries for comparable workers. Similar regularities are found for gender, age group and occupation.

The extreme position on the demand side is taken by Thurow (1975) who argued that marginal productivity resides in the job rather than with the worker. His so-called job competition model assumes that employers use personal characteristics including education as criteria for hiring workers, simply on the supposition that employing more educated workers in a job will require a lower investment in training by the firm. In the extreme, education simply serves to obtain the job, and there is a zero return to human capital beyond that required to do the job, as all workers in a given job are paid the same wage. Thus

$$\text{Log } W_t = \alpha_0 + \alpha_1 q^r + \varepsilon \tag{2.1}$$

where q^r equals the qualifications required to do the job. Any qualifications in excess of q^r are essentially unrewarded, so that we may regard the Mincer model and the Thurow model as the two extreme cases, being on the one hand purely supply side driven and on the other purely demand side driven.

A third strand of the literature is based on the job assignment model which goes back to Roy (1951) and Tinbergen (1956) and was developed further by Hartog (1977) and Sattinger (1993). This model is based on the proposition that there is an allocation problem in assigning heterogeneous workers to jobs that differ in their complexity. Hartog, for example, views labour supply and demand as consisting of a bundle of capabilities, and suggests that up to 40 per cent of the income variance can be attributed to capability variables. Following Tinbergen, let us suppose that s_i equals the degree to which a skill i is required and t_i the degree to which it is present among potential employees. On the demand side, employers will specify a frequency distribution $M(s_1, s_2{\_}{\_}{\_})$ of the number of employees they require in each region of the variable s_i. On the supply side, a similar frequency distribution $N(t_1, t_2{\_}{\_}{\_})$ describes the availability of skills among potential employees. In practice, the frequency distributions are unlikely to match and overeducation may be a persistent problem if the job structure is relatively unresponsive to changes in relative supplies of educated labour. Earnings are then a function of both worker and job characteristics. We can encompass both the Mincer and Thurow models in a more general equation (sometimes referred to as the Duncan and Hoffman or the ORU model).

$$\text{Log } W_t = \beta_0 + \beta_1 q^r + \beta_2 q^s + \beta_3 q^u + \varepsilon^1 \tag{2.2}$$

in which actual educational qualifications are (q) decomposed into required (q^r), surplus (q^s) and deficit (q^u) qualifications in relation to those necessary to do the job. The human capital specification implies that $\beta_1 = \beta_2 = -\beta_3$ and the job competition specification that $\beta_2 = \beta_3 = 0$. The hypothesis of earnings equations restricted to the human capital and job competition models can be tested with an F-test on the residual sum of squares. Such tests have been conducted on Dutch data (Hartog, 1988; Hartog and Oosterbeek, 1988) and by Sloane, Battu and Seaman (1999) using British data. In each case it was found that the job assignment model outperformed both the standard human capital and job competition models.

Using such an assignment approach, Sicherman (1991) suggests that there are two stylised facts relating to the earnings of over- and undereducated workers. The first is that earnings of overeducated workers are less than the earnings of those with the same level of education but who are in jobs with the required level of education, but more than those in their current occupation with the required level of education. The second stylised fact is that the earnings of the undereducated workers are more than the earnings of those with the same level of education but who work in jobs which require that level of education, but less than the earnings of their co-workers who have the required but higher level of education. These stylised facts have been found in a number of studies, but it is far from clear why and how employers are able to differentiate the pay of their workforces in this way. One possible explanation relates to the internal labour market. Workers may be initially hired for jobs below their educational capabilities with the expectations of internal promotion (Sicherman and Galor, 1990). This has been studied for the US, where seniority is particularly important, by Hersch (1993), for Spain by Garcia-Serrano and Malo-Ocana (1996) and for the Netherlands by Dekker, de Grip and Heijke (2002). The Spanish study found, in fact, controlling for personal characteristics in a logistic regression model that overeducated workers have a lower probability of being promoted than properly matched workers. The Dutch study also found, contrary to expectations, that upward mobility was not significantly higher in the internal labour market than in the 'supplementary' market. While overeducation has the expected positive effect on upward mobility in general the coefficient is not significant for the internal labour market. Another possibility is that formal education is a substitute for other forms of human capital investment. That is, over- or undereducation may be a substitute for experience, tenure and on-the-job training, but this does not necessarily lead to the stylised facts referred to above. A third possibility is that overeducated workers are of inferior quality than matched employees with the same qualifications, but again it is not clear why such workers should attract a wage premium.

Recently, Bulmahn and Kräkel (2000) have offered a novel explanation. Employers hire overeducated workers as an insurance against the breakdown of the production process, since such workers are capable of improvisation. They tested this using firm data in Westphalia, and speculated that the implication of their model is that, if firms hire overeducated workers for insurance purposes this will lead to a lower average salary per white-collar worker and a positive correlation between material stock per white-collar worker and the average salary per white-collar worker. While their results are consistent with their model, the test does not appear to be particularly strong. Furthermore, the alternative of buying in external help when needed would seem likely to be much more cost effective. Answers to these questions seem to require a detailed study of employers to ascertain what their precise recruitment and promotion strategies are, but such studies are presently lacking.

2.3 MEASUREMENT ISSUES

Three main alternative measures have been used to estimate the degree of over-education:

(i) Systematic job evaluation, which states the level of qualifications required to perform a particular job. This is referred to as an *objective measure* though it is better regarded as an objective measure based on subjective values. It ignores the possibility that there may be a distribution of educational levels suitable for performing different tasks within a broad occupation and may become inappropriate over time as the nature of a job alters.

(ii) Worker self-assessment is referred to as a *subjective measure* and suffers from the fact that different questions may be asked, such as 'how much education is required to get a job like yours?' or 'what level of education is required in order to perform the job?' If there is credentialism, firms may specify a higher level of education to obtain the job than is required to perform it adequately, thereby leading to skill under-utilisation.

In both these measures reference is made to the level of education rather than the type of education. Thus a worker may still be mismatched if the level of education is appropriate, but its type inappropriate, such as a graduate in English being hired as a statistician.[4] There is also disagreement over whether (i) or (ii) is more accurate in practice in defining the true educational requirements of jobs. Thus, van der Velden and van Smoorenburg (1997) favour (ii) on the grounds that the job evaluation method systematically over-estimates the level of overeducation, while Hartog and Oosterbeek (1998) suggest worker assessment may lead to an upward bias.

(iii) The third method is used where there is no direct question on overeducation and is referred to as *the empirical* method. Mismatching is said to occur when the level of education is more than one standard deviation above or below the mean. This cannot be directly compared with the above measures as it ignores minor differences between actual and mean education. This difference is more striking when the question asked under (i) and (ii) requires a simple yes or no response. It also implies a symmetry between over- and undereducation, which is rarely found in practice and thus is likely to provide biased estimates. Indeed, it is doubtful whether we should refer to over- or undereducation in this context. If we consider individual occupations some will require rigid qualifications, such as in the professions, whilst in others educational qualifications may be relatively unimportant. It is, however, useful to consider whether the distribution of educational qualifications within particular occupations is narrow or broad. The analysis of overeducation by occupation is, however, a relatively neglected issue in the literature.

Notwithstanding the above, given asymmetry between over- and undereducation it seems more appropriate to use the modal rather than the mean measure of education. This also has the advantage of being less sensitive to outliers or technological change. Such a measure has been used, for example, amongst others, by Alpin, Shackleton and Walsh (1998), Kiker, Santos and De Oliveira (1997), De Oliveira, Santos and Kiker (2000) and Bauer (2002). De Oliveira, Santos and Kiker noted that in some occupations the number of workers may be so small or the dispersion of actual qualifications so wide that any measure of central location is likely to be unreliable. Thus, as a rule of thumb they limited their analysis to cases where the modal number of years of education was shared by at least 60 per cent of the workers in that occupation.

The frequent omission of any measure of ability in studies of overeducation is particularly serious because we do not know whether the overeducated worker is in this state simply because of low ability given the level of education. It is usually assumed in the literature that the more able an individual, the longer he or she will stay on at school. This would result in an upward bias in the ordinary least squares (OLS) estimated return to years of schooling (or qualifications dummies) and, therefore, an over-estimation of the rate of return to schooling. Hartog (2001) interpreted the literature as suggesting that the schooling coefficient would be reduced by no more than a third if ability variables such as IQ test scores were included, with a central tendency perhaps in the range of 10 to 15 per cent.[5] At least four procedures have been used to deal with this problem—IQ tests, identical twins or siblings data, panel data, which treats ability as a constant over time and an instrumental variable technique, which purges schooling of any ability relationship. Without such a correction the overeducation literature implicitly assumes not only that ability bias is not a problem, but also that there is no ability variation within a particular education qualification level.

Few authors compare the results of using different measures of overeducation on the same dataset. One exception is Battu, Belfield and Sloane (2000). Using data from two cohorts of UK graduates they found that the scale of overeducation varies with measurement techniques, with only weak correlations between their three measures (answers to a yes/no question on whether a degree was a job requirement in current main employment, a measure of whether the modal worker was a non-graduate and answers to a question on how dissatisfied the graduate was with the match between work and qualifications). The effects of overeducation as measured in the three cases on earnings and job satisfaction are similar, despite the fact that each measure identifies different individuals as being overeducated (see Table 2.1, which provides correlation coefficients between different measures of overeducation with individuals as data points). Similar results were obtained for the Netherlands by Groot and Maassen van den Brink (2000b). Their three measures are the standard empirical method, a comparison between the education level and job level of the worker and worker self reports. They found that only a small fraction of those workers counted as overeducated when any of the three measures is counted as so by all three. Further, unlike Battu, Belfield and Sloane they found that the estimated rates of return to over- and

Table 2.1 The correlation between different measures of overeducation for graduates

| | Degree requirements | | | | Occupational skill level | | | |
| | 1985 | | 1990 | | 1985 | | 1990 | |
	men	women	men	women	men	women	men	women
Degree requirements	–	–	–	–	–	–	–	–
Occupational skills level	0.25	0.45	0.37	0.35	–	–	–	–
Work match (mid cut)	0.21	0.37	0.31	0.31	0.20	0.39	0.29	0.41
Work match (third cut)	0.21	0.42	0.31	0.35	0.24	0.49	0.33	0.34

Degree requirement:	Yes/no response to question: 'Was the degree gained in 1985 or 1990, a requirement in the job specification for your current main employment (including self employment)?'
Occupational skills level:	More than 50 per cent of workers have a highest qualification below degree level.
Work match (mid cut):	Individual responses to the question: 'How satisfied are you with the match between your work and your qualifications (in your current main job)?'
Work match (third cut):	A mid way cut-off corresponds to a satisfaction score of 3 or less on a 6-point scale and a third cut corresponds to a satisfaction level of 1 or 2.

Source: Battu, Belfield and Sloane (2000).

undereducation varied markedly among the three definitions. Thus, one must conclude that the validity and reliability of mismatching measures is poor and any results from such studies should be treated with a degree of caution.

The key issue is, however, to what extent do perceived mismatches represent labour market sorting on the basis of the varying quality of labour within educational levels. This should be viewed in the context of increasing numbers of qualified individuals. If educational standards have fallen, the employer response might be to upgrade entry qualifications to ensure that new entrants have appropriate skills (grade-drift). Alternatively, employers may take advantage of a larger pool of qualified applicants by upgrading some traditionally lower-level jobs or recruiting, say graduates to previously non-graduate jobs (qualifications inflation).[6] Little is known about the extent to which employers have gone down these paths, if at all, and if demand for highly qualified manpower has increased at least as fast as supply there would not necessarily be a surplus of qualified manpower to make such choices feasible.

Assuming that the heterogeneity of graduates has increased Chevalier (2000) distinguished between two categories of overeducated graduates by making a distinction between *apparently* overeducated and *genuinely* overeducated graduates (Table 2.2).[7] In the former case, where mismatch is minor, these individuals should receive more initial training than matched workers to offset their inferior quality, whereas in the latter case they should receive less initial training, since their superior quality means they learn faster. He then proposed an alternative measure of overeducation based on the answer to a job satisfaction question, namely, 'how dissatisfied are you with the match between your work and your qualifications?'[8] This was then used to form a dichotomous variable with satisfied workers classified as being apparently overeducated and dissatisfied as genuinely overeducated.[9] We have two types of graduates—high-skilled (g) and low-skilled (type 1) and three classifications of jobs—graduate (G), upgraded (U) and non-graduate (L). All graduates who are in graduate jobs are defined as matched whatever their satisfaction, with all others dissatisfied described as overeducated. Chevalier estimated that two-thirds of the overeducated are only apparently so. However, this is dependent on both the classification of jobs according to expert opinion, the division of graduates into two types and the interpretation of the job satisfaction question.

A similar type of approach has been adopted, using a 1991 survey of graduates from Dutch universities and vocational institutes as part of the Higher Education and Graduate Employment in Europe project, by Allen and van der Velden (2000), who allowed job levels to vary for a given educational level match. They distinguished a formal education mismatch (referred to as educational mismatch) from a mismatch between acquired and required skills (skill mismatch). Their dataset included two key questions.[10] First, whether the current job offers sufficient scope to use acquired knowledge and skills

Table 2.2 Genuine and apparent overeducation

	Skilled graduate (g)	Less skilled graduate (type 1)
Graduate job (G)	Perfect match (Gg)	X
Upgraded job (U)	Genuine overeducation (Ug)	Apparent overeducation (U1)
Non-graduate job (L)	X	Genuine overeducation (L1)

Source: Chevalier (2000).

(utilisation). Second, whether the graduate would perform better in their current job if additional knowledge and skills had been acquired (skill deficit). About 15 per cent of all graduates in their sample experienced under-utilisation, but a much larger proportion experienced high levels of skill deficits; and this measure was only weakly related to educational mismatches. Furthermore, their results casted doubt on one of the key assumptions of the assignment theory, namely, that a mismatch between education and jobs necessarily implies a serious mismatch between available and required skills. Skill mismatches have a strong negative impact on job satisfaction, unlike educational mismatches. One interpretation of their results is that graduates with the same level of education but differing abilities are efficiently sorted into the labour market according to their abilities, so that the apparent effects of over- and undereducation are spurious, masking unmeasured ability differences.

A third approach is to test directly whether the overeducated are less able than those who are properly matched. This was attempted by Green, McIntosh and Vignoles (1999) using the National Child Development Survey (NCDS),[11] which, unusually, has questions on both aspects. Their results indicated that individuals who had higher scores in a maths test when aged 16 were significantly less likely to be overeducated later in their working lives, and this effect was substantial. This is also consistent with the finding that there are higher returns to numerate degrees.[12] Further results from their analysis of the International Literacy Survey (ILS) support the argument that those individuals who lack good quantitative skills are more likely to be overeducated. Using the German Life History Study (GLHS), Büchel and Pollmann-Schult (2001) found that a poor grade in the school-leaving certificate had a strong effect on the later risk of overeducation for those graduating with a vocational degree, after controlling for selectivity effects.

Taking these results together, it seems clear that a substantial part of what is referred to in the literature as overeducation simply reflects the heterogeneity of individual abilities and skills within particular educational qualifications. Far from representing inefficient allocation this indicates that the labour market is functioning effectively in allocating workers to jobs which match their abilities and skills.

2.4 THE IMPACT ON PAY

As we saw earlier, there are certain stylised facts with regard to the impact of over- and undereducation on pay although, as Hartog (2000) pointed out, it would, in view of the previous discussion, be more informative if we knew the impact on productivity rather than on pay. Tsang (1987) had studied this, finding that reductions in job satisfaction lower productivity, with the implication that overeducation must do so too. This would seem to lead to the expectation that overeducation should lower pay rather than increase it relative to those who are properly matched. However, Büchel (2000) analysed several firm-related aspects of worker productivity using the German Socio-Economic Panel (GSOEP) over the period 1984 to 1995. He found, in fact, that overqualified workers were healthier, more strongly work orientated, more likely to participate in training and had longer tenure than their matched colleagues. This he interpreted as consistent with the payment of a wage premium for surplus education.

In fact, Groot and Maassen van den Brink (2000a) in their meta-analysis summarised 25 studies as producing unweighted average rates of return of 5.6 per cent for attained years of education, 7.8 per cent for required years of education, 3.0 per cent for years of overeducation and minus 1.5 per cent for years of undereducation, confirming Sicherman's stylised facts (referred to in Section 2) and suggesting a real impact on pay. Whilst they find no tendency for overeducation to increase or decrease over time they suggested that overeducation has increasingly been concentrated among lower ability workers for whom the pay-off to a year of education is low. Likewise, Cohn and Ng (2000) found for Hong Kong that the wage benefits of overeducation decline as one gains more labour market experience. This is consistent with the existence of sheepskin effects. Workers are sorted into their most appropriate jobs after several years or so on the basis of actual performance rather than their educational qualifications. Again, this may be picked up by researchers without having such information as mismatching, when in reality productivity has been maximised. Evidence consistent with the presence of sheepskin effects had been found, for example, by Belman and Heywood (1997) and Denny and Harmon (2001).

The earlier discussion suggests that the returns to education for overeducated workers will vary according to their ability and skills, and there is some evidence for this. Thus, Chevalier (2000) found a pay penalty for overeducated graduates compared to matched graduates, which is 7 per cent for apparently overeducated graduates and 26 per cent for genuinely overeducated graduates, the latter suffering a pay penalty, which virtually wipes out the advantage of having a degree. However, this 7 per cent penalty for apparently overeducated graduates suggests that not all their overeducation is apparent as opposed to genuine. Allen and van der Velden (2001) found that skill under-utilisation reduced earnings by 6 per cent when over- and undereducation were excluded from their estimating equation as independent variables and 3.2 per cent when they were included, in both cases with significant coefficients. Battu, Belfield and Sloane (1999) found that class of degree had a significant effect on graduate earnings both one year and six years after graduation, with a first class degree having a premium of 8–13 per cent over lower-second class honours. Similarly, the type of institution from which one graduated mattered, with those graduating from more established universities earning 8–11 per cent more than those graduating from former polytechnics, holding constant a measure of overeducation. Using a different dataset (the 1980 National Survey of Graduates and Diplomates) Dolton and Vignoles (2000) found, however, no evidence that overeducated workers with good degrees earned more than those with poorer degrees. They did, however, find that those with better degree classifications and those from more established universities, as opposed to polytechnics, were less likely to be overeducated.

Wage effects of overeducation are unlikely to be constant over all education levels or occupations. Thus, Vahey (2000) found for Canada that overeducated men only received a wage premium over properly matched workers in their job when the required level of education was a first degree. For undereducated males a wage penalty compared to properly matched workers only applies at lower required levels of education. For women, however, overeducation and undereducation have no impact on earnings, in contrast to findings in other countries. In one of few studies including an occupation-specific model, Verdugo and Verdugo (1989) found that the earnings of over-, adequately and undereducated workers do vary substantially by broad occupational group. Of nine occupational categories overeducation has significant effects on earnings in five cases and for undereducation significant effects in only three.

There is some recent evidence that returns to education may be affected by the education levels of co-workers, and this could be one explanation why employers pay a premium to overeducated workers if indeed this is really the case. Workers do not generally work autonomously—many tasks require team work, so that the productivity of workers is influenced by the performance of their colleagues. These positive effects may also be produced by information sharing, co-training, monitoring and more general support.[13] In order to test these propositions matched samples of employers and employees are required. Battu, Belfield and Sloane (2002) have tested these hypotheses on the 1998 establish-ment-based British Workplace Employment Relations Survey, using random effects generalised least squares. It was found that workplace education levels had strong effects on own earnings, only slightly reducing the return to own education, when introduced into a conventional human capital model. Thus, in one formulation an across-the-workplace increase in education of 1.2 years (one standard deviation) raised own earnings by 11.3 per cent.[14] Further support for these propositions was found in an unpublished paper by Barth (2000), using two types of matched employer/employee data from Norway. He found that the independent effect on own pay, from raising the average level of education within the workplace, ranged from 1 to 4 per cent per year of average education. Although these studies do not have direct measures of worker productivity, they are consistent with positive spillovers from more education in the workplace, which may make it worthwhile to hire workers with more education than a narrow interpretation of the job would imply.

All the above studies have been cross-section in nature and it is possible that estimates are biased as a result of unobserved heterogeneity. Bauer (2002) used panel data—the GSOEP over the period 1984 to 1998, which enabled him to control for innate ability.[15] He was able to replicate earlier findings when using the standard OLS formulation. The results change dramatically when using panel estimation techniques. For men the estimated returns to years of required education fall and become very similar to those of actual education using a random effects model based on a modal index and the Duncan and Hoffman (1981) model. For overeducated women, but not undereducated women, rather different results are obtained and for women the human capital model cannot be rejected. These results suggest at least for men that ability can explain why overeducated workers receive a premium over their colleagues with the required level of education, in line with the findings in Section 3 (Allen and van der Velden, 2001; Chevalier, 2000).

Finally, the above literature assumes that mismatch is essentially exogenous, occurring as part of a random process. This has been challenged by Dolton and Silles (2001), noting in particular that graduates who are overeducated in their first job have difficulty in entering graduate jobs later. They hypothesise that overeducation results from labour market rigidities caused by geographical immobility on the part of workers, family commitments, trade union restrictions and imperfect information. They utilised instrumental variable techniques to allow for simultaneity between earnings and type of job entered by graduates, treatment effects models to deal with ability bias and a Heckman type model to deal with the possibility that the overeducated are drawn from a non-random subset of the population. Using a sample drawn from a 1998 postal questionnaire to Newcastle University graduates with data provided at five specific time intervals, they found inter alia that the overeducation process may be endogenous to the determination of wages. Their instrumental variable (IV) estimates suggested that labour market mobility, certain family commitments and the level of student debt[16] all impact significantly on the likelihood of overeducation, whilst not being correlated with wages. Surprisingly, given their arguments, there is no gender difference in the likelihood of being overeducated. The IV estimates of this impact of overeducation on pay in first jobs are identical to the OLS estimates with a pay penalty of 18 per cent. However, when attention moves to current employment the OLS estimate rises to 30 per cent in contrast to an IV estimate of 17 per cent, and the Heckman selection type model for current employment produces estimates varying between 81 and 87 per cent. According to these pay penalty results there is no return at all to surplus education.[17]

Taken together, the above studies imply that overeducation has long-run as well as short-run effects on wages. There appeard to be scarring effects for those workers who do not obtain a good match early on in their careers.

2.5 THE IMPACT ON ADDITIONAL TRAINING

If initial education and industrial training are substitutes, overeducated workers will be less likely to participate in additional training than workers who are adequately educated. Less training will be required to perform the job because their education gives them additional skills, which can compensate for the lack of training. If, in contrast, initial education and industrial training are complements, perhaps because graduates learn faster, initial differences will be increased by the additional training and overeducated workers are likely to be promoted faster than adequately educated workers. In the case of undereducated workers, the substitutability hypothesis suggests that this group will acquire more training to offset the lack of formal education. Since such workers are less likely to quit than other workers they also provide the employer with more continuity in the labour force.

Strong evidence in favour of the substitutability hypothesis was found by Alba-Ramírez (1993) using Spanish data, Sloane, Battu and Seaman (1996) using British data and Büchel and Mertens (in press) using German data. The first of these found that undereducated workers were more likely to be men and to hold jobs associated with higher required job training and experience than overeducated workers. These findings tend to confirm the hypothesis that experience and on-the-job training allow workers to improve their job match over their working lives. Likewise, Sloane, Battu and Seaman (1996) found that undereducated workers had more experience, longer tenure with the firm and took longer to become fully proficient on-the-job than adequately educated workers, while the reverse was true for overeducated workers. In their multinomial logit model estimates designed to explain mismatch, these three variables were significant for both under- and overeducated workers, but with opposite signs. Büchel and Mertens, using the GSOEP, found a very strong correlation between formal and informal training and mismatch, with overeducated workers having far less access to on-the-job training and undereducated workers far more than adequately educated workers. In the US Robst (1995b) found, as did Büchel and Mertens, that overeducated workers had fewer opportunities to learn things that they considered useful for their future career, while Hersch (1995), for an individual firm, found likewise that training time for entry-level jobs was inversely related to overqualification and overqualified workers received less training and more promotions. Van Smoorenburg and van der Velden (2000), using Dutch data, found also that overeducated workers were less likely to participate in firm training than properly matched workers, although an earlier Dutch study (Groot, 1993) could find no such relationship. Yet, they could not detect any relationship between undereducation and the likelihood of participating in training, whereas the earlier Groot study found that undereducated workers had the lowest probability of such participation. Interestingly, Smoorenberg and van der Velden found that school leavers who held a job outside their field of study were more likely to participate in training than those who were employed in their 'own' field.

What these and other studies appear to show is that formal education is but one form of human capital and deficits in it can be remedied by a number of means, one of which is on-the-job training. On the other hand, overeducated workers may be attractive to the employer precisely because less on-the-job training is required in their case than in the case of properly matched workers. For some, the difference may simply be shorter on-the-job training periods.

2.6 THE REGIONAL DIMENSION

One explanation for overeducation is restricted geographical job search. This includes two elements—the amount of time and effort that individuals are willing to spend on commuting and their willingness to migrate to another region. Frank (1978) noted in particular that for a married couple the search for a pair of jobs would be constrained geographically and only by coincidence would the best job offer for both spouses occur in the same location. If the family's objective is to select the pair of jobs in a single location that maximises joint family income, husbands are likely to make smaller compromises than wives to the extent that they possess more human capital or are prepared to work longer hours in the labour market. In such circumstances a wife has three choices—non-participation, accepting a job below her level of qualification or commuting over longer distances.

One version of the above is the 'tied stayers' model in which the husband has already optimised and is unwilling to move to obtain another job. This was tested for the US by McGoldrick and Robst (1996). They did find partial support for the differential overqualification hypothesis, since married women had a higher probability of overqualification than married men.[18] However, there was no support for Frank's related proposition that overqualification would be greater the smaller the size of the labour market. An alternative version is the 'tied mover' model in which the husband decides to move location in order to obtain a better job and the wife is forced to move with him. This was tested for Britain by Battu, Seaman and Sloane (2000), using Social Change and Economic Life Survey (SCELI) data.[19] They found that migrant married women were less likely to remain employed than other groups, and more likely to suffer a reduction in pay when they retained employment, but they were no more likely to be overqualified than single women or non-migrants. However, Büchel (2000) using German data found support for both versions. Non-migrant married women, particularly in small local labour markets had a higher risk of overqualification than unmarried women or men of either type. Also migrant married women, especially those moving to smaller labour markets than in their former place of residence, faced a substantial risk of overqualification. Büchel and Battu (2003) made due allowance for the possibility that commuting may offer the likelihood of improving job matches, finding that higher commuting distances strongly reduced the possibility of being overqualified, both for married women and for men living in rural areas. Recently, Büchel and van Ham (in press) have adopted a broader framework, postulating that spatial restrictions (i.e., the location of residence in relation to the spatial configuration of employment opportunities) were likely to affect the labour market outcomes of *all* workers. This may explain why, using the 1998 wave of the GSOEP and correcting for sample selection, they found that women living with a partner and with children were no more likely to be overeducated than single women or men. Spatial flexibility in the form of having a car for personal use or increasing commuting time reduces the probability of overeducation. The size of the labour market is also important, since job search in a larger market increases the probability of finding a job, regardless of underlying supply and demand conditions.

It appears, therefore, that some workers are overeducated because they are prepared to trade off being properly matched for locational advantage, in terms of their place of residence and a shorter journey to work.[20] More research is required, however, in order to determine, more clearly, what proportion of overeducation can be explained by spatial factors.

2.7 OVEREDUCATION AND SKILL BUMPING

If the proportion of the workforce with various educational qualifications rises given the level of demand, it is possible that some of the educated will move into lower prestige jobs (generating overeducation) and that the less educated will be crowded out or bumped down into lower prestige jobs than they currently occupy, so that the mean education level rises in all occupations and presumably some of the uneducated lose their jobs. The increase in the number of unemployed workers seeking jobs would have the effect of widening wage differentials at the lower end of the occupational distribution, thus offsetting the tendency for the wage differential of educated workers over the uneducated to fall with the increase in supply of qualifications.[21] For this to happen there are certain requirements. Thus, Nickell and Bell (1995) noted that skilled workers can perform many of the tasks undertaken by the unskilled, which makes it easier to hoard skilled workers during recessions. A lack of specific skills will reduce the attachment to the firm of unskilled workers and raise their rate of turnover. These effects will be increased the higher the unemployment benefit replacement ratio and the higher the wage floor imposed by minimum wage legislation. There are, however, two distinctive explanations for the relatively high cyclical unemployment rates for lower educated workers. The hoarding model suggests that employers invest more in job specific capital for highly educated workers, leading to them being hoarded in recessions, with lower educated workers being laid off. This contrasts with the crowding out explanation in which lower-educated workers are replaced by higher-educated workers in recession. This would be reinforced where it is costly to adjust wages, as this would encourage firms to raise hiring standards for lower-level occupations. Both models are associated with flows into and out of the labour market, with the hoarding model focusing on outflows and the crowding out model focusing on inflows. Outflows into lower-level jobs have, at least in the case of Britain, been found to be surprisingly large. Thus, Evans (1999), taking a relatively prosperous year (1989) found that the annual flow out of full-time jobs for men aged between 20 and 60 as a percentage of total employment consisted of 3.16 per cent into no job, 5.11 per cent into a job at the same level, 3.06 per cent into a higher level job and 2.47 per cent into a lower-level job. Surprisingly, he found that both downward and upward movements are pro-cyclical. In their study of graduates, Dolton and Silles (2001) found that of those entering graduate or post-graduate jobs, initially 13 per cent switch out of these jobs into lower-level jobs. Also, 8.4 per cent of graduates in sub-degree jobs move down further into lower-level jobs. In another study using unemployment flow data for Wallonia over the period 1989 to 1994, Cockx and Dejeineppe (2002) found that 43 per cent of dismissed workers who found a new job were overeducated. According to these studies unemployment, therefore, appears to be the catalyst for skill bumping.

There have been relatively few formal tests of skill bumping. Some studies are contained in the edited book *The Overeducated Worker* (Borghans and de Grip, 2000a), thus Battu and Sloane (2000) matched the 1986 SCELI dataset with the British Household Panel Survey (BHPS) 1991 and 1995, utilising the fact that both datasets incorporated the Hope/Goldthorpe scale for the social desirability of jobs. They found clear evidence of skill bumping at the higher educational levels, but this did not extend down to the less or no educational qualifications categories, so that there was no evidence that the unqualified had been forced out of the labour market as a consequence of an increase in the proportion of the workforce who were overeducated. Asplund and Lilja (2000) examined skill bumping in the context of the Finnish labour market over the period 1975 to 1995. Over this period the overall probability of remaining in the same occupation declined rapidly, but the negative consequences for the least educated were dealt with mainly through the retirement system and to a lesser extent by pushing the least educated into unemployment. For Belgium, Nicaise (2000) found consistent with the bumping down theory, that men's wages lie far below potential earnings. As a consequence, mainly low-skilled workers are displaced and the burden of unemployment is shifted more to the bottom end of the labour market. However, in the case for women no such effects are found.

A substantial amount of work on crowding-out has been undertaken, however, by Dutch economists, largely based on matching models[22] and recognising that a direct test of the crowding-out hypothesis must focus on the composition of new hires over the cycle.[23] In an early study using indirect methods, Teulings and Koopmanschap (1989) focused on the relative change in the proportion of employees with a higher than required level of education in various occupations across regions in Holland. Finding that this was higher in regions with high unemployment they concluded there was crowding out. Van Ours and Ridder (1995) focused on new hires by computing unemployment vacancy ratios for different educational levels using data collected by the Dutch Central Bureau of Statistics between 1980 and 1988. Their results showed that crowding-out is limited to those with academic and higher vocational education, with no job competition at lower levels of education, in line with the UK evidence. In a recent paper, Gautier et al. (2002) utilised a matched employer/employee sample based on Dutch Ministry of Social Affairs and Employment data for 1992 to 1996, which enabled them to distinguish six job complexity categories and seven education levels. They use this to test whether the difference in years of schooling between the inflow and outflow of workers for a given job level in a particular firm is larger during low employment years. In fact, they found the reverse to be true.[24] Further, their data enabled them to estimate a wage equation including fixed match specific effects. Their results suggest that the wage differential between new workers with excess qualifications and their matched colleagues in simple jobs is close to zero, in contrast to Sicherman's stylised facts and consistent with Dolton and Silles (2001). When they take out fixed match specific effects to make their models comparable to other studies they obtained the traditional results of a positive and significant return to over-

education. Together, these results suggest that the overeducated self select
themselves into high wage firms, and the results of earlier studies are mainly
driven by uncontrolled selectivity effects. The main conclusion, however, is
that the evidence for crowding out is rather thin, being limited to outflows
rather than inflows of workers with relatively low levels of education.[25]

It is interesting to speculate on how far such skill bumping as occurs is permanent. That is, are workers who move down to lower-level jobs able to return
to their previous level jobs when economic conditions become more favour-
able? Further work is needed also to establish the extent to which jobs have
been modified to take advantage of the influx of highly educated manpower
into intermediate level occupations. Mason (1996) suggested that in Britain the
increase in new graduate supply has been so rapid that many employers are
only just beginning to adjust in this way. In a later paper (Mason, 1997), he reported that British managers found there to be a number of advantages in employing graduate engineers alongside traditional shopfloor-trained supervisors.
These included the greater ability of graduates to develop and improve computer systems used on the shop floor and to keep up with technological developments elsewhere and their key role in some plants in planning and imple-
menting new cellular work systems in conjunction with other highly qualified
staff in production engineering departments. This suggests that this kind of
apparent under-utilisation of skills should be seen as a natural part of the process of technological advance and as a permanent rather than a temporary phenomenon.

2.8 ARE PARTICULAR GROUPS VULNERABLE?

There is reason to expect that groups likely to suffer from discrimination will
find it more difficult to compete in the labour market and overeducation may
be one consequence of this.

Young workers are likely to be particularly vulnerable as new entrants into
the labour market, and the finding that overeducation is linked to lack of work
experience supports this. Thus, Dekker, de Grip and Heijke (2002) found that
in their Dutch sample the proportion of overeducated decreased from 41.7 per
cent for the 15–19 age group to 27 per cent for the 30–44 age group and 18 per
cent for the 49–64 age group.

As we saw earlier, there is reason to expect that married women in particular are likely to be vulnerable to overeducation (Frank's 1978 theory of differential overqualification), although support for this theory is rather mixed.
Another reason may be the presence of fixed costs of employment and a higher
quit rate for women than for men, implying that employers may require higher
ability from women relative to men at the hiring stage for a given job. Using

Dutch data to test this model, Renes and Ridder (1995) found that on average women require almost six months more work experience than men to be hired for the same job, implying that they are overqualified taking a broader view of human capital. In their meta-analysis, Groot and Maassen van den Brink (2000a) suggested that overeducation is more frequent among female workers than among male workers, while the opposite holds true for undereducation. Examination of those studies in Table A2.1, which differentiate their results by gender, suggests, however, that the likelihood of overeducation is not very different for men and for women, although exceptions can be found. Thus, in their study of young French workers aged 18 to 29, Forgeout and Gautie (1997) found that 24 per cent of the women, as opposed to 18 per cent of the men, were overeducated, and in the case of undereducation for Germany Bauer (2002) found that 15.6 per cent of the women as opposed to 10.4 per cent of the men (using a mean index), were undereducated.[26] Why these differences should arise across different countries and different groups is quite unclear.

Ethnic minorities may be more prone to overeducation than the white majority if there is hiring discrimination. Analysis of the relative position of ethnic minorities is, however, rare. However, Duncan and Hoffman (1981) found that about 49 per cent of black men were overeducated compared to 42 per cent of the male workforce as a whole. For the UK, Alpin, Shackleton and Walsh (1998) found that 30 per cent of non-white graduates were overeducated compared to 27 per cent of white graduates. Yet, it is important to distinguish between those ethnic minorities who are native-born and those who are foreign-born as well as the different ethnic groups. Battu and Sloane (2002) found such differences to be important. In fact, foreign qualifications, being native-born and language fluency all raise the likelihood of being both overeducated and undereducated, which does not conform to the predictions of the assimilation theory.

The analysis of particular labour market groups seems, therefore, to raise as many questions as it is able to answer.

2.9 IS OVEREDUCATION A TEMPORARY PHENOMENON?

If individuals were overeducated due to a temporary bad match or because they were substituting extra-education for other forms of human capital this may be regarded as the natural operation of the labour market and the only concern might be that these processes were taking too long.[27] If, in contrast, overeducation was a permanent phenomenon but workers were only apparently overeducated this again would not necessarily be regarded as sub-optimal, as attempting to match workers at the lower end of the ability distribution for their level of education in the sort of job that traditionally used that level of education may well lower productivity or leave such workers unemployed. Of more concern would be those who were permanently and *genuinely* overeducated, and we do not know the precise proportion of the overeducated that falls into this category.

The notion that overeducation is a temporary phenomenon is implicit in the theory of career mobility proposed by Sicherman and Galor (1990), and briefly referred to already in Section 2, which holds that part of the returns to education takes the form of a higher probability of occupational upgrading. Hence, individuals may be prepared to accept jobs with low direct returns to education if this is accompanied by a higher probability of promotion. Sicherman's (1991) own empirical tests using panel data confirmed the expectation that overeducated workers had a greater probability of promotion in terms of career moves than adequately educated workers in the US. Robst's (1995a) analysis, referred to in Section 5, found contrary to the career mobility hypothesis that overeducated workers were no more likely than adequately educated workers to receive the sort of training that would assist in the process. Büchel and Mertens (in press) tested the hypothesis for Germany on the basis of wage mobility as originally proposed in the theory developed by Sicherman and Galor (1990). Using the GSEOP they found that overeducated German workers had substantially lower rates of wage growth than adequately educated workers, as well as less access to formal and informal on-the-job training. Evidence for the career mobility model is, therefore, mixed.

What is not in doubt is that for some workers overeducation is a long-run phenomenon. Thus, for British graduates Dolton and Vignoles (2000) found that 38 per cent of 1980 graduates were overeducated in their first job and 30 per cent still were six years later in 1986. Battu, Belfield and Sloane (1999) examined panels of UK graduates from 1985 and 1990 at career points one year, six years and eleven years after graduation. They found that over these time spans about 30 per cent of graduates had never had a job that required a degree and at any given time 40 per cent were in work that did not require a degree. Both studies found that those graduating with more vocational degrees, such as engineering, science and law were more likely to be matched. Examining the whole range of occupations, Sloane, Battu and Seaman (1999) utilising work history data found again for Britain that job changes did not ensure a permanently improved match for overeducated workers, since such workers may simply move from one state of overeducation to another or fail to hold on to any short-term progress they make, in line with the notion that overeducated workers are less employable than their matched counterparts. In order to unravel these issues with more certainty we require panel datasets, which include direct questions on over- and undereducation and which are presently lacking.

2.10 CONCLUSIONS

In the introduction a series of questions were raised. In relation to the first of these—challenges to human capital theory—perhaps the major contribution of the overeducation literature has been to emphasise that it matters precisely where a worker is employed both in terms of current and future earnings and of job satisfaction. In that sense, assignment type models, which generally outperform both the unaugmented Mincer human capital model and the job competition model, serve to broaden the human capital framework. Further, it is clear that education is but one form of human capital and there are many possibilities of substitution of one type of human capital by another.

As regards the second question of measurement, interpreting labour market outcomes requires detailed knowledge of the abilities and skills of individual workers, and by themselves neither years of education completed or qualifications achieved can measure adequately worker productivity. Yet, few datasets contain direct information on both imperfect matching and worker abilities. There are also severe measurement problems which bedevil comparisons across datasets, since different measures of overeducation are poorly correlated, which results in individuals being classified differently in terms of whether they are properly matched. The use of the mode rather than the mean as a central measure for determining matching should be obligatory given asymmetry between over- and undereducation. The distinction between *apparent* and *genuine* overeducation is a fruitful line of approach, as is the incorporation of job satisfaction measures to determine the goodness of match.

Given the above, it seems that a substantial part of what is referred to in the literature as overeducation simply reflects unobserved heterogeneity of abilities and skills within given educational levels and in no way represents market failure. For policy purposes, measured overeducation should not be taken as a clear indicator of an over-production of graduates or other levels of qualifications. Part of it may, indeed, reflect measurement error through sheepskin effects. However, a question does arise as to whether some individuals are receiving too much education, considered from an investment rather than a consumption perspective. However, if overeducated workers are of low quality it is possible that the additional education compensates for the lack of their skills valued in the market and serves to gain employment, which otherwise might have been more difficult.

As for the impact of overeducation on earnings in the short- and the long-run, Sicherman's stylised fact that there is a positive wage premium to overeducation has been challenged by those studies that have been able to control adequately for worker heterogeneity, so that it appears that there is a substantial penalty on workers who are unable to find a job commensurate with their level of education. The bulk of studies that have examined the impact of mismatching on training have supported the substitutability hypothesis, with overeducated workers receiving less and undereducated workers more training than those who are properly matched. Turning to the regional dimension, it does appear that some workers are overeducated because they are prepared to trade-off labour market matching against location advantages with respect to place of residence and commuting time, but the precise size of this effect is unknown. The work on skill bumping and crowding out has shown that the effects are far from uniform over the range of skills and over the cycle. Overeducation declines with age, affects ethnic minorities to a greater degree than the majority of employees, but does not appear to affect women more than men to any marked extent. Certainly for a large group of overeducated workers this state is likely to be more a permanent than a temporary feature of their working lives.

There are many areas in which further research is required. For example, precisely how employers behave strategically in hiring workers with particular qualifications for particular jobs in the internal labour market is poorly understood. What is the significance of human capital spillovers for the job matching process? What proportion of overeducation arises from spatial factors? Is skill bumping substantial and is it a temporary or a permanent feature of the labour market? Why do the proportions of over- and undereducated workers vary so much across different countries? This is by no means an exhaustive list of questions and one which can only be answered by further research.

Would it be fair then to categorise the overeducation literature as much ado about nothing? This depends in part on the extent to which the results from those studies, which control for ability, utilise matched employer/employee samples or panel data generalise to other datasets over different time periods and across countries. Even if that were true, the overeducation literature has served to shift the focus of attention in human capital analysis away from an undue reliance on supply side issues and towards a recognition that demand side forces are no less important in determining labour market outcomes. It also suggests that the job matching process is much more complex than the earlier literature implied.

NOTES

1   Sheepskin effects are returns specific to educational credentials in contrast to accumulated years of education. The origin of the term lies in the Asian tradition in the second century BC of presenting diplomas or parchments made out of sheepskins. They are based on the hypothesis that education serves as a credential, which signals high innate productivity, with the expectation that returns to the credential decline as workers gain increased experience and employers become better informed about their actual productivity.
2   Using a unique dataset covering five countries, Denny and Harmon (2001) tested for non-linearity of schooling in a conventional earnings equation. They found that the imposition of a linear relationship in the earnings equation was not robust and that there are well-deter-

mined positive returns to the completion of educational levels, having controlled for years of schooling.

3 Mincer (1974) was well aware of this. On page 137 he states: 'The model of worker self-investment as the basic determinant of earnings might be criticised as giving undue weight to the supply of human capital while ignoring the demand side of the market. Certainly demand conditions in general and employer investments in human capital of workers in particular, affect wage rates and time spent in employment, and thereby affect earnings.' He goes on to state '... the present approach is an initial and simple one and greater methodological sophistication is clearly desirable.'

4 Dolton and Silles (2001), for example, found that arts and humanities (including languages) graduates are more likely to be overeducated than graduates from other faculties.

5 A confounding factor in the context of the overeducation literature is clear evidence of interlocking heterogeneities. That is, the relevance of factors such as abilities and personalities will differ by type of occupation.

6 Dolton and Silles (2001) suggested that one can capture this effect using two separate questions on overeducation, which distinguish between qualifications required for entering a job and qualifications required to actually do the job. In their sample of graduates only 58 per cent believed that a degree was necessary actually to do the job, while 67 per cent of them needed a degree to acquire the job, with respect to first employment.

7 Borghans and de Grip (2000b), in contrast, refer to a genuine under-utilisation of skills occurring when workers are employed in jobs in which they have lower productivity than others with the same educational background.

8 This is similar to one of the three measures used by Battu, Belfield and Sloane (2000), using the same dataset.

9 It has generally been found that overeducated graduates express lower job satisfaction than those graduates who are properly matched. Whilst confirming this, Belfield and Harris (2002) were unable to detect any relationship between degree quality and job satisfaction.

10 Unusually, they also have a question on which field of education is most appropriate for the job, finding that 20 per cent of graduates were in jobs for which their own field was not the most appropriate. However, in their regressions this variable has no significant effect on wages, job satisfaction or job search.

11 The NCDS is not ideal for this purpose, however, as it suffers from the problem of missing values and the fact that the explanatory power of the models is relatively low.

12 Thus, Dolton and Vignoles (2000) found for the UK that individuals with GCE Advanced Level Mathematics qualifications earn between 7 and 10 per cent more than similarly educated workers without this qualification, after controlling for ability.

13 Negative externalities are also possible. Thus, if co-workers are overeducated, leading to lower job satisfaction, this may have negative effects on performance or if co-workers have different amounts of human capital this could lead to skills incompatibility.

14 They also show that own earnings are higher the wider the workplace dispersion of earnings. This seems more consistent with the tournament theory in which a wider earnings spread tends to lead to greater effort, in contrast to those theories, which suggest a narrower earnings dispersion is beneficial to cooperative behaviour.

15 As Martins (2001) noted this particular dataset contains relatively few controls and is of relatively small size, which may raise the importance of unobserved heterogeneity and decrease the precision of the estimates respectively.

16 If students incur substantial debt during their course, as is increasingly the case in the UK, this may increase the pressure on them to find employment quickly and this may lead them to accept a job with educational requirements below those that they possess.

17 Given the small sample size and questions about the instruments used for identification, a degree of caution is required in interpreting these results.

18 Vahey (2000) tested the theory for Canada and likewise found only partial support for the theory.

19 The SCELI 1986 is a household survey including work histories of 6,000 individuals in six different local labour markets in the UK.

20 This is comparable to the suggestion that some workers will be underpaid because information about jobs is costly to acquire, because searchers have positive discount rates and because they also have finite time horizons. Hofler and Murphy (1992) using a stochastic frontier regression approach found for the US that workers' potential wages exceeded their actual wages for such reasons by roughly 10 per cent.

21 This, however, is not inevitable (see Borghans and de Grip, 2000).

22 For a similar approach analysing the labour market for youths in Spain see Dolado, Jimeno and Felgueroso (2000).

23 These studies ignore the possibility of crowding-out occurring through intra-firm mobility.

24 More particularly, their separate estimates for inflows and outflows show that when employment is low the average educational level of the inflow does not rise, though the average educational level of the outflow does fall. Thus, the upgrading of the skill level of the workforce results from an outflow of workers with relatively low educational qualifications.

25 For an attempt to analyse skill bumping in the context of the competing human capital and job competition models see Groot and Hoek (2000).

26 The corresponding figures for the mode index were 37.0 and 20.6 per cent respectively.

27 Timing may be critical here. Those graduating at a low point in the business cycle or when the output of graduates is relatively high are likely to face greater problems than those graduating when these conditions are reversed.

REFERENCES

Ahn, J., Sook-Jae, M., and Lee, Y.S. (2001). *Mismatch and job satisfaction of Korean workers.* Unpublished manuscript (draft version).

Alba-Ramírez, A. (1993). Mismatch in the Spanish labor market: Overeducation? *Journal of Human Resources, 27* (2), 259–278.

Allen, J., and Velden, R. van der. (2001). Educational mismatches versus skill mismatches: Effects on wages, job satisfaction and on-the-job search. *Oxford Economic Papers, 53* (3), 434–452.

Alpin, C., Shackleton, J.R., and Walsh, S. (1998). Over- and under-education in the UK graduate labour market. *Studies in Higher Education, 23* (1), 17–34.

Arkes, J. (1999). What do educational credentials signal and why do employers value credentials? *Economics of Education Review, 18*, 133–141.

Asplund, R., and Lilja, R. (2000). Has the Finnish labour market bumped the least educated? In L. Borghans and A. de Grip (Eds.), *The overeducated worker? The economics of skill utilization* (pp. 57–76). Cheltenham: Edward Elgar.

Bakker, B., Tijdens, K., and Winkels, J. (1994). Gender, occupational segregation, overeducation and wages in the Netherlands. *Netherlands Official Statistics, 14*, 36–41.

Barth, E. (2000). *External effects of education: Evidence from the wage structure.* Unpublished manuscript, Institute for Social Research, Oslo.

Batenburg, R., and de Witte, M. (2001). Underemployment in the Netherlands: How the Dutch poldermodel failed to close the education-jobs gap. *Work, Employment and Society, 15* (1), 73–94.

Battu, H., Belfield, C.R., and Sloane, P.J. (1999). Overeducation among graduates: A cohort view. *Education Economics, 7* (1), 21–38.

Battu, H., Belfield, C.R., and Sloane, P.J. (2000). Over-education: How sensitive are the measures? *National Institute Economic Review, 171*, 82–93.

Battu, H., Belfield, C.R., and Sloane, P.J. (2002). *Human capital spillovers in the workplace: Evidence for Great Britain.* Unpublished manuscript.

Battu, H., Seaman, P., and Sloane, P.J. (1999). Are married woman spatially constrained: A test of gender differentials in labour market outcomes. *European Research in Regional Science,* **9**, 91–110.

Battu, H., Seaman, P., and Sloane, P.J. (2000). The impact of regional migration on the earnings, employment and overeducation of married women in the UK. In S. Gustavsson and D. Meulders (Eds.), *Gender and the labour market: Economic evidence on obstacles in achieving gender equality.* London: Macmillan.

Battu, H., and Sloane, P.J. (2000). Overeducation and crowding out in Britain. In L. Borghans and A. de Grip (Eds.), *The overeducated worker? The economics of skill utilization* (pp. 157–174). Cheltenham: Edward Elgar.

Battu, H., and Sloane, P.J. (2002). To what extent are ethnic minorities in Britain overeducated? *International Journal of Manpower,* **23** (3), 192–208.

Bauer, T. (2002). Educational mismatch and wages: A panel analysis. *Economics of Education Review,* **21**, 221–229.

Belfield, C.R., Bullock, A.D., Chevalier, A.N., Fielding, A., Siebert, W.S., and Thomas, H.R. (1997). *Mapping the careers of highly qualified workers.* Bristol: Higher Education Founding Council for England (Research Series M10/97).

Belfield, C.R., and Harris, R.D.F. (2002). How well do theories of job matching explain variations in job satisfaction across education levels? Evidence for UK graduates. *Applied Economics,* **34** (5), 535–448.

Belman, D., and Heyward, J.S. (1997). Sheepskin effects by cohort: Implications of job matching in a signalling framework. *Oxford Economic Papers,* **49**, 623–637.

Beneito, P., Ferri, J., Molto, M.L., and Uriel, E. (1996). *Over/undereducation and on the job training in Spain: Effect on pay returns.* Paper presented at EALE, Chania, Crete.

Beneito, P., Ferri, J., Molto, M.L., and Uriel, E. (1997). *Over/undereducation and specific training in Spain: Complementary or substitute components of human capital?* Paper presented at Applied Econometrics Association, Maastricht.

Borghans, L., and de Grip, A. (Eds.). (2000a). *The overeducated worker? The economics of skill utilisation.* Cheltenham: Edward Elgar.

Borghans, L., and de Grip, A. (2000b). Skills and low pay: Upgrading or over-education? In M. Gregory, W. Salverda and S. Bazen, *Labour market inequalities* (pp. 198–224). Oxford: Oxford University Press.

Borghans, L., de Grip, A., and Sloane, P.J. (1998). Under-utilisation of skills, bumping down and low wages. In C. Lucifora and W. Salverda (Eds.), *Policies for low wage employment and social exclusion* (pp. 92–98). Milan: Franco Angeli.

Borghans, L., and Heijke, H. (1996). Forecasting the educational structure of occupations: A manpower requirement approach with substitution. *Labour,* **10** (1), 151–192.

Borghans, L., and Smits, W. (1997). *Underutilisation and wages of HVE graduates.* Unpublished manuscript, Research Center for Education and the Labour Market, Maastricht University.

Bowles, S., Gintis, H., and Osborne, M. (2001). The determinants of earnings. A behavioral approach. *Journal of Economic Literature,* **XXXIX**, 1137–1176.

Büchel, F. (1994). Overqualification at the beginning of a non academic working career. The efficiency of the German Dual System under test. *Konjunkturpolitik,* **40** (3–4), 342–368.

Büchel, F. (2000). Tied movers, tied stayers: The higher risk of overeducation among married women in West Germany. In S.S. Gustafsson and D.E. Meulders (Eds.), *Gender and the labour market* (pp. 133–146). London: Macmillan (Applied Econometrics Association Series).

Büchel, F. (2001). Overqualification: Reasons, measurement issues, and typographical affinity to unemployment. In P. Descy and M. Tessaring (Eds.), *Training in Europe: Second report on vocational training research in Europe 2000* (Vol. 2, pp. 453–560). Luxembourg: Office for Official Publications of the European Communities.

Büchel, F. (2002). The effects of overeducation on productivity in Germany: The firm's viewpoint. *Economics of Education Review,* **21**, 263–276.

Büchel, F., and Battu, H. (2003). The theory of differential overqualification: Does it work? *Scottish Journal of Political Economy,* **50**, 1–16.

Büchel, F., and Mertens, A. (in press). Overeducation, undereducation and the theory of career mobility. Applied Economics.

Büchel, F., and Pollmann-Schult, M. (2001). *Overeducation and skill endowments: The role of school achievement and vocational training quality.* Bonn: Forschungsinstitut zur Zukunft der Arbeit (IZA Discussion Paper 337).

Büchel, F., and van Ham, M. (in press). Overeducation, regional labour markets and spatial flexibility. *Journal of Urban Economics.*

Bulmahn, G., and Kräkel, M. (2000). Over-educated workers as an insurance device. *Labour,* **16** (2), 383–402.

Burris, V. (1983). The social and political consequences of overeducation. *American Sociological Review,* **48**, 454–467.

Chevalier, A. (2000). *Graduate over-education in the UK.* London: Centre for the Economics of Education (CEE Discussion Paper 7).

Cockx, B., and Dejeineppe. M. (2002). *Do the higher educated unemployed crowd out the lower educated ones in a competition for jobs?* Bonn: Forschungsinstitut zur Zukunft der Arbeit (IZA Discussion Paper 541).

Cohn, E. (1992). The impact of surplus schooling on earnings. *Journal of Human Resources,* **27** (4), 679–682.

Cohn, E., and Kahn, S. (1995). The wage effects of overschooling revisited. *Labour Economics,* **2**, 67–76.

Cohn, E., and Ng, Y.C. (2000). Incidence and wage effects of overschooling and underschooling in Hong Kong. *Economics of Education Review,* **19**, 159–168.

Daly, M., Büchel, F., and Duncan, G. (2000). Premiums and penalties for surplus and deficit education: Evidence from the United States and Germany. *Economics of Education Review,* **19**, 169–178.

De Jong, G.F., and Madamba, A. (2001). The double disadvantage? Minority group, immigrant status, and underemployment in the United States. *Social Science Quarterly,* **82** (1), 117 –130.

De Oliveira, M., Santos, M.C., and Kiker, B.F. (2000). The role of human capital and technological change in overeducation. *Economics of Education Review,* **19**, 199– 206.

Dekker, R., de Grip, A., and Heijke, H. (2002). The effects of training and over-education on career mobility in a sequential labour market. *International Journal of Manpower,* **23** (2), 106–136.

Denny, K.J., and Harmon, C.P. (2001). Testing for sheepskin effects in earnings equations: Evidence for 5 countries. *Applied Economics Letters,* **8** (9), 635–637.

Dickens, W., and Katz, L. (1986). Inter industry wage differences and industry characteristics. In K. Lang and J. Leonard (Eds.), *Unemployment and the structure of labour markets* (pp. 48–89). London: Blackwell.

Dolado, J.J., Jimeno, J.F., and Felgueroso, F. (2000). Youth labour markets in Spain: Education, training and crowding out. *European Economic Review,* 44, 943–956.

Dolton, P., and Silles, M. (2001). *Over-education in the graduate labour market: Some evidence from alumni data.* London: Centre for the Economics of Education (CEE Discussion Paper 9).

Dolton, P., and Vignoles, A. (1997). *Overeducation duration: How long did graduates in the 1980s take to get a graduate job?* Unpublished manuscript.

Dolton, P., and Vignoles, A. (2000). The incidence and effects of overeducation in the U.K. graduate labour market. *Economics of Education Review,* 19, 179–198.

Duncan, G.J., and Hoffman, S.D. (1981). The incidence and wage effects of overeducation. *Economics of Education Review,* 1, 75–86.

Evans, P. (1999). Occupational downgrading and upgrading in Britain. *Economica,* 66 (261), 79–96.

Forgeout, G., and Gautie, J. (1997). *Overeducation in the youth labour market in France.* Paper presented at Applied Econometrics Association, Maastricht.

Frank, R.H. (1978). Why women earn less: The theory and estimation of differential overqualification. *American Economic Review,* 68 (3), 360–373.

Freeman, R. (1976). *The overeducated American.* New York: Academic Press.

García-Serrano, C., and Malo-Ocana, M. (1996). *Educational mismatch and internal labour markets: Is there any relationship?* Essex: ESRC Research Centre on Micro-Social Change (Working Paper 96–12).

García-Serrano, C., and Malo-Ocana, M. (2001). *Educational mismatch and expected promotions.* Unpublished manuscript (draft version).

Gautier, P.A., van den Berg, G.S., van Ours, J.C., and Ridder, G. (2002). Worker turnover at the firm level and crowing out of less educated workers. *European Economic Review,* 46 (3), 523–538.

Gottschalk, P., and Hansen, M., (2000). *Is the proportion of college workers in 'non-college' jobs increasing?* Unpublished manuscript (draft version).

Green, F., McIntosh, S., and Vignoles, A. (1999). *Overeducation and skills: Clarifying the concepts.* London: Centre for Economic Performance (Discussion Paper 435).

Groot, W. (1993). Overeducation and the returns to enterprise-related schooling. *Economics of Education Review,* 12 (4), 299–309.

Groot, W. (1996). The incidence of, and returns to overeducation in the UK. *Applied Economics,* 28, 1345–1350.

Groot, L., and Hoek, A. (2000). Job competition in the Dutch labour market. In L. Borghans, and A. de Grip, *The overeducated worker? The economics of skill utilisation* (pp. 231–252). Cheltenham: Edward Elgar.

Groot, W., and Maassen van den Brink, H. (2000a). Overeducation in the labor market: A meta analysis. *Economics of Education Review,* 19, 149–158.

Groot, W., and Maassen van den Brink, H. (2000b). Skill mismatches in the Dutch labour market. *International Journal of Manpower,* 21 (8), 584–595.

Groshen, E.L. (1991a). Sources of inter-industry wage dispersion: How much do employers matter? *Quarterly Journal of Economics,* CVI (3), 869–884.

Groshen, E.L. (1991b). Five reasons why wages vary across employers. *Industrial Relations,* 30 (3), 350–381.

Gurgaud, H.C. (1999). *Schooling and unemployment: Is there job competition on the French labour market?* Unbublished manuscript, CREST, Paris.

Hartog, J. (1977). On the multicapability theory of economic distribution. *European Economic Review,* **10**, 157–171.

Hartog, J. (1986). Earnings functions: Beyond human capital. *Applied Economics,* **18**, 1291–1309.

Hartog, J. (1988). Allocation and the earnings function. *Empirical Economics,* **11** (2), 97–110.

Hartog, J. (1997). *On returns to education: Wandering along the hills of Oru Land.* Paper presented at Applied Econometrics Association, Maastricht.

Hartog, J. (2000). Over-education and earnings: Where are we, where should we go? *Economics of Education Review,* **19**, 131–147.

Hartog, J. (2001). On human capital and individual capabilities. *Review of Income and Wealth,* **47** (4), 515–540.

Hartog, J., and Oosterbeek, H. (1988). Education, allocation and earnings in the Netherlands: Overschooling? *Economics of Education Review,* **7** (2), 185–194.

Hartog, J., and Oosterbeek, H. (1998). Health, wealth and happiness: Why pursue a higher education? *Economics of Education Review,* **17** (3), 245–256.

Hartog, J., Perreira, P.T., and Veira, J.A.C. (2001). Changing returns to education in Portugal during the 1980s and early 1990s: OLS and quantile regression Estimators. *Applied Economics,* **33** (8), 1021–1037.

Hersch, J. (1993). Education match and job match. *Review of Economics and Statistics,* **73**, 140–144.

Hersch, J. (1995). Optimal mismatch and promotions. *Economic Inquiry,* **33**, 611– 624.

Hofler, R.A., and Murphy, K.J. (1992). Under-paid and over-worked: Measuring the effect of imperfect information on wages. *Economic Inquiry,* **XXX**, 511–529.

Kiker, B.F., Santos, M.C., and De Oliveira, M. (1997). Overeducation and under-education: Evidence for Portugal. *Economics of Education Review,* **16** (2), 111–125.

Krueger, A.B., and Summers, L.H. (1987). Reflections on the inter-industry wage structure. In K. Lang and J. Leonard (Eds.), *Unemployment and the structure of labour markets* (pp. 17–47). London: Blackwell.

Lassibille, G., Gomez, L.N., Ramos, L.A., and Sanchez, C.D. (2001). Youth transition from school to work in Spain. *Economics of Education Review,* **20** (2), 139–149.

Lissenburgh, S., and Bryson, A. (1996). *The returns to graduation.* London: Department for Education and Employment (DfEE Research Series).

Madamba, A., and De Jong, G.F. (1997). Job mismatch among Asians in the United States: Ethnic group comparisons. *Social Science Quarterly,* **78** (2), 524–542.

Martins, P. (2001). *Wage impacts of schooling mismatches: Evidence from a matched employer-employee panel.* Unpublished manuscript, University of Warwick.

Mason, G. (1996). Graduate utilisation in British industry: The initial impact of mass higher education. *National Institute Economic Review, May,* 93–101.

Mason, G. (1997). *Back from the dead again? Production supervisors in the United States, Britain and Germany.* London: National Institute of Economic and Social Research (Discussion Paper 120).

McGoldrick, K., and Robst, J. (1996). Gender differences in overeducation, a test of the theory of differential overqualification. *American Economic Review,* **86** (2), 280–284.

McGuinness, S. (2002). Private sector post graduate training and graduate under-employment: Evidence from Northern Ireland. *International Journal of Manpower,* **23** (6), 527–541.

Meer van der, P., and Wielers, R. (1996). Educational credentials and trust in the labour market. *Kyklos,* **49**, 29–46.

Mincer, J. (1974). *Schooling, experience and earnings.* New York: Columbia University Press.

Mincer, J. (1983). *Over-education or under-education.* New York: Columbia University (Discussion Paper 248).

Muysken, J., and Ruholl, J. (2001). *The impact of education and mismatch on wages: The Netherlands, 1986–1998.* Maastricht: MERIT Research Memorandum 2001-030.

Nicaise, I. (2000). The effects of bumping down on wages: An empirical test. In L. Borghans and A. de Grip (Eds.), *The overeducated worker? The economics of skill utilization* (pp. 175–190). Cheltenham: Edward Elgar.

Nickell, S., and Bell, B. (1995). The collapse in demand for the unskilled and unemployment across the OECD. *Oxford Review of Economic Policy,* **11** (1), 40–62.

Oosterbeek, H. (2000). Introduction to special issue on overschooling. *Economics of Education Review,* **18** (2), 129–131.

Patrinos, H.A. (1997). Overeducation in Greece. *International Review of Education,* **43** (2–3), 203–224.

Renes, G., and Ridder, G. (1995). Are women overqualified? *Labour Economics,* **2**, 3–18.

Robinson, P. (1995). *Qualifications and the labour market: Do the national training and education targets make sense?* London: Centre for Economic Performance (Working Paper 736).

Robst, J. (1995a). Career mobility, job match, and overeducation. *Eastern Economic Journal,* **2** (4), 539–550.

Robst, J. (1995b). College quality and overeducation. *Economics of Education Review,* **14** (3), 221–228.

Roy, A.D. (1951). Some thoughts on the distribution of earnings. *Oxford Economic Papers,* **3**, 135–146.

Rumberger, R.W. (1981a). *Overeducation in the US labor market.* New York: Praeger.

Rumberger, R.W. (1981b). The rising incidence of overeducation in the US labor market. *Economics of Education Review,* **1** (3), 293–314.

Rumberger, R.W. (1987). The impact of surplus schooling on producitivity and earnings. *The Journal of Human Resources,* **22** (1), 24–50.

Sattinger, M. (1993). Assignment models of the distribution of earnings. *Journal of Economic Literature,* **LXXXI**, 831–880.

Shockey, J.W. (1989). Over-education and earnings: A structural approach to differential attainment in the US labour force (1970–1982). *American Sociological Review,* **54**, 856–868.

Sicherman, N. (1991). Overeducation in the labor market. *Journal of Labor Economics,* **9** (2), 101–122.

Sicherman, N., and Galor, O. (1990). A theory of career mobility. *Journal of Political Economy,* **98** (1), 169–192.

Sloane, P.J., Battu, H., and Seaman, P. (1996). Overeducation and the formal education/experience and training trade-off. *Applied Economics Letters,* **3**, 511–515.

Sloane, P.J., Battu, H., and Seaman, P. (1999). Overeducation, undereducation and the British labour market. *Applied Economics,* **31**, 1437–1453.

Smith, H.L. (1986). Over-education and under-employment: An agnostic view. *Sociology of Education,* **59**, 85–89.

Teulings, C., and Koopmanschap, M. (1989). An econometric model of crowding out of lower education levels. *European Economic Review,* **33**, 1653–1664.

Thurow, L.C. (1975). *Generating inequality.* New York: Basic Books.

Tinbergen, J. (1956). On the theory of income distribution. *Weltwirtschaftliches Archiv,* **LXXVII**, 156–175.

Tsang, M.C. (1987). The impact of underutilization on productivity: A case study of the U.S. bell companies. *Economics of Education Review,* **6**, 239–254.

Tsang, M.C., and Levin, H.M. (1985). The economics of over-education. *Economics of Education Review,* **4** (2), 93–104.

Tsang, M.C., Rumberger, R.W., and Levin, H.M. (1993). The impact of surplus schooling on workers productivity. *Industrial Relations,* **30** (2), 209–228.

Vahey, S.P. (2000). The great Canadian training robbery: Evidence on the returns to education mismatch. *Economics of Education Review,* **19**, 219–227.

Van der Velden, R. K.W., and van Smoorenburg, M.S.M. (1997). *The measurement of overeducation and undereducation: Self-report versus the job-analyst method.* Mimeo, University of Maastricht.

Van de Werfhorst, H.G., and Andersen, R. (2002). *Social background, credential inflation, and education Strategies.* Unpublished manuscript (draft version).

Van Ours J.C., and Ridder, G. (1995). Job making and job competition: Are lower educated worker at the back of job queues? *European Economics Review,* **39**, 1717–1731.

Van Smoorenburg, M.S.M., and van der Velden, R.K.W. (2000). The training of school leavers, complementarity and substitution. *Economics of Education Review,* **19**, 207–217.

Verdugo, R.R., and Verdugo, N.T. (1989). The impact of surplus schooling on earnings: Some additional findings. *The Journal of Human Resources,* **24** (4), 629–643.

Verhaest, D., and Omey, E. (2002). *Overeducation in the Flemish youth labour market.* Gent: University of Gent (Working Paper 141).

Wachtel, M.H., and Betsey, C. (1972). Employment at low wages. *Review of Economics and Statistics,* **54** (2), 121–129.

Winter-Ebmer, R., and Zweimueller, J. (1997). Unequal assignment and promotion in job ladders. *Journal of Labor Economics,* **15** (1), 43–71.

APPENDIX

Table 2A.1 Summary of mismatch estimates

Author(s)	Country	Time Period	Dataset	Measure(s)	Estimates and Comments
Duncan and Hoffman (1981)	US	1976	PSID	Subjective	46.1% AE, 11.9% UE, 42.0% OE
Burris (1983)	US	1977–1978	National Sample Survey	Objective	21.7% OE, 22.7% (men), 20.1% (women)
Rumberger (1987)	US	1969, 1973, 1977	Quality of Employment Surveys	Objective	OE 1969: 35%, 1973: 27%, 1977: 32%
Hartog and Oosterbeek (1988)	Netherlands	1960, 1971, 1974	Dutch Census and Labour Force Surveys	Objective—job analyst (ARB1 code) and subjective	Objective 1960: OE 7%, UE 35.6%, AE 57.5% 1971: OE 13.6%, UE 27.1%, AE 59.3% Subjective 1974: 17% OE, 30% UE, 53% AE
Verdugo and Verdugo (1989)	US	1980	US Census	Standard deviation	10.9% OE, 9.9% UE, 79.2% AE
Sicherman (1991)	US	1976, 1978	PSID	Subjective	44% AE, 16% UE, 40% OE
Alba-Ramírez (1993)	Spain	1985	The Living and Working Conditions Survey (ECVT)	Subjective	60% AE, 23% UE, 17% OE
Groot (1993)	Netherlands	1983	Brabant Survey	Standard deviation	16.3% UE, 67.5% AE, 16.1% OE
Robst (1995)	US	1976, 1978, 1985	PSID	Subjective	Pooled estimates for 3 years: 36% OE, 20% UE, 44% AE
Hersch (1995)	US	1991	Survey of Private Firm in Wyoming	Self-assessment and subjective	Self-assessment: 58% AE, 29% OE, 13% UE Subjective:
Cohn and Kahn (1995)	US	1984	PSID	Subjective and standard deviation	Subjective: 33% OE, 20% UE, 47% AE Standard dev.: 13% OE, 12% UE, 75% AE
García-Serrano and Malo-Ocana (1996)	Spain	1991	Survey of Class Structure (ECBC)	Subjective	26.9% OE, 33% UE, 40.1% AE

Table 2A.1 Summary of mismatch estimates continued

Author(s)	Country	Time Period	Dataset	Measure(s)	Estimates and Comments
Groot (1996)	UK	1991	BHPS	Standard deviation	11% OE, 9% UE, 80% AE Men: 13% OE, 10% UE, 77% AE Wemen: 10% OE, 8% UE, 82% AE
Kiker, Santos and de Oliveira (1997)	Portugal	1991	Personnel Records collected by Ministry of Labor	Standard deviation; modal; objective	Combined: OE 9.4%, 25.5%, 33.1% UE 5%, 17%, 37.5% AE 85.6%, 57.5%, 29.4% Men: OE 10.9%, 25.5%, 28.8% UE 5.3%, 16.0%, 44.2% AE 83.8%, 58.4%, 27.0% Women: OE 6.9%, 25.3%, 40% UE 4.7%, 18.7%, 25.9% AE 88.4%, 56.0%, 33.7%
Dolton and Vignoles (1997, 2000)	UK	1980, 1986	1980 National Survey of Graduates and Diplomates	Subjective	38% of graduates OE in first job and 30% OE in final job
Forgeout and Gautie (1997)	France	1995	French Employment Survey	Objective	OE in French youth (18–29 years old). 18% of young men OE and 24% of young women OE
Beneito et al. (1997)	Spain	1985, 1990	Survey of Class Structure (ECBC)	Standard deviation, subjective (both 1990 and self-classification) (1985)	OE: 15.2%, 25.6%, 27.9% AE: 69.4%, 58%, 61.3% UE: 15.3%, 16.5%, 10.9%
Alpin, Shackleton and Walsh (1997)	UK	1995	Labor Force Survey (graduates only)	Two objective measures—degree required (yes/no) modal	55.2% AE, 17.8% UE, 27% OE 53.9% AE, 8.4% UE, 37.7% OE

Table 2A.1 Summary of mismatch estimates continued

Author(s)	Country	Time Period	Dataset	Measure(s)	Estimates and Comments
Battu, Belfield and Sloane (1999)	UK	1986, 1991, 1996	Careers of Highly Qualified Workers Surveys (graduates)	Degree required (yes/no)	1985 Graduates 37.6% OE in 1986 (men), 46.4% (women) 39.6% OE in 1991 (men), 39.0% (women) 41.5% OE in 1996 (men), 40.1% (women) 1990 Graduates 41.6% OE in 1991 (men), 45.3% (women) 41.3% OE in 1996 (men), 39.3% (women)
Sloane, Battu and Seaman (1999)	UK	1986	SCELI	Subjective	17% OE, 31% UE, 52% AE
Green, McIntosh and Vignoles (1999)	UK	1995	National Child Development Survey	Subjective	47.4% OE, 1.9% UE, 35.1% AE
Chevalier (2000)	UK	1986, 1991, 1996	Careers of Highly Qualified Workers Survey	(1) Objective, (2) Subjective, degree required (yes/no), (3) Subjective, based on satisfaction	OE Cohort (1) (2) (3) Male 1985 13.0% 33.8% 12.7% 1990 18.9% 33.8% 20.0% Female 1985 14.7% 30.9% 14.4% 1990 21.6% 30.9% 17.4%
Groot and Maassen van den Brink (2000)	Netherlands	1994	Sixth Wave of the Dutch; OSA Labor Market Survey	(1) Standard deviation (2) Objective (3) Subjective	Men Women (1) 11.5% OE 12.2% OE (2) 12.3% OE 19.5% OE (3) 8.7% OE 13.6% OE (1) 16.7% UE 14.3% UE (2) 13.3% UE 5.7% UE (3) 3.8% UE 2.1% UE (1) 71.8% AE 73.5% AE (2) 74.4% AE 74.8% AE (3) 87.5% AE 84.3% AE

Table 2A.1 Summary of mismatch estimates continued

Author(s)	Country	Time Period	Dataset	Measure(s)	Estimates and Comments
Daly, Büchel and Duncan (2000)	US, Germany	1976, 1985, 1984	Panel Study of Income Dynamics; German Socio-Economic Panel	Subjective	1976 US 1985 US 38.5% OE (men) 31.8% OE (men) 36.8% OE (women) 33.5% OE (women) 16.3% UE (men) 21.2% UE (men) 11.3% UE (women) 16.8% UE (women) 45.2% AE (men) 47.0% AE (men) 52.0% AE (women) 49.7% AE (women) 1984 Germany 14.3% OE (men) 20.7% OE (women) 6.9% UE (men) 7.4% UE (women) 78.8% AE (men) 71.9% AE (women)
De Oliveira, Santos and Kiker (2000)	Portugal	1991	Ministry of Employment Survey of Business Firms	Adequate = level shared by at least 60% of workers in that occupation (modal value)	Mean years of adequate schooling: 4.040 Mean years of over schooling: 1.106 Mean years of under schooling: 0.132
Van Smoorenburg and van der Velden (2000)	Netherlands	1996	STOA (School leavers) Survey	Subjective	26% OE, 2% UE, 72% AE
Vahey (2000)	Canada	1982	National Survey of Class Structure and Labour Process	Subjective	30% OE men, 32% OE women 24% UE men, 17% UE women For those aged under 26 57% AE men, 33% AE women

44

Table 2A.1 Summary of mismatch estimates continued

Author(s)	Country	Time Period	Dataset	Measure(s)	Estimates and Comments
Cohn and Ng (2000)	Hong Kong	1986, 1991	Hong Kong by Census 1986 and Census 1991	Standard deviation (modal value)	Men 1986 38% OE, 28% UE, 35% AE; Women 1986 32% OE, 24% UE, 44% AE; Men 1991 37% OE, 28% UE, 35% AE; Women 1991 31% OE, 23% UE, 44% AE
Dolton and Silles (2001)	UK	1998 (variable dates)	University of Newcastle Alumni Survey	Subjective	42% OE first job in terms of degree being 22% OE current job necessary to do the work (33% did not require a degree to *get* a job)
Allen and van der Velden (2001)	Netherlands	1998	High Education and Graduates Employment in Europe Survey	Subjective	33% OE total sample, 14% UE higher vocational education graduates, 8% UE University graduates
Bauer (2002)	Germany	1984–1998	German Socio-Economic Panel	Standard deviation using both mean and modal values	Mean index: Men 12.3% OE, 10.4% UE; Women 10.7% OE, 15.6% UE. Mode index: Men 30.8% OE, 20.6% UE; Women 29.9% OE, 37.0% UE
McGuinness (2002)	Northern Ireland	1997–2000	Telephone Survey of Graduates	Subjective	29% OE first job 24% OE current job
Dekker, de Grip and Heijke (2002)	Netherlands	1992	Labour Supply Survey (OSA)	Subjective	OE by age groups 15–19 = 41.7%, 30–44 = 27.0%, 49–64 = 18.0%, overall 30.6%

PART ONE

Mobility

3. The Dynamics of Skill Mismatches in the Dutch Labour Market

Wim Groot and
Henriëtte Maassen van den Brink

3.1 INTRODUCTION

There is a growing literature on the incidence and returns to overeducation. Groot and Maassen van den Brink (2000) provide a meta-analysis of overeducation studies. The overall incidence of overeducation in all studies included in this meta-analysis is about 26 per cent. The incidence of overeducation also appears to be stable over time: The percentage of workers that are overeducated does not seem to have changed significantly over the past decades.

Most of the research on overeducation is motivated by the concern that the rise in the educational attainment of the labour force may have outpaced the growth in jobs for higher-educated workers. If so, higher-educated workers may have displaced lower-skilled workers. Workers are overeducated if the skills they bring to their job exceed the skills required for that job. With overeducation the allocation of skills over jobs is less than optimal. The result is that educational skills are under-utilised. From an educational policy point of view this may implicate that too many resources are spent on (higher) education.

Two possible explanations can be given for the existence of overeducation. First, overeducation may be a compensation for the lack of other human capital endowments, such as ability, on-the-job training or experience. This hypothesis is empirically tested in Groot (1993). In this paper it is found that correctly allocated workers have the highest probability of participation in firm-related training, while this probability is lowest for undereducated workers. No evidence is found for overeducation and firm-related training being either substitutes or complements. These findings do not seem to support the compensation hypothesis.

Support for the compensation hypothesis is found in Groot and Maassen van den Brink (1996). This study finds that workers who have experienced a career interruption—such as women with dependent children—are more likely to be in jobs for which they are overeducated. This also suggests that over-education compensates for the lack of other productive skills (in this case loss of human capital due to career interruptions). Similar conclusions can be drawn from Groot (1993, 1996) and Sicherman (1991). These studies find that over-educated workers have less experience, tenure and on-the-job training than correctly allocated workers. In Groot and Maassen van den Brink (1997) it was found that on balance misallocations on the labour market tend to decrease with labour market experience. Simulations indicate that an increase in age and ex-perience of all workers in the labour market decreases both years of over-education and years of undereducation. This also suggests that overeducation is for many workers a temporary phenomenon.

The second explanation is that overeducation is part of a career mobility or insertion process in the labour market. Workers may enter the labour market in jobs for which they are overeducated and later on move to jobs that better match their educational attainment. Sicherman (1991) hypothesises that over-education may be part of a career mobility process. Workers temporarily accept jobs for which they are overeducated in exchange for training that helps them in their future career.

Robst (1995), Dekker, de Grip and Heijke (2002) and Büchel and Mertens (in press) provide a test for the career mobility hypothesis. Robst (1995) found that overeducated workers were more likely to move to better jobs over time. However, contrary to the career mobility hypothesis, overeducated workers are less likely to state that the skills that they acquire will help them in their future jobs. In Sicherman (1991) it was also found that overeducated workers change jobs more frequently. This supports the hypothesis that over-education is part of a phase of insertion and adaptation in the early stages of the working life.

Dekker, de Grip and Heijke (2002) analysed the effects of overeducation and training on promotion within the firm. It was found that overeducation had a positive effect on the probability of being promoted to a higher-level job. They concluded from this that overeducation is partly a temporary phe-nomenon. Contrary to this, Dolton and Vignoles (2000) found that a signifi-cant portion (30%) of university graduates are overqualified six years after graduation.

The findings in Büchel and Mertens (in press) also point at rejection of the career-mobility hypothesis. Using data for Germany this study found that over-educated workers are less likely to experience upward occupational mobility or above average wage growth than correctly allocated workers. This study fur-ther found that overeducated workers are less likely to receive on-the-job train-ing and are less likely to learn skills that are beneficial for promotion.

Groot and Maassen van den Brink (1997) found evidence that supported the career mobility or insertion hypothesis. This study concludes that the incidence of overeducation is higher among younger age cohorts, but that this effect is offset by the fadening of overeducation with years of labour market experience. Groot (1996) and Groot and Maassen van den Brink (1996) found that—after controlling for experience—younger workers are more likely to be over-educated than older workers.

In conclusion, the evidence on the career mobility hypothesis is mixed. There is some indirect evidence to support this hypothesis. However, more direct tests point at a rejection of the career mobility hypothesis.

With internal labour market and hiring on the external labour market for entry positions only, workers may enter the labour market in a job for which they are overqualified, gradually move to a job which matches their qualifica-tions and eventually—after acquiring the necessary human capital through experience and on-the-job training—end in a job for which they are under-qualified. If this is true, we may expect that overeducation decreases with internal mobility (promotion) and tenure at the firm. In that case, overeducation is only a temporary state of affairs and can be seen as part of an insertion process in the labour market.

Persistent overeducation—on the other hand—may reflect a cohort effect. If the growth in the education level of the labour force is greater than the growth in the educational quality of jobs, higher-educated workers may displace lower-educated workers and overeducation will increase. For the younger, higher-educated cohorts there are relatively less high qualified jobs than for the older cohorts. Younger cohorts are, therefore, more likely to be permanently in jobs for which they are overeducated.

The question addressed in this paper is what determines the dynamics of job-skill mismatches in the labour market? To answer this question we look both at the determinants of the incidence of overeducation and the determinants of the entry in and exit from overeducation. The data we use are taken from a large longitudinal sample for the Netherlands, the Organisation for Strategic Labor Market Research (OSA) survey 1994 to 1996. The availability of longi-tudinal data allow us to control for unobservable individual heterogeneity in the incidence of overeducation. We account for unobservable individual hetero-geneity in the incidence of overeducation by estimating random effects probit models. Some light is shed on the dynamics of overeducation by testing whether the impact (i.e., the coefficients) of some essential variables—such as job-to-job mobility and internal mobility within the firms—on the incidence of overeducation varies between individuals.

Next, we analyse the determinants of the entry in and the exit from over-education. Transitions in and out of overeducation are estimated with a Markov type model. These analyses allow us to answer whether the determinants of the transition into overeducation (conditional on not being overeducated) differ from the determinants of the transition out of overeducation (conditional on being overeducated). This gives us another perspective on the dynamics of overeducation.

Thirdly, we distinguish between different degrees of overeducation, that is, workers who are overeducated in one of the two periods we observe, workers who are overeducated in both periods and workers who are overeducated in neither of the two periods. We use a multinomial logit model to analyse the determinants of the persistence of overeducation.

Finally, we look at the reverse effects: Does overeducation have an impact on labour market dynamics? Probit equations are estimated to determine the impact of overeducation on the chance of job-to-job mobility and promotion.

3.2 DATA AND DEFINITION OF OVEREDUCATION

The data for the empirical analysis are taken from the sixth and the seventh wave of the Dutch OSA-Labour Market Survey, conducted in the Fall of 1994 and 1996 respectively. The OSA-Labour Market Survey is, in part, a longitudinal survey of individuals who participated in one of the five previous waves, which were conducted bi-annually between 1985 and 1996. Because of sample attrition, the longitudinal part of each wave of the survey is supplemented by observations from a cross section of the population aged 15 to 65 years.

We select individuals who are in paid employment at the time of the interview. The total sample size is 3,917 observations. In the transition models only the respondents who participated in both the 1994 and the 1996 wave of the survey are included. This reduces the sample size to 1,861 observations.

Overeducation is based on a self-report on skill mismatches by the respondents of the OSA survey. Workers are first asked to assess the quality of the match between the job and their education. ('How do you evaluate the match between your work and your education?' Is this 'good,' 'reasonable,' 'poor' or 'bad'?) Workers who do not qualify the match as being 'good' are then asked in what respect the match is less than optimal. They can indicate if their education level is higher than required for the job and if their education level is lower than required for the job.

3.3   RESULTS

3.3.1 Descriptive Analyses

In Table 3.1 some descriptive statistics are presented on the dynamics of skill mismatches. From this Table we can conclude that the incidence of overeduca-

Table 3.1 Cross tabulation of overeducation in 1994 and overeducation in 1996 (in %)

	Not overeducated in 1996	Overeducated in 1996	Total
Not overeducated in 1996	85.1	5.0	90.1
Overeducated in 1996	5.8	4.1	9.9
Total	90.9	9.1	100.0

tion is fairly stable over time: both in 1994 and 1996 around 10 per cent of the workforce classified themselves as being overeducated.

Underlying this stability in the incidence of skill mismatches is a fair amount of dynamics, however. Table 3.1 shows that more than 40 per cent of the workers who were overeducated in 1994 were no longer overeducated in 1996. Of the workers who were not overeducated in 1994, a little over 5 per cent classified themselves as overeducated two years later.

Next, we turn to the explanatory analyses. In the equations we control for a number of individual, job- and firm-related characteristics. We include seven dummy variables for the highest education level attained. Other individual characteristics include: gender, marital status, hours of work, age, tenure and a dummy for the year of observation (when applicable). The job-related characteristics include dummy variables for the amount of induction training required for the job, the number of workers supervised and whether the worker received firm-related training during the two years preceding the interview. We also include a variable for the job level. This variable runs from 1 (simple work) to 5 (complex and specialised work). The firm-related characteristics are seven dummy variables for industry and a variable for firm size. Finally, we include two variables for mobility: one for job-to-job mobility and one for mobility within the firm.

We expect the incidence of overeducation to increase with education level and to decline with job level. Other indicators of the complexity of the job—such as the amount of induction training needed and the number of workers supervised—are also expected to have a negative effect on the incidence of overeducation. If overeducation is a substitute for the lack of other productive characteristics, we expect negative effects from hours of work, tenure, age and participation in firm-related training. If mobility is toward a better allocation between skills supplied and skills required, we expect that job-to-job mobility and internal mobility both have a negative effect on the incidence of overeducation.

3.3.2 Random Effects Model

To analyse the determinants of overeducation a random effect ordered probit model is estimated. A random effects model allows us to assess whether the impact of relevant variables—such as job-to-job mobility, internal mobility within the firm, job level and tenure—on the incidence of overeducation varies between individuals. It also gives us an estimate of the inter-temporal correlation of overeducation.

The random effects model is estimated by a maximum marginal likelihood estimation (see Agresti and Lang, 1993). For details about the maximum marginal likelihood estimation procedure, see Hedeker and Gibbons (1994). The estimation was done with MIXOR, a Fortran-based computer programme for mixed-effects ordinal regression analysis (Hedeker and Gibbons, 1996).

The parameter estimates of the random effects probit equations on overeducation are found in Table 3.2. The probability of being overeducated increases with the level of education and decreases with job level as expected. We further find that the incidence of overeducation decreases with hours of work and tenure at the current firm. If part-time workers are less productive than full-time workers and productivity increases with tenure these findings are consistent with the view that overeducation compensates for the lack of other productive characteristics. Relative to workers in jobs that require more induction training, workers in jobs that require only one day of induction training are more likely to be overeducated than workers in jobs that require more induction training. However, this finding is conditional on the complexity of the job as measured by the job level. We further find no statistically significant differences in the incidence of overeducation between industries, by firm size and between male and female workers. We do find a statistically significant effect of marital status: Workers who are married or cohabiting are less likely to be overeducated. A possible explanation for this is that married workers have more financial obligations and are, therefore, more keen on searching for a better paid job that match their skills.

If we look at our mobility variables we find that neither a change of employers in the two years prior to the interview *(job-to-job mobility)*, nor a change of jobs with the same employer during this period *(internal mobility)* has a statistically significant effect on being overeducated.

We further find that the intercept term and the coefficients for tenure and job level should be treated as random effects, that is, the impact of these variables on overeducation varies over individual workers. The inter-temporal correlation coefficient is 0.54, indicating that overeducation in the first period is strongly, but not perfectly, correlated with being overeducated in the second period as well.[1]

Both for tenure and job level we find that the variance terms are about the same size as the coefficients for tenure and job level. This indicated that the dif-

Table 3.2   *Parameter estimates (random) effects probit equation on the incidence of overeducation (standard errors in brackets)*

	I		II		III		IV	
Intercept	0.344	(0.244)	0.379	(0.370)	0.534	(0.370)	0.361	(0.384)
Highest education level (reference category: lower vocational education)								
Primary education	−0.251*	(0.116)	−0.324	(0.186)	−0.365*	(0.180)	−0.318	(0.188)
Lower secondary education	0.185	(0.100)	0.239	(0.161)	0.256	(0.159)	0.236	(0.164)
Intermediate secondary edu.	0.439**	(0.166)	0.527*	(0.247)	0.646**	(0.240)	0.486*	(0.256)
Higher secondary education	0.739**	(0.149)	1.045**	(0.262)	1.053**	(0.286)	1.035**	(0.268)
Intermediate vocational edu.	0.393**	(0.089)	0.492**	(0.142)	0.556**	(0.140)	0.494**	(0.143)
Higher vocational education	0.711**	(0.113)	0.883**	(0.180)	0.997**	(0.196)	0.874**	(0.183)
University	1.021**	(0.164)	1.282**	(0.254)	1.257**	(0.295)	1.271**	(0.262)
Other individual characteristics								
Male	0.085	(0.077)	0.099	(0.124)	0.127	(0.128)	0.084	(0.127)
Married	−0.196**	(0.075)	−0.241*	(0.120)	−0.186	(0.121)	−0.236*	(0.121)
Hours of work	−0.020**	(0.004)	−0.028**	(0.006)	−0.027**	(0.006)	−0.027**	(0.006)
Age	−0.002	(0.004)	−0.006	(0.006)	−0.006	(0.006)	−0.005	(0.006)
Tenure	−0.012*	(0.005)	−0.019*	(0.008)	−0.047**	(0.017)	−0.019*	(0.008)
Year	−0.198	(0.140)	−0.226	(0.205)	−0.237	(0.205)	−0.221	(0.207)
Job-related characteristics								
No induction training	−0.179	(0.115)	−0.271	(0.169)	−0.236	(0.169)	−0.276	(0.171)
One-day induction training	0.361**	(0.098)	0.429**	(0.150)	0.430**	(0.150)	0.413**	(0.153)
Does not supervise others	−0.036	(0.073)	−0.029	(0.109)	−0.042	(0.115)	−0.024	(0.111)
Received firm-related training	0.008	(0.011)	0.010	(0.018)	0.011	(0.020)	0.012	(0.018)
Job level	−0.355**	(0.039)	−0.452**	(0.057)	−0.675**	(0.111)	−0.444**	(0.060)
Firm-related characteristics (reference category: public services)								
Metal and chemical industry	0.120	(0.121)	0.157	(0.190)	0.160	(0.193)	0.157	(0.193)
Other industry	0.017	(0.169)	−0.015	(0.239)	0.005	(0.238)	−0.027	(0.242)
Construction	0.045	(0.176)	0.074	(0.249)	0.039	(0.253)	0.071	(0.253)
Trade	0.039	(0.142)	0.025	(0.206)	0.009	(0.202)	0.028	(0.208)
Transportation	−0.097	(0.133)	−0.134	(0.186)	−0.128	(0.191)	−0.139	(0.189)
Banking	−0.061	(0.178)	−0.044	(0.244)	−0.018	(0.247)	−0.058	(0.247)
Commercial services	0.018	(0.139)	0.040	(0.196)	0.037	(0.200)	0.030	(0.198)
Firm size/100	−0.009	(0.005)	−0.012	(0.007)	−0.013*	(0.007)	−0.012	(0.007)
Mobility								
Job-to-job mobility	−0.104	(0.115)	−0.088	(0.158)	−0.173	(0.138)	0.101	(0.329)
Internal mobility	0.076	(0.085)	0.071	(0.134)	0.059	(0.138)	0.000	(0.264)
σ intercept			1.078**	(0.108)	0.599**	(0.263)	1.052**	(0.118)
σ tenure					0.048**	(0.015)		
σ job level					0.310**	(0.080)		
σ job-to-job mobility							0.573	(1.128)
σ internal mobility							0.423	(0.620)
Log likelihood	−1,128.23		−1,085.61		−1,080.03		−1,085.66	
Inter-temporal correlation coefficient					0.537			

* significant at 5% level; ** significant at 1% level.

ferences in the impact of tenure and job level between individuals are relatively large.

The variances of the coefficients for job-to-job mobility and internal mobility are both statistically not significant, indicating that there is little variation in the effects of both variables on overeducation.

3.3.3 Fixed Effects Model

Next, we estimate some fixed effects probit equations on the transition in and out of overeducation (Markov model). With the fixed effects model, all variables that do not change over time drop out of the equation. We therefore only include variables that (may) change during the period 1994 to 1996, that is, whether the worker received firm-related training between 1994 and 1996, whether the worker changed employers *(job-to-job mobility)* and whether the worker changed jobs within the firm *(internal mobility)*.

The parameter estimates are found in Table 3.3. The only variable with a statistically significant effect is *job-to-job* mobility in the equation from overeducation in 1994 to another state in 1996. The coefficient indicates that for workers who were overeducated in 1994 a change of employers increased the probability of *not* being overeducated in 1996 by 36 per cent.

We estimate transition equations in and out of overeducation that include a larger number of explanatory variables as well. All explanatory variables are taken in their 1994 values. The parameter estimates are found in Table 3.4.

We find that a higher education level increases the probability of a transition *into* overeducation and decreases the probability of an exit *from* overeducation. Longer working hours (a full-time job), a longer tenure at the current firm and a higher job level decrease the probability of becoming overeducated. Older workers who were overeducated in 1994 are less likely to exit this state than younger workers. A higher job level in 1994 increases the probability of exiting from the state of overeducation.

Finally, if we look at the two mobility variables we find a positive effect of job-to-job mobility on the probability of exiting from overeducation (this is similar to the effect found in Table 3.3, although the size of the coefficient is somewhat smaller). We further find that internal mobility increases the probability of becoming overeducated.

Table 3.3 Parameter estimates fixed effects probit equations on entry in and exit from overeducation (standard errors in brackets)

	From: not overeducated in 1994 To: overeducated in 1996		From: overeducated in 1994 To: not overeducated in 1996	
Intercept	−1.650**	(0.108)	−0.107	(0.182)
Received firm-related training	0.063	(0.120)	0.279	(0.208)
Job-to-job mobility	−0.138	(0.181)	0.964**	(0.327)
Internal mobility	0.162	(0.148)	0.247	(0.296)
Log likelihood	−358.06		−119.80	
LRT zero slopes	2.34		10.95	

** significant at 1% level.

Table 3.4   Parameter estimates fixed effects probit equations on entry in and exit from overeducation (standard errors in brackets)

	From: not overeducated in 1994 To: overeducated in 1996		From: overeducated in 1994 To: not overeducated in 1996	
Intercept	−0.257	(0.409)	0.841	(0.774)
Highest education level (reference category: lower vocational education)				
Primary education	−0.003	(0.190)	−0.093	(0.518)
Lower secondary education	0.275	(0.174)	−0.638	(0.348)
Intermediate secondary edu.	0.072	(0.347)	−2.245**	(0.671)
Higher secondary education	0.959**	(0.256)	0.182	(0.666)
Intermediate vocational edu.	0.448**	(0.166)	−0.738*	(0.316)
Higher vocational education	0.442*	(0.231)	−1.322**	(0.447)
University	0.865**	(0.311)	−1.325*	(0.585)
Other individual characteristics				
Male	0.283	(0.149)	0.036	(0.276)
Married	−0.222	(0.140)	0.287	(0.269)
Hours of work	−0.024**	(0.007)	−0.003	(0.012)
Age	0.003	(0.007)	−0.033*	(0.015)
Tenure	−0.019*	(0.009)	0.017	(0.020)
Job-related characteristics				
No induction training	0.396	(0.238)	−0.359	(0.427)
One-day induction training	0.298	(0.218)	−0.214	(0.306)
Does not supervise others	−0.026	(0.131)	0.052	(0.290)
Received firm-related training	0.032	(0.018)	−0.075	(0.052)
Job level	−0.323**	(0.078)	0.340*	(0.165)
Firm-related characteristics				
Firm size/100	−0.004	(0.007)	0.093	(0.049)
Mobility				
Job-to-job mobility	−0.035	(0.146)	0.736**	(0.294)
Internal mobility	0.312*	(0.160)	0.291	(0.398)
Log likelihood	−323.60		−103.65.	

* significant at 5% level; ** significant at 1% level.

There are some differences between the results of the random effects estimates on the incidence of overeducation (Table 3.2) and the fixed effects estimates in Table 3.4. For example, the random effects estimates do not show that job-to-job mobility or internal mobility have a statistically significant effect on overeducation, while the fixed effects estimates show that job-to-job mobility significantly increases the probability of exiting from the state of overeducation while internal mobility increases the probability of becoming overeducated. A possible explanation for these seemingly contradictory findings is misspecification of random effects equation. If the individual specific effect in the overeducation equation is correlated with job-to-job or internal mobility, estimates of the random effect equations may be biased. It may well be that the individual specific effect that increases the likelihood of being overeducated also increases or decreases the chance of mobility.

3.3.4 Multinomial Logit Model on the Persistence of Overeducation

For more insight into the persistence of overeducation, we created a new variable that distinguishes between workers who were neither in 1994 nor in 1996 overeducated, workers who were overeducated in only one of these two years, and workers who were overeducated in both of these years (persistent overeducated workers). A little over 4 per cent of the workers in our sample are classified as long-term or persistent overeducated. About 11 per cent were overeducated in only one of the two years of observation, while 85 per cent were overeducated in neither of the two years. For the explanatory analyses, we estimate a multinomial logit model to determine what affects persistent overeducation. All explanatory variables are taken in their 1994 values.

Table 3.5 Parameter estimates multinomial logit equations at the persistence of overeducation (standard errors in brackets)

	Overeducated in 1994 or in 1996		Overeducated in 1994 and in 1996	
Intercept	1.055	(0.582)	−0.284	(0.943)
Highest education level (reference category: lower vocational education)				
Primary education	−0.458	(0.307)	−1.123	(0.688)
Lower secondary education	0.160	(0.260)	1.070*	(0.445)
Intermediate secondary edu.	−0.567	(0.626)	2.541**	(0.561)
Higher secondary education	1.851**	(0.363)	1.540	(1.890)
Intermediate vocational edu.	0.701**	(0.237)	1.788**	(0.425)
Higher vocational education	1.080**	(0.323)	3.106**	(0.531)
University	1.922**	(0.435)	3.793**	(0.713)
Other individual characteristics				
Male	0.234	(0.211)	0.218	(0.341)
Married	−0.251	(0.207)	−0.668*	(0.320)
Hours of work	−0.034**	(0.010)	−0.035*	(0.015)
Age	−0.014	(0.010)	0.015	(0.016)
Tenure	−0.025	(0.014)	−0.035	(0.024)
Job-related characteristics				
No induction training	0.786*	(0.331)	1.052*	(0.498)
One-day induction training	0.996**	(0.271)	1.512**	(0.369)
Does not supervise others	−0.148	(0.195)	0.164	(0.354)
Received firm-related training	0.051	(0.029)	0.019	(0.053)
Job level	−0.635**	(0.114)	−1.106**	(0.184)
Firm-related characteristics				
Firm size/100	−0.020	(0.014)	−0.129*	(0.056)
Mobility				
Job-to-job mobility	−0.045	(0.209)	−0.807*	(0.362)
Internal mobility	0.335	(0.249)	−0.000	(0.443)
Observed frequency	0.109		0.041	
Log likelihood		−818.58		

* significant at 5% level; ** significant at 1% level.

The results in Table 3.5 show that persistent overeducation (i.e., being over-educated in both 1994 and 1996) increases with education, is higher for workers in jobs that require little or no induction training and is lower for workers who are married and for workers in larger firms and in higher job levels. Finally, we find that job-to-job mobility in the two years prior to 1994 reduces the probability of persistent overeducation.

3.3.5 Does Overeducation Affect Mobility?

So far, we have focused our attention on the effects of internal and external mobility on the incidence of overeducation. It may well be that there also is a reverse effect. On the one hand, overeducated workers may be more inclined to search for another job. On the other hand, if overeducation indicates that the worker's performance is below average or if overeducation is taken as a signal by other employers of sub-standard performance, overeducation may impede job mobility.

First, we look at the relation between job search and overeducation. We combine information on overeducation and job search of both the 1994 and 1996 sample. In both samples workers are asked whether they are currently actively searching for another job. The cross-tabulation of job search and over-education is found in Table 3.6.

A little over 8 per cent of the workers state that they are actively searching for another job. Overeducated workers are searching for another job more frequently than workers who are not overeducated. Of the overeducated workers 19.5 per cent were searching for another job, while this is only 7.0 per cent among workers who are not overeducated.

Next, we analyse whether overeducation has an effect on job mobility. We look at both external and internal mobility in the period 1994 to 1996. All explanatory variables—including overeducation—are taken in their 1994 values. The results of some probit equations on job mobility are found in Table 3.7. The results show that overeducation neither has a statistical significant effect on ex-

Table 3.6   Cross tabulation of overeducation and job search in 1994 and 1996 (in %)

	Not overeducated	Overeducated	Total
Not actively searching for another job	83.7	8.1	91.8
Actively searching for another job	6.3	1.9	8.2
Total	90.0	10.0	100.0

Table 3.7 Parameter estimates probit equations on the incidence of job-to-job and internal mobility from 1994 to 1996 (standard errors in brackets)

	Job-to-job mobility				Internal mobility			
Intercept	0.173	(0.330)	0.168	(0.325)	−1.471**	(0.316)	−1.493**	(0.317)
Highest education level (reference category: lower vocational education)								
Primary education	−0.027	(0.163)	−0.026	(0.163)	−0.188	(0.156)	−0.187	(0.156)
Lower secondary education	−0.100	(0.144)	−0.099	(0.144)	0.094	(0.126)	0.091	(0.126)
Intermediate secondary edu.	−0.155	(0.224)	−0.160	(0.223)	0.291	(0.190)	0.276	(0.190)
Higher secondary education	−0.023	(0.264)	−0.026	(0.263)	0.293	(0.202)	0.292	(0.202)
Intermediate vocational edu.	0.050	(0.127)	0.047	(0.126)	0.030	(0.122)	0.021	(0.123)
Higher vocational education	−0.284	(0.185)	−0.287	(0.184)	0.007	(0.153)	−0.002	(0.154)
University	−0.059	(0.256)	−0.062	(0.254)	0.146	(0.215)	0.134	(0.216)
Other individual characteristics								
Male	0.011	(0.111)	0.010	(0.111)	−0.104	(0.104)	−0.111	(0.104)
Married	−0.178	(0.109)	−0.175	(0.109)	0.269*	(0.114)	0.274*	(0.115)
Hours of work	0.005	(0.006)	0.005	(0.006)	0.005	(0.005)	0.006	(0.005)
Age	−0.030**	(0.006)	−0.030**	(0.006)	−0.007	(0.005)	−0.007	(0.005)
Tenure	−0.059**	(0.009)	−0.058**	(0.009)	−0.005	(0.006)	−0.004	(0.006)
Job-related characteristics								
No induction training	0.204	(0.218)	−0.022	(0.108)	−0.273	(0.255)	−0.275	(0.256)
One-day induction training	0.213	(0.167)	0.202	(0.218)	−0.219	(0.198)	−0.238	(0.200)
Does not supervise others	−0.024	(0.108)	0.212	(0.166)	0.055	(0.092)	0.053	(0.092)
Received firm-related training	−0.009	(0.020)	−0.009	(0.020)	0.044**	(0.013)	0.043**	(0.013)
Job level	0.016	(0.062)	0.017	(0.061)	0.017	(0.056)	0.021	(0.056)
Firm-related characteristics								
Firm size/100	−0.002	(0.006)	−0.002	(0.006)	0.006	(0.005)	0.006	(0.005)
Overeducation								
Overeducated in 1994	−0.043	(0.143)	0.009	(0.193)	0.081	(0.134)	0.279	(0.182)
Duration of overeduc. in 1994			−0.001	(0.003)			−0.004	(0.003)
Log likelihood	−518.248		−518.167		−630.500		−629.138	

* significant at 5% level; ** significant at 1% level.

ternal mobility, nor on internal mobility. We also estimated some specifications including the length of time workers have been overeducated. This variable is zero for workers who are not overeducated. For workers who are overeducated it represents the length of time in their current job. It might be expected that a longer spell of overeducation reduces the likelihood of obtaining another job, as longer spells of overeducation serve as a signal of below average capabilities. As is shown in Table 3.7, the length of the spell of overeducation does not have a statistically significant effect on job mobility.

3.4 CONCLUSION

In this paper we have looked at the dynamics of overeducation. Three conclusions emerge from the analyses. First, the dynamics in overeducation is high. Over a two-year period, the outflow rate out of overeducation is about 40 per cent, while the inflow rate is about 5 per cent. Only 4 per cent of the workers in the sample are classified as long-term persistently overeducated. It appears that job-to-job mobility provides a way out of overeducation. Young workers are more likely to escape from overeducation than older workers. We also find that job mobility reduces the probability of persistent or long-term overeducation. Internal mobility does not seem to provide an escape from overeducation. However, we do find that the probability of *being* overeducated decreased with tenure at the current firm. Therefore, although changing jobs with the current employer has no statistically significant effect on overeducation, the length of tenure has. A possible explanation for this—seemingly contradictory—finding is that workers perceive the match between their work and their education more positively the longer they are with their current employer and the longer the time since they left school.

Secondly, we find evidence to support the hypothesis that overeducation is a compensation for the lack of other productive skills. Contrary to some other studies we find no gender differences in overeducation. We do, however, find a strong effect of hours of work. Part-time workers are more likely to be overeducated than full-time workers. Also since more than two-thirds of all part-time workers are women, the gender difference found in earlier studies may simply be an artifact for hours of work. The negative effect of hours of work on the probability of being overeducated suggests that overeducation compensates for the lack of (full-time equivalent) work experience and the lower productivity and higher employment costs of part-time workers.

A third conclusion we draw is that overeducated workers are almost three times as likely to search for work than workers who are not overeducated. Nearly 20 per cent of the workers who are overeducated state that they are actively searching for other work. This active search behavior of overeducated workers does not appear to have a positive effect on their probability of job mobility. We find that overeducation does not have a statistically significant effect on internal or external mobility. Therefore, although overeducation increases the likelihood of searching for other work, it does not improve the chance of actually finding another job. This may suggest that overeducated workers are perceived as less capable by other employers.

Whether overeducation is a cause for concern depends on whether overeducation for individual workers is a persistent phenomenon or rather a temporary state of affairs. The results in this paper clearly suggest that for many workers overeducation is a temporary rather than a permanent phenomenon. Even if overeducation is part of an adjustment period in the labour market and disappears with years of experience, overeducation may be a permanent feature in Western economies and create an inefficiency. Some workers experience an employment spell in which they bring more education to their job than they—at least initially—require for their work. This raises the issue of the optimal timing of educational investments. By the time the skills, which initially are under-utilised, can be made productive they may have become obsolete, or have been forgotten. When there are opportunities for lifelong learning, it may be argued that it is more efficient to train workers 'just in time.' Further, there is also the issue of the financing of these educational investments. Skills learned at school are usually (at least partly) publicly financed. If these skills are learned later at the workplace, employers may pay part of the costs of these investments. If so, overeducation is, in part, a public subsidy for skill investments which would otherwise have been paid by firms. However, we have also found evidence for the hypothesis that overeducation compensates for the lack of other productive skills, such as experience. Rather than an inefficiency, overeducation may even create a social benefit. If without this surplus education workers find it more difficult to find any employment and are more likely to be unemployed, overeducation may lead to savings in unemployment benefits and active labour market policies aimed at the insertion of workers in the labour market.

NOTE

1 The inter-temporal correlation coefficient is calculated as: $\sigma / (1 + \sigma)$, where σ is the variance of the intercept term.

REFERENCES

Agresti, A., and Lang, J. (1993). A proportional odds model with subject-specific effects for repeated ordered categorical responses. *Biometrika,* **80,** 527–534.
Büchel, F., and Mertens, A. (in press). Overeducation, undereducation, and the theory of career mobility. *Applied Economics.*
Dekker, R., de Grip, A., and Heijke, H. (2002). The effects of training and overeducation on career mobility in a segmented labour market. *International Journal of Manpower,* **23,** 106–125.
Dolton, P., and Vignoles, A. (2000). The incidence and effects of overeducation in the UK graduate labour market. *Economics of Education Review,* **19,** 179–198.
Groot, W. (1993). Overeducation and the returns to enterprise-related training. *Economics of Education Review,* **12,** 299–309.
Groot, W. (1996). The incidence of, and returns to overeducation in the UK. *Applied Economics,* **28,** 1345–1350.
Groot, W., and Maassen van den Brink, H. (1996). Overscholing en verdringing op de arbeidsmarkt. *Economisch Statistische Berichten,* **4042,** 74–77.
Groot, W., and Maassen van den Brink, H. (1997). Allocation and the returns to overeducation in the United Kingdom. *Education Economics,* **5,** 169–183.
Groot, W., and Maassen van den Brink, H. (2000). Overeducation in the labor market: A meta-analysis. *Economics of Education Review,* **19,** 149–158.

Hedeker, D., and Gibbons, R. (1994). A random-effects ordinal regression model for multilevel analysis. *Biometrics,* **50**, 933–944.

Hedeker, D., and Gibbons, R. (1996). MIXOR: A computer program for mixed-effects ordinal regression analysis. *Computer Methods and Programs in Biomedicine,* **49**, 157–176.

Robst, J. (1995). Career mobility, job match and overeducation. *Eastern Economic Journal,* **21**, 539–550.

Sicherman, N. (1991). Overeducation in the labour market. *Journal of Labour Economics,* **9**, 101–122.

4. Types of Job Match, Overeducation and Labour Mobility in Spain[1]

Alfonso Alba-Ramírez and Maite Blázquez

4.1 INTRODUCTION

Spain has experienced a remarkable increase in the educational level of its population, which has been accompanied by more jobs for higher-educated workers and the upgrading of skills needed to perform jobs adequately. In this context, we can ask ourselves whether the increase in the demand for higher-educated workers has been able to fully absorb the increase in the supply. If the answer is no, then overeducation can emerge and become a problem.

Using data from the European Community Household Panel (ECHP)[1] we address several questions regarding overeducation: How do we measure it? What was its incidence in the Spanish labour market in the 1990s? What are the determinants of and the returns to overeducation? To what extent is overeducation a temporary or a permanent phenomenon? What is the empirical relationship between overeducation and job mobility?

Our conceptual framework is based on the occupational mobility theory. This theory predicts that workers may temporarily work in jobs for which they are overeducated because they obtain skills that can be used in different higher-level positions or jobs. Thus, it might be beneficial for individuals to work in jobs where they are overqualified.

In this paper, we are particularly interested in investigating whether mobility depends on the extent to which formal training or education is related to the job held by workers who perceive themselves as overeducated. To this end, we characterise the job match according to workers' reports on the relationship between their formal training or education and the work they do.

In Section 2 we review the conceptual frameworks that have been proposed for studying overeducation in the labour market; in Section 3 we outline overeducation in Spain; in Section 4 we describe the dataset; in Section 5 we analyse the determinants of and the returns to overeducation; in Section 6 we study job-match transitions; in Section 7 we explore the relationship between job match and mobility; finally, in Section 8 we conclude.

4.2 THE CONCEPTUAL FRAMEWORK

In a model of job competition, where the number of job seekers is higher than the number of vacancies, employers select workers from a group of workers with little or no experience by relying on their level of education. This can lead to the so-called 'crowding-out' of less-educated workers by the higher-educated workers. Workers are willing to accept jobs in which they are overeducated if the wage plus the economic value of the skills that can be acquired exceeds the reservation wage. Work experience and human capital accumulation leads to promotion or better outside opportunities. That is why most senior workers usually perform jobs for which they are adequately qualified.

The concept of overeducation was introduced by Freeman (1976) and Thurow (1975) in the context of the American economy of the 1970s. Competition for the same scarce jobs among workers with different educational attainments can induce a higher unemployment rate among less-educated workers through the crowding-out effect.

Different points of view about the overeducation problem are represented in the literature. From the standpoint of the neoclassical theory, changes in the population structure, in the sense of an unordered increase in the numbers of people investing in higher education, prompt firms and workers to adjust their educational requirements and their investments in education respectively. This adjustment by both firms and individuals implies that overeducation will be no more than a short-term imbalance.

Matching theory (Jovanovic, 1979a) also supports the view that overeducation is a temporary phenomenon. In this framework, overeducation represents a poor match for workers because they are educated to perform a higher-level job. Over time, however, workers are expected to improve their job match; therefore, overeducation will be temporary.

Another theory that approaches overeducation as a short-term phenomenon is occupational mobility theory (Rosen, 1972; Sicherman and Galor, 1990), which states that overeducation is a temporary mismatch because overeducated workers soon get promoted or move to more demanding jobs. This theory predicts that it may be beneficial for individuals to temporarily occupy jobs for which they are overeducated because they gain skills needed to perform higher-level jobs.

However, other theories consider overeducation as a more serious and long-lasting problem. In Spence's job-screening model (1973), the labour market is characterised by imperfect information. The focus of attention of this theory is on the uncertainty surrounding the hiring decision. This uncertainty stems from the fact that the employer does not know, prior to hiring, how productive a particular employee will turn out to be. In this context, individuals will invest in education in order to signal high productivity.

The job-competition theory (Thurow, 1975) also views overeducation as a rather permanent phenomenon. The job competition model describes a queue of workers in the labour market competing for jobs, with those at the head of the queue being hired first. A worker's position in the queue is determined by their costs for the firm in terms of training. In this framework, education is a proxy for training costs, with the highly educated being seen as more able and, therefore, requiring less training. It is assumed that productivity and wages are fixed in relation to jobs so that overeducated workers have identical productivity and receive the same wages as those who are in jobs with the required level of education.

4.3 OVEREDUCATION IN SPAIN

Overeducation can arise as a result of an increase in the population's average level of education and a consequent change in the composition of labour supply. This phenomenon has appeared to grow in importance since the mid-1980s in some European countries and particularly in Spain. Over the last two decades the Spanish labour market has experienced a progressive expansion of post-compulsory education, mainly orientated toward higher education (university/ tertiary degrees). This tendency has been reinforced by a steady rise in women's demand for formal education. In this context, transitions from school to work in Spain typically involve young workers accepting jobs for which the required level of education is lower than the level they have attained. Thus, overeducation is considered an explanatory factor in the high and persistent unemployment of less-educated young workers in Spain (Dolado, Felgueroso and Jimeno, 2000; García-Serrano and Malo, 1996).

As documented in Dolado, Felgueroso and Jimeno (2000), the proportion of the Spanish population with an upper secondary education is among the largest in the OECD countries. The proportion of the population with higher education is about 75 per cent of the OECD average. However, when comparing the relative educational attainments of cohorts aged 25 to 34 and 55 to 64 years old, the proportion of people who have completed tertiary/university education in the first group is 4.5 times larger than in the second group. This figure reflects the intense educational efforts that have been made by the Spanish youth labour force over the last two decades. However, in spite of this rapid educational upgrading, the Spanish labour market has one of the highest unemployment rates in the OECD area. Women and young people are most affected by unemployment, with unemployment rates of about 10 and 20 percentage points higher than the average.

It appears that the impressive evolution of the supply of high-educated labour has not been matched by an equal increase in the supply of skilled vacancies (Dolado, Felgueroso and Jimeno, 2000), thus resulting in overeducation. There seems to be some evidence for crowding-out, in the sense that high-educated workers have taken jobs that would otherwise be occupied by low-educated workers.

4.4 THE DATASET

The data used comes from the ECHP.[2] We use a sample of wage and salary workers, meaning that self-employed and unpaid family-employed workers are not considered. We exclude individuals still at school at the time of the first interview and those occupied in the agricultural sector. We use information contained in the ECHP to assess the type of job match and, more particularly, to identify overeducated workers.

Four different definitions of overeducation can be distinguished in the literature and classified into 'objective' and 'subjective' definitions. The subjective definitions are based on individual workers' self-reports on their level of skill utilisation. Either workers are asked directly whether they are overeducated or undereducated for the work they do, or they are asked what minimum education is required for their job. The self-reported level of required education is compared with the worker's actual educational level to assess the job match. The objective definitions can be classified into two types. In the first type, overeducation is assessed by comparing years of education with the average educational level in the worker's current occupation. Workers are classified as overeducated if they have more than the average years of education for their occupation plus one standard deviation (Groot and Maassen van den Brink, 1997; Verdugo and Verdugo, 1989). Finally, the fourth definition of overeducation is based on a comparison between the actual educational level and the job-level requirements (Hartog and Oosterbeek, 1988; Thurow and Lucas, 1972).

Most research on overeducation has used a measure of overeducation that is based on comparing the worker's educational attainment with educational requirements of the job—either to obtain it (Cohn and Kahn, 1995; Duncan and Hoffman, 1981; Sicherman, 1991) or to perform the job (Alba-Ramírez, 1993; Hartog and Oosterbeek, 1988; Rumberger, 1987).

Although the ECHP does not provide direct information on the educational requirements of jobs, it contains several questions that provide us with enough information to assess the type of job match from a subjective perspective. Workers are allocated to the different types of job match according to their responses to the following three questions:

Q1 *Do you consider you have skills or qualifications to do a more demanding job than the one you have now?*

Q2 *Has your formal training or education provided you with the skills needed to perform your current job?*

Q3 *To what extent is your formal training or education related to your current job?*

The response to the first question allows us to split the sample into two initial groups. People reporting that they have the skills or qualifications to do a more demanding job will be considered *overeducated,* whereas people reporting that they do not have such skills or qualifications will be considered *non-over-educated.*

Starting from this initial classification of the sample, workers can be further classified according to their answers to questions (2) and (3). Table 4.1 contains the classification of the sample for the 1995 survey based on participants' responses to these questions. We identify the following subcategories within the overeducated group: those reporting that their educational attainments have not provided them with the skills needed to perform their current job (Type 3 over-educated workers, *OV3*), those whose formal training or education has provided them the skills needed to perform the job, though this formal training or educa-tion is not related very closely or at all to their work (Type 1 overeducated work-ers, *OV1*) and finally, those whose formal training or education has provided them with the skills needed to perform their work and is quite or very closely related to that work (Type 2 overeducated workers, *OV2*). As an illustration of the different types of job match, consider a lawyer in the three following situations:

(1) Employed as a *clerk*. In this case, the law graduate might be included in the *OV1* category if their university degree allowed them to obtain and perform the job, though the individual might feel that theiy have the skills or qualifica-tions for a more demanding job.

(2) Employed as a *paralegal*. Although working in a job in which their for-mal training or education is quite or very relevant, this lawyer may feel that they have the skills or qualifications for a more demanding job. Therefore, they could be included in the *OV2* category.

(3) Employed as a *salesman*. In this situation, the individual would report that their formal training or education has not provided them with the skills needed for the job, in the sense that they would not have needed a university degree to obtain and perform the job. At the same time, they would state that they have the skills or qualifications for a more demanding job. This individual would thus be included in the *OV3* category.

Non-overeducated workers, on the other hand, are classified as Type 1 ad-equately educated workers *(AD1)* if their formal training or education has pro-vided them with the skills needed to perform their job, though it is not related very closely or at all to that job,[3] and as Type 2 adequately educated workers *(AD2)* if their formal training or education is quite or very closely related to their work. Finally, Type 3 non-overeducated workers *(NOV3)* are those whose formal train-ing or education has not provided them with the skills needed for their current job.

Table 4.1   Sample distribution (1995 survey)

		Q2		Total
	No	Yes		
		Q3 = 1 Quite or very	Q3 = 2 Not much or not at all	
Q1 Yes (over- educated)	OV3 (Type 3 overeducated) 896 (21.02%)	OV2 (Type 2 overeducated) 1,027 (24.10%)	OV1 (Type 1 overeducated) 371 (8.71%)	2,294 (53.84%)
No (non- over- educated)	NOV3 (Type 3 non- overeducated) 1,023 (24.01%)	AD2 (Type 2 adequately educated) 677 (15.89%)	AD1 (Type 1 adequately educated) 267 (6.26%)	1,967 (46.16%)
Total	1,919 (45.03%)	1,704 (39.99%)	638 (14.97%)	4,261 (100.00%)

Notes:
Type 1: overeducated   = OV1+OV2+OV3 = 53.84%
Type 2: adequately educated = AD1+AD2 = 22.15%
Type 3: non-overeducated   = NOV3 = 24.01%

Thus, we have divided the sample into six different types of job match *(OV1, OV2, OV3, AD1, AD2* and *NOV3)* based on workers' self-reports about their job. Although workers' responses to the three questions are subjective, they are based on the characteristics of the jobs they hold. As workers were asked about their current job in each wave of the panel, we are able to study job match transitions as well as employment transitions.

Table 4.2 describes the main characteristics of the selected sample. The variables, used later as explanatory variables to study the determinants of the job match, relate to personal and job characteristics: sex, marital status, age, educational attainments, type of firm, type of contract,[4] on-the-job training, seniority in the current job and experience of unemployment during the last five years.

Some points are worth mentioning with regard to the explanatory variables relating to educational attainments. Data from the 1995 survey show that 50.88 per cent of the entire sample left the educational system with a lower secondary education diploma, 20.89 per cent of the total sample reported upper secondary education as the highest level of education completed and the remaining 28.23 per cent had completed tertiary/university education. When comparing over-educated, adequately and non-overeducated workers, clear differences become apparent. A higher proportion of overeducated and adequately educated people whose formal training or education is quite or very closely related to their work have completed tertiary/university education than in the sample as a whole

Table 4.2 Relation of variables and sample means (1995 survey)

Log wage	Entire sample	Overeducated			Adequately educated		Non-overeduc. (Type 3)
		OV1	OV2	OV3	AD1	AD2	NOV3
Male	65.61	65.50	59.30	68.86	67.41	61.00	71.75
Married	64.42	58.76	64.65	57.03	73.78	70.46	66.27
Age	37.64	34.21	37.67	34.59	40.99	40.64	38.68
Education							
Tertiary	28.23	23.72	58.81	14.73	8.99	43.87	5.67
Upper Secondary	20.89	33.96	22.49	27.12	18.35	20.09	10.26
Lower Secondary	50.88	42.31	18.69	58.15	72.66	36.04	84.07
Type of firm							
Public	27.46	27.49	44.69	15.40	24.72	39.73	13.29
Private (< 20)	36.68	37.73	22.98	46.32	37.83	24.67	49.27
Private (20–500)	25.88	22.10	22.69	29.13	26.59	22.75	29.52
Private (> 500)	9.95	12.67	9.54	9.15	10.86	12.85	7.92
Permanent contract	64.02	60.38	73.42	48.99	73.41	79.32	56.50
Seniority							
< 1 year	17.79	26.68	13.73	27.45	13.11	9.30	17.01
1–5 years	28.07	29.92	25.22	33.26	22.47	20.97	31.87
5–10 years	14.83	15.36	18.30	14.06	16.10	12.70	12.90
> 10 years	39.31	28.03	42.74	25.22	48.31	57.01	38.22
Training	30.51	28.30	48.29	20.76	26.59	42.83	14.86
Unemployment							
No unemployment	66.11	55.79	73.61	53.35	72.66	79.47	62.95
Once	17.88	22.64	16.55	21.76	15.35	11.52	18.96
More than once	16.00	21.56	9.83	24.88	11.98	9.01	18.08
Sample size	4,261	371	1,027	896	267	677	1,023
Distribution (in %)	100.00	8.71	24.10	21.02	6.26	15.89	24.01

(58.81% of people at *OV2* and 43.87% of people at *AD2* report having tertiary/ university education). In contrast, people at *AD1* and *NOV3* are more likely to report a lower secondary education diploma as the maximum educational level completed. Regarding the age variables, it can be observed that both adequately educated workers and Type 3 non-overeducated workers tend to be older than overeducated workers.

With regard to job characteristics, there are clear differences in the sample means for each type of job match. Over- and adequately educated workers whose formal training or education is quite or very closely related to their jobs are more likely to be occupied in the public sector. Workers with these two types of job match are also more likely to receive on-the-job training provided by the employer and not to have experienced unemployment in the last five years.

In contrast, overeducated workers whose formal training or education has not provided them with the skills needed to perform their jobs *(OV3)* and Type 3 non-overeducated workers tend to be occupied in private firms with less than 20 employees and are also less likely to receive on-the-job training provided by the employer.

Finally, Type 1 and Type 3 overeducated workers are more likely to have experienced unemployment more than once in the last five years.

4.5 THE DETERMINANTS OF AND THE RETURNS TO JOB MATCH

In this section we aim at analysing the determinants of the different types of job match and the relationship between the job match and earnings. We use a multinomial logit model to analyse the determinants of the different types of job match. The dependent variable is a six-point variable indicating the respondent's allocation to one of the six different types of job match considered in our analysis. Five sets of coefficients (one for each type of job match other than AD2) are estimated.[5] The probability of being at each of the five types of job match other than AD2 is estimated conditional on a vector of explanatory variables that includes personal and job characteristics.

The full empirical results are reported in Table 4.3. We find that the educational level exerts a strong influence on the probability of being at each of the five types of job match. People with tertiary/university education are most likely to be Type 2 overeducated workers. In contrast, people at *OV1, OV3, AD1* and *NOV3* are much less likely to have completed tertiary/university education than people with the best match *(AD2)*.

We also find that Types 1 and 3 overeducated workers and Type 3 non-overeducated workers receive less on-the-job training than Type 2 adequately educated workers. By contrast, there is no difference between Type 2 over- and adequately educated workers in this respect.

The estimation also reveals a negative and significant influence of seniority on the likelihood of being overeducated. The estimated coefficients of the dummy variable indicating more than ten years' seniority in the current job are negative and significant for all three types of overeducated workers.

Finally, Types 1 and 3 overeducated workers are most likely to have experienced unemployment more than once in the last five years.

A stringent assumption of the multinomial logit models is that outcome categories for the model have the property of independence of irrelevant alternatives (IIA assumption). This assumption requires that the inclusion or exclusion of categories does not affect the relative risks associated with the regressors in the remaining categories. Thus, under the IIA assumption we would expect no

Table 4.3   Multinomial logit estimates (1995 survey)

	$\log\left[\dfrac{Pr(OV1)}{Pr(AD2)}\right]$		$\log\left[\dfrac{Pr(OV2)}{Pr(AD2)}\right]$		$\log\left[\dfrac{Pr(OV3)}{Pr(AD2)}\right]$		$\log\left[\dfrac{Pr(AD1)}{Pr(AD2)}\right]$		$\log\left[\dfrac{Pr(NOV3)}{Pr(AD2)}\right]$	
	RRR	t	RRR	t	RRR	t	RRR	t	RRR	t
Male	1.048	0.30	1.066	0.55	1.292	1.98	1.036	0.20	1.124	0.88
Married	1.060	0.34	0.906	–0.78	0.965	–0.26	1.202	0.94	1.108	0.73
Age	1.042	0.79	1.054	1.32	1.024	0.61	1.028	0.53	0.946	–1.44
Age (squared)	0.999	–1.57	0.999	–1.59	0.999	–1.34	0.999	–0.51	1.000	1.20
Education										
Tertiary	0.638	–2.42	2.600	6.86	0.375	–6.41	0.124	–8.07	0.103	–12.75
Upper Secondary	1.343	1.65	2.012	4.51	0.931	–0.48	0.463	–3.71	0.269	–8.15
Lower Secondary	–	–	–	–	–	–	–	–	–	–
Type of firm										
Public	1.248	0.86	1.278	1.32	0.866	–0.67	0.971	–0.10	0.674	–1.84
Private (< 20)	–	–	–	–	–	–	–	–	–	–
Private (20–500)	0.980	–0.10	1.142	0.86	1.001	0.01	0.937	–0.31	0.808	–1.43
Private (> 500)	1.132	0.48	0.775	–1.22	0.860	–0.71	0.756	–0.94	0.663	–1.91
Perm. contract	1.344	1.40	0.847	–0.98	0.767	–1.55	1.211	0.78	0.723	–1.88
Seniority										
< 1 year	–	–	–	–	–	–	–	–	–	–
1–5 years	0.515	–2.89	0.766	–1.33	0.746	–1.52	0.852	–0.56	1.235	1.05
5–10 years	0.594	–1.65	0.890	–0.45	0.886	–0.46	1.286	0.67	1.459	1.40
> 10 years	0.319	–3.61	0.553	–2.31	0.483	–2.80	0.710	–0.93	0.993	–0.03
Training	0.627	–2.85	1.096	0.80	0.685	–2.80	0.753	–1.54	0.574	–3.95
Unemployment										
No unemployment	–	–	–	–	–	–	–	–	–	–
Once	1.664	2.22	1.179	0.88	1.318	1.45	1.324	1.02	1.175	0.83
More than once	1.777	2.33	0.906	–0.47	1.575	2.23	1.207	0.62	1.208	0.90
Sample size					4,261					
Log likelihood					6,152					

Note:
16 industry and 6 region dummies were included in each estimation. Relative Risk Ratios (RRR) reported.

systematic change in the coefficients if one of the outcomes is excluded from the model.

One of the most common tests for the IIA assumption is the Hausman test. This entails re-estimating the model excluding each outcome and then performing a Hausman test against the fully efficient model. The results of the Hausman tests are reported in Table 4.4). For the cases where we exclude the outcome categories *OV1* and *OV3*, the Hausman test provides strong evidence in favour of the null hypothesis. That is, there is no evidence that the IIA assumption has been violated. For the cases where we exclude the outcome categories *OV2*, *AD1* and *NOV3*, the χ^2 is actually negative. We might interpret this as strong

Table 4.4   Hausman test for IIA assumption[1]

Omitted category	$\chi^2 (k)$	Prob. $> \chi^2$
OV1	5.05	1.000
OV2	−21.40	–
OV3	4.60	1.000
AD1	−8.20	–
NOV3	−28.71	–

Note:
[1] H_0: Difference in coefficients not systematic (IIA assumption).

evidence that we cannot reject the null hypothesis. Such results are not unusual for the Hausman test.

Having analysed the determinants of the type of job match, we aim at studying the returns to the different types of job match. The standard approach to estimating the returns to education dates back to Becker (1962) and Mincer (1974) and has its roots in the neoclassical theory. The economic theory of human capital views education as an investment. Like investments in physical assets, investments in human capital have an internal rate of return that may be estimated, using earnings data for a sample of individuals with different levels of education.

One would expect these returns to education to vary according to demand and supply conditions. On the supply side, the expansion of higher education and, in consequence, the presence of overeducation might induce a change in the returns to education.

A straightforward way to examine the economic effects of overeducation is to estimate an earnings equation in which the individual's actual educational attainment is decomposed into the number of years of education required and years of surplus or deficit education.

Much research into overeducation has focused on one key question: Do overeducated workers earn less than their peers who find jobs commensurate with their schooling? The wage-reducing effect of under-utilisation has often been investigated in the literature. Most researchers have found that there is a positive return to surplus education, but that it is less than the return to required education. Duncan and Hoffman (1981), Alba-Ramírez (1993), Hartog (2000), Rumberger (1987), Hartog and Oosterbeek (1988) and Sloane et al. (1999) all found that the rate of return to surplus education was approximately half the rate of return to required education. Thus, years of education that are not utilised still yield returns, but these returns are lower than they would have been if an appropriate job had been obtained.

In the earnings equation, we allow education to affect wages in a non-linear way by including dummy variables for the highest completed educational level.

The reference group consists of individuals with only lower secondary education. This also leads us to measure the returns to the different types of job match by introducing dummy variables for the type of job match to the earnings equation instead of the years of required education and years of surplus or deficit education.

It is true that the six different types of job match considered in our analysis might not be exogenous to the determination of earnings. However, like most of the findings reported in the related literature, our results are going to be based on the assumption that the type of job match is an exogenous variable when estimating the earnings function.[6]

The dependent variable in the estimation of the earnings function is the log of hourly net wages. Since the possibility that employees may not be a random subset of the total population could bias our results, the earnings equation is corrected for sample selection. The likelihood ratio test clearly justifies the Heckman selection equation for the data. A parsimonious specification for the variables in the selection equation is chosen, including marital status, age, education, number of people over 65 years old in the household and a dummy variable indicating whether the individual has a physical or psychological disability.

Table 4.5 reports the estimation results of the earnings function for the 1995 survey controlling for sample selection. Our primary interest is in differences between the estimated coefficients of the dummy variables indicating the type of job match. Since the job match is dependent on the way workers are sorted among jobs, we need to control for characteristics of the job. Thus, apart from some personal characteristics (sex, marital status, age and educational attainments), we include a set of explanatory variables relating to characteristics of the job (type of firm, type of contract, seniority, previous unemployment experience and industry). The results reported in Table 4.5 indicate that most of the variables chosen are statistically significant explanatory factors for the hourly net wage. The likelihood ratio test for sample selection clearly confirms that it is necessary to control for sample selection when estimating the earnings function.

Our results show that the classification of the sample made in this article is clearly justified in terms of earnings. Significant differences are apparent in the estimated coefficients of the dummy variables indicating the type of job match. As can be seen, Types 1 and 3 overeducated workers both earn significantly less than Type 2 adequately educated workers. This result indicates that individuals who report having skills or qualifications for a more demanding job and whose formal training or education has not provided them with the skills needed to perform their current job, or has provided them with skills that are not related very closely or at all to that job, earn significantly less than individuals who report that they do not have the skills or qualifications to do a more demanding job than their current one and whose formal training or education has provided

Table 4.5 Wage equation (1995 survey) controlling for sample selection

Log wage	Coefficient	t
Male	0.141	11.63
Age	0.003	0.67
Age (squared)	0.000	1.08
Education		
Tertiary	0.178	9.69
Upper Secondary	0.079	4.88
Lower Secondary	–	–
Type of firm		
Public	0.260	12.99
Private (< 20)	–	–
Private (20–500)	0.134	9.80
Private (> 500)	0.262	12.50
Permanent contract	0.125	8.08
Training	0.079	6.10
Seniority		
< 1 year	–	–
1–5 years	0.071	4.30
5–10 years	0.045	1.96
> 10 years	0.129	5.52
Unemployment		
No unemployment	–	–
Once	–0.058	–3.40
More than once	–0.050	–2.78
Type of job match		
OV1	–0.099	–4.43
OV2	0.007	0.40
OV3	–0.105	–5.80
AD1	–0.035	–1.44
AD2	–	–
NOV3	–0.085	–4.74
Constant	6.356	58.06
Sample size	15,662	
Log likelihood	–8,629.468	

Note:
16 industry and 6 region dummies were included in this estimation.

them with the skills needed to perform the current job and that are quite or very closely related to it. However, no earning differences are observed between people at *OV2* and *AD2*. This suggests that the extent to which formal training or education is related to the job is of paramount importance in determining earnings.

4.6 JOB MATCH TRANSITIONS

In the research on the determinants and economic effects of overeducation, authors have proposed several explanations for this phenomenon.[7] One explanation is that overeducation is a compensation for a lack of experience or of other human capital endowments, such as ability or on-the-job training. Groot (1993, 1996) and Sicherman (1991) found that overeducated workers have less experience, tenure and on-the-job training than correctly allocated workers. In the same way, Alba-Ramírez (1993) showed how overeducated workers have less experience, less on-the-job training and higher turnover rates than otherwise comparable workers. Groot and Maassen van den Brink (1997) found that workers who have experienced a career interruption are more likely to be in jobs for which they are overeducated.

Another explanation for overeducation is that it is part of a career path or insertion process in the labour market. Workers may enter the labour market in jobs for which they are overeducated and later on move to jobs that better match their educational attainments. Groot (1996) and Groot and Maassen van den Brink (1997) found that—after controlling for experience—younger workers are more likely to be overeducated than older workers. Further, Sicherman (1991) found that overeducated workers change jobs more frequently.

For overeducation to be a serious long-lasting problem it must hold that changes in the relative supplies of different educational levels have little or no effect on the skill composition of the labour demanded by firms. However, if firms regularly adapt their production techniques to minimise production costs as relative labour supplies and input prices change, then overeducation could simply be a short-term phenomenon resulting from a lack of coordination between firms and individuals.

Young workers tend to have particular difficulty in obtaining their first job. This has applied to the Spanish labour market over recent decades and has led young workers to temporarily accept jobs for which they are overeducated while continuing to look for better jobs.[8] Under the occupational mobility framework, schooling increases the likelihood of occupational upgrading. This would again mean that overeducation would just be a temporary phenomenon.

Although workers entering the labour market perform jobs for which they are overeducated, they later tend to move to higher-level jobs. Once we have classified workers according to how closely their formal training or education is related to the job they do, we are able to show that this plays an important role in determining the probability of a good job match.

To this end, we first analyse job transitions between the six possible types of job match considered in our analysis. The sample used for this analysis is composed of workers at any of the six different types of job match or in a non-employment situation in the 1995 survey. Starting from this initial state, we analyse the transitions to other types of job match or to a non-employment situation, with self-employment, unpaid family work, jobs of less than 15 hours per week, unemployment and inactivity being considered non-employment situations. Moreover, in order to restrict our analysis to one observation per worker, once an individual makes a transition they are no longer considered in the following interviews. The results are reported in Table 4.6. An important finding that should be emphasised is that most transitions take place within the same group, either the overeducated or the non-overeducated group. The most frequent transitions between the two groups take place between individuals giving the same answer to questions (2) and (3). We can thus infer that the degree to which formal training or education is related to the job plays an important role in explaining transitions from overeducation to non-overeducation. Comparing the percentages of people moving from *OV2* to *AD2* with those of people moving from *OV1* and *OV3* to *AD2* indicates the extent to which formal training or education is related to work and its relevance for future promotions or job opportunities.

To test this hypothesis, we use an econometric model of career mobility following Sicherman and Galor (1990, p. 180). These authors run a multinomial logit model in which the dependent variable may adopt three different states described by *j*: move to a higher level occupation across firms *(j = 1)*, promotion to a higher level occupation within the firm *(j = 2)*, or neither *(j = 0)*. The estimation is also made by aggregating the two types of upward transition into one category 'career mobility' in such a way that the model collapses to a standard logit model.

Büchel and Mertens (in press) also analysed the career mobility theory. Using data from the German Socio-Economic Panel (GSOEP), they explored different measures of upward career mobility. Like Sicherman and Galor (1990), they analysed the effect of being over- or undereducated on the probability of moving to a higher-ranked occupation. The ranking of occupations is based on the mean levels of human capital needed to work in the different occupations. Apart from this approach, these authors consider an alternative measure of upward career mobility, which consists of moving to a higher status position where the status definition is based on the German coding for status position of the worker. Following Sicherman's approach they find that both over- and undereducated workers are more likely to move to occupations with higher human capital requirements than the reference group of correctly allocated workers. However, using the second approach to upward career mobility (move to a higher status position), Büchel and Mertens found that overeducated workers show the highest mobility to higher status positions of all workers and that undereducated workers are least likely to make an upward career step, that is, compared to correctly allocated workers, overeducated workers are more likely to move up the career ladder, whereas undereducated workers are less likely to do so.

In contrast to the cited authors, we consider promotion as a job match improvement within the firm rather than occupational upgrading within the firm.

Table 4.6 Job match transition

a)

	Overeducated			Non-overeducated			Non-employ-ment	Sample size
	OV1	OV2	OV3	AD1	AD2	NOV3		
Overeducated								
OV1	10.15	26.46	40.62	1.23	1.85	4.00	15.69	325
OV2	11.02	45.63	14.41	0.54	16.93	1.85	9.62	916
OV3	18.40	17.63	25.35	3.09	4.12	10.43	20.98	777
Non-overeducated								
AD1	4.91	6.25	6.25	6.70	24.11	43.75	8.03	224
AD2	1.02	21.63	2.90	7.67	36.29	19.76	10.73	587
NOV3	3.81	4.71	15.69	11.10	17.94	24.78	21.97	892
Non-employment	1.18	2.21	3.14	0.41	0.99	2.13	89.94	7,377
Sample size				11,098				

Note:
This transition matrix leads to the following percentages of people at the six different job matches in the steady state.

b)

		Per cent	Per cent of total salary workers
Overeducated	OV1	4.45	11.05
	OV2	11.15	27.68
	OV3	8.90	22.09
Non-overeducated	AD1	2.05	5.09
	AD2	7.21	17.90
	NOV3	6.52	16.19
Non-employment[1]	NE	59.73	–
Salary workers	OV1 + OV2 + OV3 + AD1 + AD2 + NOV3	40.28	

Note:
[1] Non-employment includes the following categories: self-employment and unpaid family work, jobs of less than 15 hours per week, unemployed and inactive workers.

We estimate a multinomial logit model, where the dependent variable is a three-point variable that takes value 1 if the individual moves to the best job match, *AD2*, within the same firm (promotion), 2 if the individual achieves the best job match by moving to another firm and 0 otherwise. The results are reported in Table 4.7. Apart from some personal and job characteristics, we include dummy variables indicating the reported job match at the previous interview as explanatory variables in the estimation. Furthermore, in order to analyse the factors that

Table 4.7 Multinomial logit model for career mobility[1]

	$log\left[\dfrac{Pr(x=1)}{Pr(x=0)}\right]$		$log\left[\dfrac{Pr(x=2)}{Pr(x=0)}\right]$	
	Coefficient	t	Coefficient	T
Male	−0.100	−0.81	0.079	0.19
Married	0.030	0.21	0.302	0.64
Age	0.040	0.90	0.078	0.53
Age (squared)	−0.000	−0.06	−0.000	−0.22
Education				
Tertiary	0.314	1.86	0.237	0.42
Upper Secondary	0.290	1.73	0.336	0.65
Lower Secondary	−	−	−	−
Type of firm				
Public	0.349	2.12	−0.251	−0.40
Private (< 20)	−	−	−	−
Private (20–500)	0.290	1.90	0.082	0.20
Private (> 500)	0.220	1.04	0.744	1.01
Permanent contract	−0.106	−0.61	−2.466	−3.82
Seniority				
> 3 years	−0.158	−0.83	−0.425	−0.76
Training	0.140	1.07	−0.737	−1.23
Unemployment				
No unemployment	−	−	−	−
Once	−0.083	−0.45	−0.352	−0.57
More than once	−0.509	−2.15	0.799	1.59
Type of job match				
OV1	−0.612	−2.61	−1.092	−1.31
OV2	−	−	−	−
OV3	−1.041	−4.96	−0.603	−1.16
AD1	0.739	3.60	−1.073	−0.96
NOV3	0.487	2.90	−0.528	−0.89
MOC	0.565	4.14	−0.768	−2.04
Constant	−4.067	−4.49	−4.492	−1.61
Sample size		2,479		
Log likelihood		−1,190		

Notes:
[1] The dependent variable x takes value 1 if the individual moves to the best job match, *AD2*, within the same firm (promotion), 2 if the individual achieves the best job match by moving across firms and 0 otherwise.

Six region dummies were included in each estimation.

affect 'career mobility' in more depth, an additional dummy variable indicating whether individuals remain in the same occupation or not (MOC)[9] is included in the regression. After deleting observations for which the occupation variable is not observed, we have a sample of 2,479 individuals. Our results indicate that of

Table 4.8 Logit model for the probability of leaving a poor match within the same firm[1]

	Coefficient	t
Male	0.062	0.46
Married	0.011	0.07
Age	0.030	0.67
Age (squared)	0.000	0.14
Education		
Tertiary	0.162	0.92
Upper Secondary	0.248	1.44
Lower Secondary	–	–
Type of firm		
Public	0.206	0.97
Private (< 20)	–	–
Private (20–500)	0.329	2.08
Private (> 500)	0.221	0.98
Permanent contract	–0.088	–0.49
Seniority		
> 3 years	1.589	2.06
Training	0.109	0.82
Unemployment		
No unemployment	–	–
Once	–0.022	–0.12
More than once	–0.448	–1.85
Type of job match		
OV1	–	–
OV2	1.838	2.44
OV3	1.059	1.38
AD1	3.167	3.95
NOV3	2.536	3.39
Job match and seniority		
OV2D3	–1.593	–2.02
OV3D3	–1.917	–2.30
AD1D3	–2.269	–2.66
NOV3D3	–1.793	–2.27
MOC	0.604	4.33
Constant	–6.050	–5.12
Sample size	2,479	
Log likelihood	–1,031	

Notes:
[1] The dependent variable in this model is a dummy variable that takes value 1 if the worker improves their job match and, at the same time, remains employed in the same firm or with the same employer and 0 otherwise.

Sixteen industry and six region dummies were included in each estimation.

the three types of overeducated workers (*OV1, OV2* and *OV3*), those who were at job match *OV2* (reference group) are most likely to be promoted.

To analyse the factors affecting promotions in more depth, and due to the lack of observations of people attaining the best job match by moving across firms, we estimate a logit model in which the dependent variable is a dummy variable that takes value 1 if the individual moves to the best job match within the same firm (promotion) and 0 otherwise. Apart from personal and job characteristics and the dummy variables for the different types of poor job match, we include a set of cross-dummy variables for the type of job and a dummy variable indicating job seniority of shorter or longer than three years. Type 1 overeducated workers with less than three years' tenure are taken as the reference group. Results are reported in Table 4.8. The estimated coefficients of the explanatory variables for the type of job match are quite similar to the previous estimation. Again, we find that Type 2 overeducated workers are much more likely to improve their job match within the same firm than the other two types of overeducated workers. If we interpret job match improvements within the same firm as a sort of 'promotion,' then Type 2 overeducated workers are most likely to be promoted within the overeducated group.

On the other hand, the estimated coefficients of the cross-dummy variables are negative and significant, indicating that workers at any of the four types of job match *OV2, OV3, AD1* and *NOV3* with more than three years' tenure are far less likely to improve their job matches within the same firm than the reference group. Finally, the positive and significant estimated coefficients of the MOC variable indicate that most job match improvements within the same firm seem to take place within the same occupation.

4.7 JOB MATCH, DURATION AND MOBILITY

Mismatch can be a temporary status in workers' career development, resulting from imperfect information and adjusted by on-the-job search. From the human capital perspective, overeducation may result from a deliberate choice, with the worker seeing the low-level job as a good investment opportunity. Sicherman (1991) tested the prediction that over-schooled workers are more likely to move to higher-level opportunities. Alba-Ramírez (1993) found that overeducated workers are more likely to change occupation when moving firms and that undereducated workers are more likely to move to a different job in the same occupation.

In this section we analyse the effect of job match on job mobility. The key question providing information on the length of job tenure is, *'When did you start your current job?'* The answer to this question provides us with the information needed to identify the duration in the current job.

A multinomial logit model is used to model the transition probabilities from job to job or to a non-employment situation. Both demand- and supply-side factors influence the transition probabilities. Therefore, the estimated multinomial logit model can be regarded as a reduced form model capturing the combined effect of both types of factors. A broad set of explanatory variables including individual and job-related characteristics is used. The individual characteristics are sex, marital status, age and the maximum level of educational attainment. The job-related characteristics include type of firm, type of contract, seniority, previous unemployment experience, satisfaction with job security, type of job match and a set of cross-dummy variables which result from interacting the dummy variables for the type of job match and the dummy variable for seniority in the current job. The results of this multinomial logit model estimation are reported in Table 4.9.

We find that overeducated workers whose formal training or education is quite or very closely related to their jobs (Type 2 overeducated workers) are more likely to change firms if they have been in their current job for longer than three years. This result is consistent with the occupational mobility theory (see Sicherman and Galor, 1990, p. 176). According to their model, the higher a worker's expected probability of promotion, the higher the effect of not being promoted on the decision to quit. We propose the following interpretation of the results contained in Table 4.9: Workers who consider themselves overeducated, but at the same time indicate that their formal training or education is quite or very closely related to what they do, seem to seek promotion within the same firm. This is consistent with the finding that Type 2 overeducated workers are more likely to improve their job match within the same firm than the other two types of overeducated workers. They are also more likely to leave the firm after three or four years of employment, presumably because their upgrading expectations have not been met. Moreover, Type 2 overeducated workers are more likely to improve their job matches and achieve the best job match than the other two types of overeducated workers. Thus, these job match improvements can be regarded as a sort of promotion within the firm. We also found that after three years of job tenure, workers at any of the four types of job match *OV2*, *OV3*, *AD1* and *NOV3* are less likely to improve their job match within the same firm than Type 1 overeducated workers with less than three years' tenure in their current job. However, as can be seen from Table 4.9, of these four types of job match, only Type 2 overeducated workers show a significant probability of leaving the job after three or four years.

As predicted by the job-matching theory, we also find a negative effect of seniority on external job mobility. Our estimations also support the predictions of human capital and job-matching theories in the sense that workers receiving on-the-job training are clearly less likely to exhibit external job mobility. Finally, the dummy variable indicating the degree of satisfaction with job

Mobility

Table 4.9 Job match and job mobility (multinomial logit estimation)[1]

	$log\left[\dfrac{Pr(y=1)}{Pr(y=0)}\right]$		$log\left[\dfrac{Pr(y=2)}{Pr(y=0)}\right]$	
	Coefficient	t	Coefficient	t
Male	0.007	0.05	−0.445	−3.55
Married	0.052	0.33	0.170	1.23
Age	−0.090	−1.91	−0.357	−10.71
Age (squared)	0.001	1.45	0.005	12.20
Education				
Tertiary	0.161	0.83	−0.521	−2.96
Upper Secondary	−0.103	−0.60	−0.119	−0.81
Lower Secondary	–	–	–	–
Type of firm				
Public	−0.704	−2.21	−0.776	−3.29
Private (< 20)	–	–	–	–
Private (20–500)	0.110	0.78	−0.255	−2.02
Private (> 500)	0.058	0.23	−0.098	−0.46
Training	−0.627	−3.40	−0.620	−4.04
Permanent contract	−1.213	−6.77	−0.915	−6.01
Satisfaction: Job security	−0.762	−5.23	−0.537	−4.53
Unemployment				
No unemployment	–	–	–	–
Once	0.187	1.09	0.208	1.37
More than once	0.394	2.20	0.387	2.36
Type of job match				
OV1	−0.463	−1.24	−0.268	−0.77
OV2	−0.667	−2.02	−0.466	−1.46
OV3	−0.159	−0.52	−0.061	−0.21
AD1	−0.353	−0.73	−0.864	−1.73
AD2	–	–	–	–
NOV3	−0.457	−1.42	−0.337	−1.09
Seniority: > 3 years	−1.396	−3.32	−0.925	−2.75
Job match and seniority[2]				
OV1D3	0.618	0.99	0.265	0.55
OV2D3	1.268	2.62	0.473	1.19
OV3D3	0.680	1.43	−0.199	−0.51
AD1D3	0.510	0.75	0.236	0.39
NOV3D3	0.487	1.00	0.126	0.34
Constant	1.272	1.42	6.399	9.30
Sample size		3,658		
Log likelihood		−2,100		

Notes:
[1] The sample used for this analysis is composed of salary workers at the time of the 1995 survey. The dependent variable 'y' takes value 1 if the worker changes jobs at any time over the following two interviews, value 2 if they move to a non-employment situation and value 0 if they continue in the same job as at the previous interview.
[2] OV1D3, OV2D3, OV3D3, AD1D3 and NOV3D3 represent the cross-dummy variables for the type of job match and more than three years' tenure in the current job.

Sixteen industry dummies were included in this estimation.

security exerts a significantly negative effect on the probability of both moving to another job or moving from employment to non-employment.

4.8 CONCLUDING REMARKS

In this paper we have tried to examine job match patterns in Spain by classifying workers according to their responses to several questions contained in the ECHP. We have been able to distinguish overeducated workers of several types. The key element in the classification is the extent to which formal training or education is related to work done in the job. We find that this relation plays an important role in both the wage equation and the probability of job match improvement among overeducated workers.

The earnings equation reveals significant differences between the three types of overeducated workers. When the formal training or education of overeducated workers is quite or very closely related to the work they do, their earnings do not significantly differ from the earnings of adequately educated workers. This is not the case for overeducated workers whose formal training or education has not provided them with the skills needed to perform their job, or where there is little or no relation between the worker's training or education and the job held.

We have found that all types of overeducated workers exhibit shorter (incomplete) job tenure than adequately educated workers. Moreover, overeducated workers with more than three years' tenure in the current job and whose formal training or education is quite or very closely related to their work are more likely to change firms. Because these same workers are more likely to improve their job match within the firm where they feel overeducated, we interpret these results as indicating that this type of overeducated workers have higher expectations of promotion and tends to leave their job as time passes and it emerges that their expectations are unlikely to be fulfilled.

A final conclusion is that by thoroughly assessing thes type of job mismatch and of overeducation in particular we can enrich our understanding of the problem at hand. In this paper we have been able to use workers' self-reports to shed light on the nature and effects of overeducation. We expect to exploit the multinational character of the ECHP dataset to investigate the extent to which institutional differences are related to the incidence and consequences of overeducation in Europe.

NOTES

1 See Appendix for details.
2 We are grateful to an anonymous referee for comments and suggestions. This work has also benefited from discussions in seminars at the University Carlos III of Madrid, the University of Salamanca and the International Conference on 'Overeducation in Europe: What do we know?' held in Berlin in November 2002.
3 See Appendix for description of the ECHP.
4 As an example of this case, we propose a lawyer holding the position of head manager in the sales department of a large book store.
5 The variable describing the type of contract in the current job is not available for the 1994 survey. Thus, our estimations are based only on the last three waves (1995, 1996, 1997).
6 We take people at *AD2* as the reference group and consider this type of job match to be optimal.
7 The exogeneity of the variables indicating the type of job match in the earnings equation might be justified, however, in the following way: It is clear that wages depend on productivity and, at the same time, productivity depends on the type of job match. However, the type of job match is not determined by wages. If this were the case, the worker would choose the preferred match once the employer has set the wage. This is far from what actually happens in the labour market performance. By this reasoning, we consider it appropriate to include dummy variables for the type of job match among the set of explanatory variables for the earnings equation.
8 For instance, see Duncan and Hoffman (1981), Groot (1993), Groot and Maassen van den Brink (1997), Hartog (2000), Hartog and Tsang (1989), Hartog and Oosterbeek (1988), Smith (1986), Tsang (1984), Tsang and Levin (1985), Verdugo and Verdugo (1989) and Alba-Ramírez (1993).
9 As pointed out by Thurow (1975), when there is a given number of job vacancies with fixed characteristics (wages included) and an excess supply of workers, it is likely that higher-educated people will not be able to find skilled jobs and that they will temporarily accept un-skilled or semi-skilled jobs for which they are overeducated. This can lead to the 'crowding-out' of less-educated workers.
10 Current occupations are reported in the Appendix.

REFERENCES

Alba-Ramírez, A. (1993). Mismatch in the Spanish labour market. Overeducation? *Journal of Human Resources,* **28**, 259–278.
Becker, G.S. (1962). Investment in human capital: A theoretical analysis. *Journal of Political Economy,* **70**, 9–49.
Büchel, F., and Mertens, A. (in press). Overeducation, undereducation and the theory of career mobility. *Applied Economics.*
Cohn, E., and Kahn, S. (1995). The wage effects of overschooling revisted. *Labour Economics,* **2**, 67–76.
Cramer, J.S., and Ridder, G. (1991). Pooling states in the multinomial logit model. *Journal of Econometrics,* **47**, 267–272.
Dolado, J.J, Felgueroso, F., and Jimeno, J.F. (2000). Youth labour markets in Spain: Education, training and crowding-out. *European Economic Review,* **44** (4–6), 943–956.
Duncan, G., and Hoffman, S. (1981). The incidence and wage effects of overeducation. *Economics of Education Review,* **1**, 75–86.
Freeman, R.B. (1976). *The overeducated American.* New York: Academic Press.
Galindo-Rueda, F. (2001). *Graduate overeducation in Spain.* Mimeo, University College London.

García-Serrano, C., and Malo, M.A. (1996). Desajuste educativo y movilidad laboral en España. *Revista de Economía Aplicada,* **11** (IV), 105–131.

Groot, W. (1993). Overeducation and the returns to enterprise-related schooling. *Economics of Education Review,* **12**, 299–309.

Groot, W. (1996). The incidence of and returns to overeducation in the UK. *Applied Economics,* **28**, 1345–1350.

Groot, W., and Maassen van den Brink, H. (1997). Allocation and the returns to overeducation in the United Kingdom. *Education Economics,* **5**, 169–183.

Hartog, J. (2000). Overeducation and earnings: Where are we, where should we go? *Economics of Education Review,* **19**, 131–147.

Hartog, J., and Oosterbeek, H. (1988). Education, allocation and earnings in the Netherlands: Overschooling? *Economics of Education Review,* **7**, 185–194.

Hartog, J., and Tsang, M. (1989). *Education, job level and earnings in the U.S. 1969, 1973–1977.* Amsterdam: University of Amsterdam, Department of Economics.

Hausman, J.A., and McFadden, D. (1984). Specification tests for the multinomial logit model. *Econometrica,* **52**, 1219–1240.

Jovanovic, B. (1979a). Job matching and the theory of turnover. *Journal of Political Economy,* **87**, 972–990.

Jovanovic, B. (1979b). Firm-specific capital and turnover. *Journal of Political Economy,* **87**, 1246–1260.

Mincer, J. (1974). *Schooling, experience and earnings.* New York: NBER.

Rosen, S. (1972). Learning and experience in the labour market. *Journal of Human Resources,* **7**, 326–342.

Rumberger, R. (1987). The impact of surplus schooling on productivity and earnings. *Journal of Human Resources,* **22** (1), 24–50.

Sicherman, N. (1991). Overeducation in the labour market. *Journal of Labour Economics,* **9**, 101–122.

Sicherman, N., and Galor, O. (1990). A theory of career mobility. *Journal of Political Economy,* **98**, 160–192.

Sloane, D.S., Battu, H.B., and Seaman, P.T. (1999). Overeducation, undereducation and the British labour market. *Applied Economics,* **31**, 1437–1453.

Smith, H. (1986). Overeducation and underemployment: An agnostic review. *Sociology of Education,* **59**, 85–99.

Spence, M. (1973). Job market signalling. *Quarterly Journal of Economics,* **87**, 355–374.

Thurow, L. (1975). *Generating inequality: Mechanisms of distribution in the U.S economy.* New York: Basic Books.

Thurow, L., and Lucas, R.E.B. (1972). *The American distribution of income: A structural problem. A study for the Joint Economic Committee, US Congress.* Washington: US Government Printing Office.

Tsang, M. (1984). *The impact of overeducation on productivity: A case study of a communication industry.* Stanford University: Stanford School of Education.

Tsang, M.C., and Levin, H.M. (1985). The economics of overeducation. *Economics of Education Review,* **4**, 93–104.

Verdugo, R., and Verdugo, N. (1989). The impact of surplus schooling on earnings: Some additional findings. *Journal of Resources,* **24**, 629–643.

APPENDIX

The European Community Household Panel (ECHP)

The ECHP forms the most closely coordinated component of the European system of social surveys. It occupies a central position in the development of comparable social statistics across Member States on income including social transfers, labour, poverty and social exclusion, housing and health, as well as various other social indicators relating to the living conditions of private households and persons.

The longitudinal panel makes it possible to follow up and interview the same private households and persons over several consecutive years. The cross-sectional survey, in contrast, supplies data on EU social dynamics and provides information on relationships and transitions over time at the micro level.

ECHP data are collected by National Data Collection Units (NDCUs), National Statistical Institutes (NSIs) or research centres depending on the country. In the first wave (1994), a sample of some 60,500 nationally representative households—that is, approximately 130,000 adults 16 years old and over—were interviewed in the 12 Member States.

The 'Community' questionnaire of the ECHP, on which the national versions are based, collects household and personal information. We focus on the personal information provided by a Spanish representative sample. The personal file contains one record for each person with a completed personal interview. Information is grouped into 13 sections: general information, demographic information, current employment, unemployment, search of job, previous job, calendar of activities, income, education and training, health, social relations, migration and satisfaction with various aspects of life. A core set of questions in each of these categories are asked each year, providing an extremely rich source of information on the characteristics of the Spanish labour market. For this study we extracted data on working men and women from the ECHP in order to analyse different types of job match and turnover among Spanish workers.

Hausman Test for IIA Assumption

The Hausman test statistic H is based on the difference between two estimates b and B. Under H_0 (IIA assumption) b is assumed to be a consistent and efficient estimate with asymptotic covariance matrix V_b. The alternative estimator B, with asymptotic covariance matrix V_B is consistent under both H_0 and the alternative hypothesis. Under the assumptions above, we have $H = (b–B)'[(V\_b–V\_B)^{(-1)}](b–B)$ which is asymptotically χ^2 distributed with $k = rank(V\_b–V\_B)$ degrees of freedom under H_0 (see Hausman and McFadden, 1984).

Cramer/Ridder Test for the Multinomial Logit Model

In practical applications of the multinomial logit model, it is an empirical question whether a subset of states can be treated as a single state or whether its members show significant differences. The distinction of separate states in a multinomial logit model can be easily tested by the Cramer/Ridder test (see Cramer and Ridder, 1991). Considering a multinomial logit model with $(S + 1)$ states and labelling the two states that are candidates for pooling as s1 and s2, the null hypothesis is that they have the same regressor coefficients apart from the intercepts: $\beta_{s1} = \beta_{s2} = \beta_{s}$.

To test this hypothesis, the following test statistic is needed: $LR = 2\{logL - logL_R\}$, where $logL$ is the maximum log likelihood of the original model and

Table 4A1 Variable description

Male	= 1 if individual is male
Married	= 1 if individual is married
Age	Sample restricted to individuals between 16 and 65 years old
Education	
Tertiary	= 1 if individual has completed tertiary education
Upper Secondary	= 1 if individual has completed upper secondary education
Lower Secondary	= 1 if individual has completed lower secondary education
Type of firm	
Public	= 1 if individual works in the public sector
Private (< 20)	= 1 if individual works in a private firm with < 20 employees
Private (20–500)	= 1 if individual works in a private firm with 20–500 employees
Private (> 500)	= 1 if individual works in a private firm with > 500 employees
Seniority	
< 1 year	= 1 if individual has worked in current job for < 1 year
1–5 years	= 1 if individual has worked in current job for 1–5 years
5–10 years	= 1 if individual has worked in current job for 5–10 years
> 10 years	= 1 if individual has worked in current job for > 10 years
Training	= 1 if individual receives on-the-job training provided by the employer
Permanent contract	= 1 if individual has a permanent contract
Type of job match	
OV1	= 1 if individual is Type 1 overeducated
OV2	= 1 if individual is Type 2 overeducated
OV3	= 1 if individual is Type 3 overeducated
AD1	= 1 if individual is Type 1 adequately educated
AD2	= 1 if individual is Type 2 adequately educated
NOV3	= 1 if individual is Type 3 non-overeducated
Unemployment	
Non-unemployment	= 1 if individual has not experienced unemployment in the last 5 years
Once	= 1 if individual has experienced unemployment once in the last 5 years
More than once	= 1 if individual has experienced unemployment more than once in the last 5 years

$logL_R$ the maximum log likelihood if the estimates are constrained to satisfy $\beta_{s1} = \beta_{s2} = \beta_s$. LR asymptotically has a χ^2 distribution with k degrees of freedom where k is the number of restrictions.

We apply this likelihood ratio test to a multinomial logit model as follows. We start from the original model (Model 1) in which only two states are considered: overeducated and non-overeducated workers. Taking this as the reference, we then consider an alternative model (Model 2) in which the overeducated group is divided into the three types of job match: *OV1, OV2* and *OV3.* Likewise, the non-overeducated group is divided into *AD1, AD2* and *NOV3.* The number of cases is 371, 1,027 and 896 for *OV1, OV2* and *OV3,* respectively, and 267, 677 and 1,023 for *AD1, AD2* and *NOV3,* respectively, Computing the likelihood ratio test, as in Cramer and Ridder (1991), we obtain *LR = 1,577.88.* This result is quite significant and we can conclude that the different types of overeducated and non-overeducated workers cannot be grouped together.

Table 4A.2 Current occupation

1112	Legislators, senior officials + corporate managers
1300	Managers of small enterprises
2122	Physical, mathematical and engineering science professionals + life science and health professionals
2300	Teaching professionals
2400	Other professionals
3132	Physical and engineering science professionals + life science and health associate professionals
3334	Teaching associate professionals + other associate professionals
4142	Office clerks + customer services clerks
5100	Personal and protective services workers
5200	Models, salespersons and demonstrators
7174	Extraction and building trades workers + other craft and related trades workers
7273	Metal, machinery and related trades workers + precision, handicraft, printing and related workers
8183	Stationary-plant and related operators + drivers and mobile-plant operators
8200	Machine operators and assemblers
9100	Sales and services elementary occupations
9200	Agricultural, fishery and related labourers
9300	Labourers in mining, construction, manufacturing and transport

PART TWO

Wages

5. The Causal Effect of Overqualification on Earnings: Evidence from a Bayesian Approach

Markus Jochmann and Winfried Pohlmeier

5.1 INTRODUCTION

Among economists overqualification is widely regarded as one important dimension of measuring the inefficiency of a labour market. The extent of the inefficient use of labour through overqualification is, however, hard to measure. The common approach so far has been to compare the returns of overqualification with the returns of required schooling based on an augmented Mincer-type earnings function.[1] Such an approach provides only limited insight into the degree of the inefficiencies due to overqualification. There are two distinct reasons for this. First, even if the returns of overqualification are lower than the returns of required schooling, as the international evidence suggests, lower return rates do not necessarily imply inefficient use of labour and/or sub-optimal behaviour of workers. This is because lower return rates of overqualification might simply be seen as evidence for decreasing returns of schooling. Second, the negative wage effects of overqualification may be due to non-random selection into overqualification, that is, a position for which one is overqualified. This situation induces spurious correlations between overqualification and earnings. In fact, ignoring self-selection into overqualification leads to a misinterpretation of the empirical results and, consequently, to misleading policy conclusions. The effect of overqualification on earnings cannot be interpreted causally.[2]

In this paper, we estimate the causal effect of overqualification on earnings using the potential outcomes approach due to Rubin (1974). This approach has been adopted in numerous econometric evaluation studies, including those of Angrist, Imbens and Rubin (1996), Heckman (1997) and Heckman, Ichimura and Todd (1997). Specifically, we focus on the estimation of the average treatment on the treated effect (TT) of overqualification on earnings, which provides us with a measure for the income loss for the overqualified as caused by overqualification. Basically, there are two alternative approaches to identifying the counter-factual outcome needed to compute this treatment effect. The basic identification condition of the matching approaches is the conditional mean independence assumption introduced by Rosenbaum and Rubin (1983). This identification condition is particularly reasonable if sufficient observable covariates are available to control for the selection process ('selection on observables'). In this study, we adopt another approach that models the selection into the treatment and the non-treatment group explicitly by means of a latent index selection equation. This equation includes observables (instruments) and unobservables ('selection on unobservables').[3] Despite the obvious advantages of structural approaches (e.g., parameters and identifying restrictions, which can easily be interpreted in economic terms, out of sample forecasting, etc.), a major drawback of this approach is the difficulty of finding plausible exclusion restrictions (instruments). Moreover, instruments, although economically reasonable, might be weak which questions the consistency and asymptotic normality of the estimator that only holds true in the case of strong instruments (see Staiger and Stock, 1997).

Here, we apply a Bayesian analysis based on Markov chain Monte Carlo (MCMC) methods in order to analyse the latent index selection model which yields small sample evidence on the average treatment effects. Moreover, the implementation of MCMC techniques is connected with further advantages as discussed below.

The sequel of the paper is organised as follows. In Section 2, we set up the standard sample selection approach for evaluating the binary treatment effects. Then we relate the treatment parameters to the selection model and to approaches, ignoring the selectivity problem. Our database is briefly described in Section 3. In Section 4, we discuss the Bayesian approach to the estimation of treatment effects following the methods by Chib and Hamilton (2000) and present the empirical findings. In particular, we determine which type of worker is affected most by income losses. Section 5 concludes and provides an outlook on future research.

5.2 THE MODEL

Following the treatment effect literature (see e.g., Cox, 1958; Fisher, 1935; Roy, 1951), we specify two potential outcomes (Y_{0i}, Y_{1i}) for each person i. The corresponding outcome equations are modelled as:

$$Y_{0i} = X_i\beta_0 + U_{0i}, \tag{5.1}$$

respectively

$$Y_{1i} = X_i\beta_1 + U_{1i}, \tag{5.2}$$

where X_i is a vector of observed random variables and U_{0i} and U_{1i}, respectively, are unobserved random variables. In our case, Y_{0i} denotes the log earnings of a person if that person has an adequate job, and Y_{1i} measures the log earnings of that person in the case of overqualification. The vector X_i contains the usual control variables, such as age, experience, etc. In this setup, the difference:

$$\Delta_i = Y_{1i} - Y_{0i}, \tag{5.3}$$

can be interpreted as the causal effect of overqualification on earnings. The basic problem now is that we cannot observe both Y_{0i} and Y_{1i} for the same individual. Instead, we observe Y_{0i} for the adequately qualified only and Y_{1i} only for overqualified persons:

$$Y_i = D_i Y_{1i} + (1 - D_i) Y_{0i}, \tag{5.4}$$

where $D_i = 1$ denotes overqualification and $D_i = 0$ denotes adequate qualification. The individual decision rule is finally specified by:

$$D_i^* = W_i \beta_D + U_{Di}, \tag{5.5}$$

$$D_i = \begin{cases} 1, & \text{if } D_i^* \geq 0, \\ 0, & \text{otherwise,} \end{cases} \tag{5.6}$$

where D_i^* is a latent variable, determining whether the individual is overqualified or not, and W_i a vector of observed random variables.

Though the individual treatment effect Δ_i cannot be calculated, we can determine the average treatment effect (ATE) and the average effect of the treatment on the treated (TT) for the sub-population with $X_i = x$, which are given by:

$$\Delta^{ATE}(x) = E[\Delta_i | X_i = x] = E[Y_{1i} | X_i = x] - E[Y_{0i} | X_i = x], \tag{5.7}$$

$$\Delta^{TT}(x) = E[\Delta_i | D_i = 1, X_i = x] = E[Y_{1i} | D_i = 1, X_i = x] - E[Y_{0i} | D_i = 1, X_i = x]. \tag{5.8}$$

In general, these two treatment effects are different due to the unobserved errors U_{0i} and U_{1i}. However, in the case that the difference Δ_i is the same for all individuals with characteristics x the two treatment effects coincide.[4] This is also true in the situation where there are idiosyncratic gains from the treatment, but individuals do not take these into account while deciding whether to participate in the programme or not, see Heckman (1997).

In this paper, we focus on unconditional estimates that we obtain by integrating equation (5.7) over the distribution of X_i for all individuals and respectively, by integrating equation (5.8) over the joint distribution of X_i and W_i for those who are in the treatment state:

$$\Delta^{ATE} = \int \Delta^{ATE}(x)\, dF(x), \tag{5.9}$$

$$\Delta^{TT} = \int \Delta^{TT} (x) \, dF (x \mid D = 1). \qquad (5.10)$$

To close the model we follow a suggestion by Aakvik, Heckman and Vytlacil (2000) and impose the following factor structure with one unobservable factor θ_i on the error terms:

$$U_{0i} = \alpha_0 \theta_i + \varepsilon_{0i}, \qquad (5.11)$$

$$U_{1i} = \alpha_1 \theta_i + \varepsilon_{1i}, \qquad (5.12)$$

$$U_{Di} = \alpha_D \theta_i + \varepsilon_{Di}, \qquad (5.13)$$

where ε_{0i}, ε_{1i}, ε_{Di} and θ_i are independently normally distributed with mean zero and are independent of X_i and W_i. In order to identify the model we finally assume $\alpha_D = 1$ and $V[\theta_i] = V[\varepsilon_{Di}] = 1$. By assuming joint normality of the error terms, this assumption completely identifies the joint distribution of U_{Di}, U_{0i} and U_{1i}.[5]

5.3 THE DATA

In our empirical analysis we use data from the 1998 wave of the German Socio Economic Panel (GSOEP). The GSOEP is a representative longitudinal survey of German households conducted by the German Institute for Economic Research in Berlin.[6]

In the literature three main strategies for measuring overqualification are found: systematic job analysis (the so-called 'objective approach,' where job analysts determine the required level of education), self-assessment by workers (the so-called 'subjective approach,' where the workers themselves specify the education that they need to perform their jobs) and the analysis of realised matches (here the required level of education is derived from the average worker's education in the considered job).[7] In this study we apply a variant of the 'subjective approach' that was proposed by Büchel and Weißhuhn (1998). They used the answer to the GSOEP question: 'What type of training is normally required for the job you do?' in order to determine the level of congruence between the actual and required education. Then they validated the result considering the occupational status of the individual. In this way, they were able to classify workers into five categories. In this study we compare individuals who are '(definitely) overqualified' with those who fall into the category with '(definite) congruence between job and education.'

Furthermore, our empirical analysis is restricted to full-time employed, prime-aged (18–60 years) men of German nationality who obtained a school-leaving certificate in West Germany. In addition, self-employed and those currently in education or training are excluded. After eliminating all observations with missing values, we obtain a final sample of 1,188 individuals with

Table 5.1   Variable definitions and summary statistics

Variable	Description	Mean	Std. Dev.
Overqual	Dummy for overqualification (1 = overqualified, 0 = adequately qualified)	0.119	
Logearn	Log of gross monthly earnings[1]	8.648	0.425
Partner	Dummy for family status (1 = married or lives with partner, 0 = otherwise)	0.798	
Age	Age (years/10)	3.817	0.824
Age (squared)	Age squared (years/100)	15.249	6.391
Firm 20	Dummy for firm size (1 = 20 ≤ Firm size < 2,000, 0 = otherwise)	0.515	
Firm 2,000	Dummy for firm size (1 = 2,000 ≤ Firm size, 0 = otherwise)	0.310	
Civil	Dummy for civil service (1 = individual is civil servant, 0 = otherwise)	0.238	
Tenure	Firm tenure (years/10)	1.098	0.901
Health	Dummy for health (1 = individual is restricted, 0 = otherwise)[2]	0.181	
Education	Years of education	12.626	2.588
UR	Regional unemployment rate[3]	4.315	3.381

Notes:
[1] Full-time equivalent based on 40 working hours per week, in DM.
[2] Person is restricted on account of health reasons in carrying out daily tasks.
[3] At time of first school graduation in the respective federal state.

Table 5.2   Summary statistics for the two groups

Variable	Adequately employed workers		Overqualified workers		p-value
	Mean	Std. Dev.	Mean	Std. Dev.	
Logearn	8.681	0.421	8.405	0.369	0.000
Partner	0.802		0.766		0.338
Age	3.830	0.826	3.721	0.808	0.133
Age (squared)	15.352	6.428	14.491	6.076	0.119
Firm 20	0.508		0.567		0.186
Firm 2,000	0.318		0.248		0.077
Civil	0.250		0.149		0.002
Tenure	1.150	0.914	0.708	0.678	0.000
Health	0.178		0.206		0.439
Education	12.762	2.626	11.617	2.012	0.000
UR	4.290	3.351	4.495	3.604	0.524

Figure 5.1 Kernel density estimates of log earnings

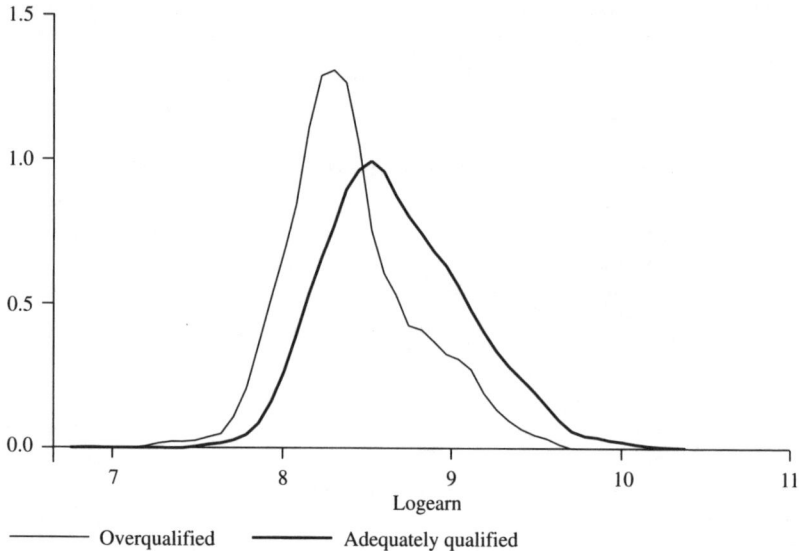

141 classified as overqualified. The variable definitions and summary statistics are reported in Table 5.1.

Table 5.2 contains the summary statistics of the covariates for the overqualified and adequately qualified individuals separately. The test of equality of the group means (last column) does not indicate significant differences for most of the covariates. The overqualified workers can be found more often in the private sector and in smaller firms. Mean tenure for the overqualified is lower than for the adequately employed workers. Note that mean schooling for the overqualified is smaller than for the adequately employed.

Figure 5.1 shows kernel density estimates of the log earnings for the two groups. Interestingly, in terms of income variation the group of the overqualified seems to be less heterogenous than the adequately employed group. Adequate employment goes along with higher average earnings, but also with a higher earnings variation.

5.4 RESULTS

We estimate the model using Markov chain Monte Carlo (MCMC) techniques. This means that we base our inference on a large sample of draws from the posterior distribution, where the sample is generated by designing a Markov chain with a transition kernel having an invariant measure equal to the posterior distribution.[8] Furthermore, we augment the parameter space by including the latent variables (following Tanner and Wong, 1987).

We chose the prior distributions to express prior ignorance. We ran the MCMC algorithm for 120,000 iterations keeping every 10th of the last 100,000 iterations. The mixing behaviour of the chain was satisfying, which means that the autocorrelations between successive draws died out quite quickly. A detailed description of the sampling scheme and the prior distributions used is given in the Appendix.

The Bayesian approach and its application via MCMC methods has several advantages. First, we can easily compute subject-specific treatment distributions by simulating the latent variables (see Chib and Hamilton, 2000). We do not report these here, but they are a great help in calculating the mean treatment effects discussed in this paper. Second, we do not have to apply numerical integration methods to evaluate the likelihood function of our model. This is of particular importance when more flexible distributions than the normal are assumed for the error terms. Finally, the Bayesian approach allows us to conduct exact small sample inference. Given the rather small number of overqualified in our data, the reliability on large sample approximations is questionable.

Although the factor structure of the error terms and the normality assumption completely identify the latent index selection model, we use the regional unemployment rate at graduation and its interaction term with age as additional instruments in the selection equation, following the reasoning put forward by Maier, Pfeiffer and Pohlmeier (see Chapter 7). They argue that times with inferior employment prospects cause students to extend their participation in the educational sector due to lower opportunity costs. In particular, the preparation year for vocational training (Berufsvorbereitungsjahr, BVJ) and the elementary vocational year (Berufsgrundbildungsjahr, BGJ) are compulsory for youths who have not received an offer for an apprenticeship training position and are below the compulsory schooling age of 18. The two institutions, therefore, serve to circumvent youth unemployment.[9] However, the argument also holds without explicit reference to the institutional setup of the BVJ and the BGJ and may also be valid for university graduates. Given that unemployment reflects opportunity costs, an individual is more likely to stay in the educational system if employment prospects are low. Clearly, this argument seems particularly relevant for the case of Germany where tuition and fees for general schooling and vocational training are rare exceptions or negligible.

Table 5.3 contains the estimation results for the selection equation. The findings are largely in accordance with the results of previous studies. The probability of being overqualified is lower for workers with a higher educational attainment. The bell-shaped effect of age on the probability of overqualification is difficult to

Wages

Table 5.3 Estimates of the selection equation

	Mean	Std. Dev.
Constant	−6.368	3.349
Partner	−0.099	0.181
Age	3.553	1.618
Age (squared)	−0.387	0.191
Firm 20	0.276	0.195
Firm 2,000	0.308	0.227
Civil	−0.188	0.193
Tenure	−0.769	0.116
Health	0.104	0.181
Education	−0.183	0.035
UR	0.468	0.220
UR × Age	−0.154	0.065

Note:
Means and standard deviations of the posterior distributions.

interpret, since our cross-section data do not allow for discrimination between age, cohort and time effects. For workers born before 1961 ($Age \geq 37$), the probability of overqualification decreases with age. A positive effect of age on the probability of overqualification can be found for younger cohorts ($Age < 37$). The coefficient estimates for the unemployment rate at the time of graduation and the interaction term with *Age* are quite precise. The sign of the effect of unemployment on the probability of overqualification is ambiguous due to the negative coefficient of the interaction term. Thus, the effect of unemployment on the probability of being overqualified is positive for younger cohorts and negative for the older ones. A positive relationship between overqualification and unemployment can be found for workers who are younger than 30 years. This will be due to the fact that the unemployment rate at the time of graduation proxies the actual unemployment rate for the younger age groups. This means that unemployment and overqualification express an excess supply of skilled workers, see Velling and Pfeiffer (1997), who found a positive correlation between the actual unemployment rate and the incidence of overqualification.

In order to analyse the robustness of earlier empirical findings that neglect sample selectivity, we present estimation results for two model specifications in the following section. One specification disregards non-random selectivity while the other takes selectivity into account through the selection equation. Table 5.4 reports on the coefficients of the earnings functions for overqualified and adequately qualified workers. The posterior means of the correlation coefficients between the earnings equations and the selection equation are −0.294 and 0.260 respectively, but are not concentrated around these values. Accounting for selectivity does not seriously affect the sign pattern of the posterior

Table 5.4   Estimates of the earnings equations

Variable	Model without selection		Model with selection	
	Overqual. = 0	Overqual. = 1	Overqual. = 0	Overqual. = 1
Constant	6.360	7.724	6.300	7.706
	(1.479)	(2.340)	(0.226)	(0.690)
Partner	0.079	0.174	0.085	0.159
	(0.192)	(0.264)	(0.029)	(0.078)
Age	0.563	0.112	0.556	0.106
	(0.782)	(1.272)	(0.116)	(0.374)
Age (squared)	–0.053	–0.016	–0.053	–0.012
	(0.101)	(0.167)	(0.015)	(0.049)
Firm 20	0.112	–0.007	0.103	0.010
	(0.204)	(0.304)	(0.030)	(0.092)
Firm 2,000	0.182	0.052	0.170	0.072
	(0.226)	(0.336)	(0.033)	(0.104)
Civil	–0.167	–0.072	–0.165	–0.067
	(0.176)	(0.314)	(0.026)	(0.093)
Tenure	–0.016	0.039	0.001	–0.002
	(0.110)	(0.179)	(0.022)	(0.080)
Health	–0.068	0.142	–0.074	0.143
	(0.187)	(0.273)	(0.028)	(0.082)
Education	0.068	0.026	0.072	0.014
	(0.030)	(0.053)	(0.006)	(0.023)
Corr			–0.294	0.260
			(0.290)	(0.342)
σ^2	0.171	0.386	0.075	0.094
	(0.024)	(0.046)	(0.036)	(0.041)

Note:
Means and standard deviations of the posterior distributions.

means. Note, however, that the parameters of the specification with selectivity are estimated with much greater precision than the model ignoring selectivity.

As expected, the parameters of the earnings equations for the overqualified are not as well determined as they are for adequately employed workers. The returns to schooling for the adequately employed are around 7 per cent, which is very similar to estimates for Germany obtained by classical methods. Overqualified workers clearly have to face lower return rates, which is consistent with previous empirical evidence (see Groot and Maassen van den Brink, 2000).

As argued above, a comparison of the coefficients on the schooling variable in the two earnings equations provides only limited information on the causal effect of overqualification on earnings. We, therefore, present the Bayesian estimates of the average treatment effect and the average effect of the treatment on the treated in Table 5.5. According to the definitions for the two treatment effects given above, a negative TT indicates that an overqualified worker, if employed adequately, can expect an increase in earnings. A negative ATE means

Table 5.5   Estimates of the ATE and the TT

	Model without selection	Model with selection
ATE	−0.230	−0.395
	(0.129)	(0.262)
TT	−0.193	−0.007
	(0.094)	(0.187)

Note:
Means and standard deviations of the posterior distributions.

that, on average, the earnings from adequate employment are larger than the earnings from a job where the worker is overqualified. This holds true when workers are randomly selected into the two types of jobs. Using the model that accounts for selectivity, the mean of the posterior distribution of the TT is close to zero with a large standard deviation of the posterior. That is, our results do not indicate that overqualified workers can expect significant earnings increases if they are placed in jobs where their educational backgrounds are adequate.

The kernel density estimates of the posterior distributions of the TT for the two specifications depicted in Figure 5.2 clarify that our results are driven by the selection on unobservables. Comparing the TT based on the two alternative specifications shows that accounting for non-random selectivity leads to an imprecise estimate of the TT.

Figure 5.2   Kernel density estimates of the TT effect

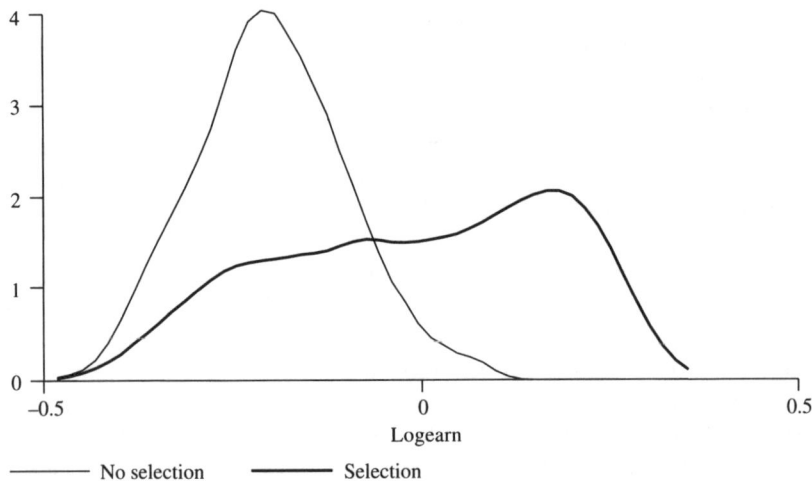

No selection   Selection

Based on the estimates presented above, we conclude with an analysis of the causal effect of overqualification on earnings for various sub-groups of the population. This is done to determine which type of worker is affected most by income losses due to inadequate employment. We differentiate types of workers according to their backgrounds in general schooling (lower secondary school, secondary school and Gymnasium, where the latter is comparable with the grammar school in Britain) and their ages by dividing them into three different age groups. The results for the TT are given in Table 5.6. The negative earnings impact of overqualification is more distinct for workers with a higher level of education and for older workers (but note the high standard deviations).

Table 5.6 Estimates of the TT for selected groups

	Model without selection	Model with selection
Lower secondary school	–0.174	0.005
	(0.106)	(0.181)
Secondary school	–0.215	–0.022
	(0.113)	(0.198)
Gymnasium	–0.330	–0.090
	(0.209)	(0.265)
Age < 30	–0.005	0.175
	(0.175)	(0.189)
30 ≤ Age < 50	–0.240	–0.053
	(0.103)	(0.189)
Age ≥ 50	–0.284	–0.089
	(0.240)	(0.216)

Note:
Means and standard deviations of the posterior distributions.

5.5 CONCLUSIONS

This chapter provides empirical evidence of the causal effect of overqualification on earnings in the sense of Rubin (1974). Using a Bayesian approach, we estimated the average treatment effect and the effect of the treatment on the treated on earnings due to overqualification based on a latent index selection model. Based on our results, we argue that the TT can serve as a benchmark for measuring labour market inefficiency caused by overqualification. Contrary to previous studies neglecting selectivity issues, we find no evidence supporting the idea that overqualification (on average) depresses earnings. If overqualified workers were placed in jobs where the job requirements were in accordance with their actual educational attainment, they could not expect significant increases in earnings.

Although an overqualified worker cannot necessarily expect an income gain if adequately employed, our findings do not imply that overqualification does not occur without any cost from the social welfare point of view. Obviously, earnings studies, such as this, do not take into account individual costs (monetary and time costs) of overqualification or the social costs of overqualification. Moreover, focusing on mean income differences between overeducated and adequately employed workers ignores the possibility of income risk being a determinant of job choice, that is, a mismatch between job requirements and the educational attainment of the worker may result in utility losses due to a higher job risk.

The Bayesian approach presented here proves to be attractive from theoretical and practical points of view. The possibility to estimate treatment effects on the individual level and exact small sample inference, are just two advantages. Moreover, the coefficient estimates based on an uninformative prior are very similar to the results obtained by classical procedures. But, computing the whole distribution of the potential outcomes creates an opportunity for analysing a range of treatment effects within the potential outcome approach. An obvious caveat of the analysis presented here is the lack of evidence for the robustness of our results. Future research using the Bayesian approach should be concerned with alternative distributional assumptions of the error terms and the robustness of the results with respect to the identifying restrictions.

NOTES

1 See, for example, Groot and Maassen van den Brink (2000) for a comprehensive survey on the international evidence.
2 Only a few studies raise the issue of selectivity in the context of overqualification, recent exceptions are Bauer (2002) and Büchel and van Ham (in press).
3 Vytlacil (2002) shows that the non-parametric version of the latent index selection model and the instrumental variable approaches estimating the local average treatment effect (LATE) proposed by Imbens and Angrist (1994) use equivalent identifying restrictions.
4 The resulting model is then called the *dummy endogenous variable model.*
5 α_0 is identified by $Cov[U_{Di}, U_{0i}]$, α_1 by $Cov[U_D, U_1]$. Thus, $Cov[U_{01}, U_{1i}] = \alpha_0\alpha_1$ is identified.
6 For more information, see SOEP Group (2001).
7 For a detailed analysis of these three strategies see Chapter 1.
8 See Chen, Shao and Ibrahim (2000) or Robert and Casella (1999) for details on MCMC methods.
9 Basically the BVJ and the BGJ serve the same purpose. The BVJ is nowadays quantitatively far more important than the BGJ. The latter can be found in larger vocational schools and often serves as a substitute for the first year within the dual vocational training system. Franz et al. (2000) give a brief description of the German vocational training system.

REFERENCES

Aakvik, A., Heckman, J.J., and Vytlacil, E.J. (2000). *Treatment effects for discrete outcomes when responses to treatment vary among observationally identical persons:*

An application to Norwegian vocational rehabilitation programs. Cambridge, MA: National Bureau of Economic Research (Technical Working Paper 262).

Angrist, J., Imbens, G.W., and Rubin, D.B. (1996). Identification of causal effects using instrumental variables (with discussion). *Journal of the American Statistical Association,* **91**, 444–472.

Bauer, T. (2002). Educational mismatch and wages in Germany. *Economics of Education Review,* **21**, 221–229.

Büchel, F. (2001). Overqualification: Reasons, measurement issues, and typographical affinity to unemployment. In P. Descy and M. Tessaring (Eds.), *Training in Europe: Second report on vocational training research in Europe 2000* (Vol. 2, pp. 453–560). Luxembourg: Office for Official Publications of the European Communities.

Büchel, F., and van Ham, M. (in press). Overeducation, regional labour markets and spatial flexibility. *Journal of Urban Economics.*

Büchel, F., and Weisshuhn, G. (1998). *Ausbildungsinadäquate Beschäftigung der Absolventen des Bildungssystems. II. Fortsetzung der Berichterstattung zu Struktur und Entwicklung unterwertiger Beschäftigung in West- und Ostdeutschland (1993–1995).* Report on behalf of the Federal Ministry of Education and Research.

Chen, M.H., Shao, Q.M., and Ibrahim, J.G. (2000). *Monte Carlo methods in Bayesian computation.* New York: Springer.

Chib, S., and Hamilton, B.H. (2000). Bayesian analysis of cross-section and clustered data treatment models. *Journal of Econometrics,* **97**, 25–50.

Cox, D.R. (1958). *The planning of experiments.* New York: Wiley.

Fisher, R.A. (1935). *Design of experiments.* London: Oliver and Boyd.

Franz, W., Inkmann, J., Pohlmeier, W., and Zimmermann, V. (2000). Young and out in Germany: On youths' chances of labor market entrance in Germany. In D.G. Blanchflower and R.B. Freeman (Eds.), *Youth employment and joblessness in advanced countries* (pp. 381–425). Chicago: The University of Chicago Press.

Groot, W., and Maassen van den Brink, H. (2000). Overeducation in the labor market: A meta-analysis. *Economics of Education Review,* **19**, 149–158.

Heckman, J.J. (1997). Instrumental variables: A study of implicit behavioral assumptions used in making program evaluations. *Journal of Human Resources,* **32**, 441–462.

Heckman, J.J., Ichimura, H., and Todd, P. (1997). Matching as an econometric evaluation estimator. *Review of Economic Studies,* **65**, 261–294.

Imbens, G.W., and Angrist, J.D. (1994). Identification and estimation of local average treatment effects. *Econometrica,* **62**, 467–476.

Robert, C.P., and Casella, G. (1999). *Monte Carlo statistical methods.* New York: Springer.

Rosenbaum, P.R., and Rubin, D.B. (1983). The central role of the propensity score in observational studies for causal effects. *Biometrika,* **70**, 41–55.

Roy, A. (1951). Some thoughts on the distribution of earnings. *Oxford Economic Papers,* **3**, 135–146.

Rubin, D.B. (1974). Estimating causal effects of treatments in randomized and non-randomized studies. *Journal of Educational Psychology,* **66**, 688–701.

SOEP Group. (2001). The German Socio-Economic Panel (GSOEP) after more than 15 years: Overview. *Vierteljahrshefte zur Wirtschaftsforschung,* **70**, 7–14.

Staiger, D., and Stock, J.H. (1997). Instrumental variables with weak instruments. *Econometrica,* **65**, 557–586.

Tanner, M., and Wong, W. (1987). The calculation on the posterior distributions by data augmentation (with discussion). *Journal of the American Statistical Association,* **82**, 528–550.

Velling, J., and Pfeiffer, F. (1997). *Arbeitslosigkeit, inadäquate Beschäftigung, Berufs-wechsel und Erwerbsbeteiligung*. Mannheim: Zentrum für Europäische Wirt-schaftsforschung (ZEW Dokumentation 97–02P).

Vytlacil, E. (2002). Independence, monotonicity, and latent index models: An equiva-lence result. *Econometrica*, **70**, 331–341.

APPENDIX

Prior Specification

Defining $\beta = (\beta_0', \beta_1', \beta_D')' : k \times 1$, $\alpha = (\alpha_0, \alpha_1)' : 2 \times 1$ and $\sigma = (\sigma_0^2, \sigma_1^2)' : 2 \times 1$ our prior distribution consists of five independent components:

- $\alpha_0 \sim N(\bar{a}_0, \bar{A}_0)$,

- $\alpha_1 \sim N(\bar{a}_1, \bar{A}_1)$,

- $\beta \sim N(\bar{b}, \bar{B})$,

- $\sigma_0^2 \propto N(\bar{g}_0, \bar{G}_0) \times \mathbb{1} \ (\sigma_0^2 > 0)$,

- $\sigma_1^2 \propto N(\bar{g}_1, \bar{G}_1) \times \mathbb{1} \ (\sigma_1^2 > 0)$,

where $\mathbb{1} \ (X \in A)$ is the indicator function which is equal to 1 if X is con-tained in the set A. In order to express prior ignorance we choose

$$\bar{a}_0 = \bar{a}_1 = \bar{b} = \bar{g}_0 = \bar{g}_1 = 0,$$

and

$$\bar{A}_0 = \bar{A}_1 = \bar{G}_0 = \bar{G}_1 = 10^4, B_0 = 10^4 \times I_k.$$

Sampling Algorithm

The posterior density is proportional to the product of the prior density and the likelihood function. The conditional distributions of the parameters and the latent variables can easily be derived. Specifically, we follow Chib and Hamilton (2000) and use a reduced blocking step in order to improve the efficiency of the algorithm.

1. Sample $(\alpha_0, \alpha_1, \sigma_0^2, \sigma_1^2)$ by first sampling (α_0, σ_0^2) from $\alpha_0, \sigma_0^2 \mid Y, D, \beta$ which is proportional to:

$$f_N(\alpha_0 \mid \bar{a}_0, \bar{A}_0) f_N(\sigma_0^2 \mid \bar{g}_0, \bar{G}_0)_\times \ (\sigma_0^2 > 0)$$

$$\times \prod_{D_i = 0} \left\{ \frac{1}{\sqrt{\alpha_0^2 + \sigma_0^2}} \exp\left[-\frac{1}{2} \frac{(Y_{i0} - X_i\beta_0)^2}{\alpha_0^2 + \sigma_0^2} \right] \right.$$

$$\times \Phi \left[\frac{-W_i\beta_D - \dfrac{a_0}{\alpha_0^2 + \sigma_0^2}(Y_{i0} - X_i\beta_0)}{\sqrt{2 - \dfrac{\alpha_0^2}{\alpha_0^2 + \sigma_0^2}}} \right] \right\}.$$

Then sample (α_1, σ_1^2) from $\alpha_1, \sigma_1^2 \mid Y, D, \beta$ which is proportional to:

$$f_N(\alpha_1 \mid \overline{a}_1, \overline{A}_1) f_N(\sigma_1^2 \mid \overline{g}_1, \overline{G}_1) \times \quad (\sigma_1^2 > 0)$$

$$\times \prod_{D_i = 1} \left\{ \frac{1}{\sqrt{\alpha_1^2 + \sigma_1^2}} \exp\left[-\frac{1}{2} \frac{(Y_{i1} - X_i\beta_1)^2}{\alpha_1^2 + \sigma_1^2} \right] \right.$$

$$\times \Phi \left[\frac{+W_i\beta_D + \dfrac{a_1}{\alpha_1^2 + \sigma_1^2}(Y_{i1} - X_i\beta_1)}{\sqrt{2 - \dfrac{\alpha_1^2}{\alpha_1^2 + \sigma_1^2}}} \right] \right\}.$$

2. If $D_i = 0$ sample the D_i^* independently for $i = 1,\dots,n$ from a $N(W_i\beta_D, 2)$ distribution truncated at the right by 0, if $D_i = 1$ sample D_i^* from a $N(W_i\beta_D, 2)$ distribution truncated at the left by 0.

3. In the case of $D_i = 1$ sample the Y_{i0}^* independently from a $N(\mu_Y, \Sigma_Y)$, where:

$$\mu_y = X_i\beta_0 + \frac{\alpha_0\alpha_1 (Y_{i1} - X_i\beta_1) + \alpha_0\sigma_1^2 (D_i^* - W_i\beta_D)}{\alpha_1^2 + 2\sigma_1^2},$$

$$\Sigma_Y = \sigma_0^2 + \frac{\alpha_0\sigma_1^2}{\alpha_1^2 + 2\sigma_1^2}.$$

If $D_i = 0$ sample the Y_{i1}^* independently from a $N(\mu_Y, \Sigma_Y)$ with:

$$\mu_y = X_i\beta_1 + \frac{\alpha_0\alpha_1 (Y_{i0} - X_i\beta_0) + \alpha_1\sigma_0^2 (D_i^* - W_i\beta_D)}{\alpha_0^2 + 2\sigma_0^2},$$

$$\Sigma_Y = \sigma_1^2 + \frac{\alpha_1\sigma_0^2}{\alpha_0^2 + 2\sigma_0^2}.$$

4. Sample β from its conditional distribution which is $\beta \sim N(\hat{\beta}, \hat{H})$, where:

$$\hat{H} = (\bar{B}^{-1} + \sum_{i=1}^{n} X_i' \Sigma^{-1} X_i)^{-1},$$

$$\hat{\beta} = \hat{H} (\bar{b}\bar{B}^{-1} + \sum_{i=1}^{n} X_i' \Sigma^{-1} Z_i),$$

and

$$\Sigma = \begin{pmatrix} \alpha_0^2 + \sigma_0^2 & \alpha_0 \alpha_1 & \alpha_0 \\ \alpha_0 \alpha_1 & \alpha_1^2 + \sigma_1^2 & \alpha_1 \\ \alpha_0 & \alpha_1 & 2 \end{pmatrix}.$$

6. The Impact of Education and Mismatch on Wages: Germany, 1984–2000[1]

Joan Muysken, Hannah Kiiver and Mombert Hoppe

6.1 INTRODUCTION

There is a growing amount of literature arguing that wages are determined by both personal characteristics and job characteristics. A theoretical motivation for this notion is provided by the assignment or allocation literature, which stresses the interaction between demand and supply when explaining earnings differentials (cf. Hartog, 1992; Sattinger, 1993). However, also search theoretical arguments and even the human capital theory can provide a motivation to include job-related variables in the widely used Mincer (1974) earnings function (Hartog, 2000a) or the theory of career mobility (Büchel and Mertens, in press; Sicherman and Galor, 1990).

Along these lines, Muysken and Ruholl (2001) showed that for the Netherlands 1986 to 1998 indeed wage differentials should be explained by both personal and job characteristics. Roughly speaking, half of the variation in wages can be explained by changes in personal characteristics, while the other half is explained by changes in job characteristics.[2] Similar results were found by Muysken, von Restorff and Weißbrich (2002) for the United States, 1986–1996. In this study we will reproduce their analysis for Germany, 1984–2000, using German Socio-Economic Panel (GSOEP) data and compare the results with those found for the Netherlands and the US.

To illustrate the relevance of different developments in these characteristics we look at education as a person-related variable and skills required as a job-related variable—these variables turn out to be important determinants of wage differentials as we show below. Figure 6.1 shows the increase in educational attainment in Germany for the period 1984–2000 from our data. During that decade the share of the working persons without further education than secondary school fell from 30.5 to 15.2 per cent. However, the share with college and full

*Figure 6.1   Share of the workforce in Germany with respect to education,
1984–2000 (in %)*[1]

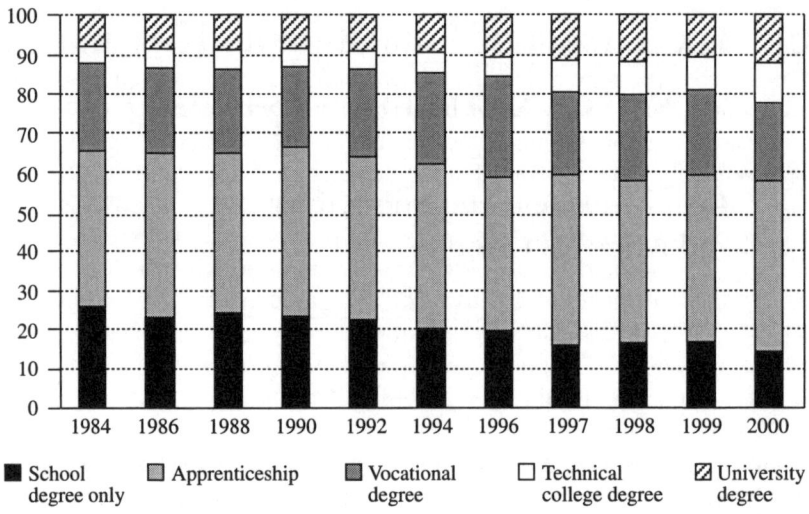

■ School   ■ Apprenticeship   ■ Vocational   □ Technical   ▨ University
degree only   degree   college degree   degree

Note:
[1] The results presented in Figures 6.1 and 6.2 are weighted to correct for sample bias.

*Figure 6.2   Share of the workforce in Germany with respect to required skills
1984–2000 (in %)*

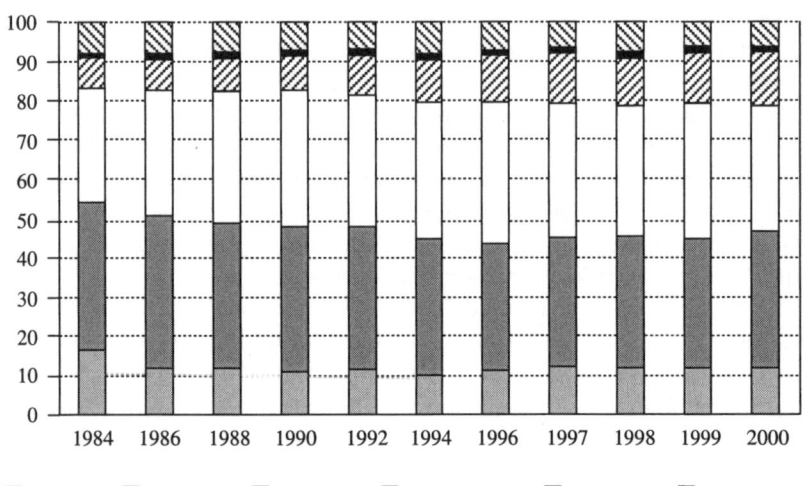

□ No collar   ■ Blue-collar   □ Low white   ▨ Medium white   ■ High white   ▨ Civil servant

academic education (Fachhochschule or University) increased from 9.5 to 20.7 per cent over that period. A similar development can be observed for the Netherlands—and to a lesser extent in the US.

Figure 6.2 shows that the share of jobs requiring high skills (high and medium white-collar jobs) increased from 6.75 to 13.5 per cent over the observation period—this is much less than the increase in the corresponding share in educational attainment. Although popular belief might suggest that the US has an abundance of low-skilled jobs compared to Europe, the share around 30 per cent in the US is hardly higher than the share around 28 per cent in the Netherlands. However, the corresponding share of low-skilled jobs in Germany is hard to identify. The share of 'no-collar' jobs is much lower: It remained stable around 12 per cent. The share of 'blue-collar' jobs dropped from 47 to 37 per cent. But, as Freeman and Schettkat (1999) argue, apparently low-skilled persons in Germany have much higher skills compared to the US. Therefore, the skill classifications in Germany are very hard to compare with those in the US. We elaborate on the classification of skills in Section 3.1.

A comparison of Figures 6.1 and 6.2 suggests that the average level of education did increase stronger over time than the average level of skills required. This is consistent with the findings of Asselberghs cs. (1998) for the Netherlands and Auerbach and Skott (2000) and Wolff (2000) for the US. Moreover, this phenomenon has been observed in many countries (cf. the survey by Groot and Maassen van den Brink, 2000).[3]

The incidence of overeducation is also well-documented for Germany. Table 6.1 summarises the findings from several studies for German men. One can see that the incidence of overeducation is about 15 per cent, whereas that of undereducation is much lower.[4] We discuss the methods used to determine job requirements in Section 3.1.

Figure 6.3, which uses our classification, demonstrates that upskilling and overeducation in Germany took place in all job categories.[5] Acemoglu (2002) explains this finding by skill-biased technological change, which has accelerated since the early 1970s. Thus, the average education of workers on jobs with a certain level of skills required has increased over time. This can be observed for each level, but the increase is higher the lower the required skill is. The

Table 6.1 Over- and undereducation for German men (shares)

Period	Overeducation	Undereducation	Source	Method
1984	14	7	Daly et al. (2000)	Subjective
1984–1998	12	10	Bauer (2002)	Mean
1984–1998	30	20	Bauer (2002)	Mode
1984–1997	12–14	2	Büchel and Mertens (in press)	Combined subjective

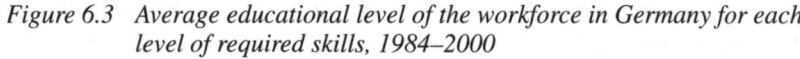

*Figure 6.3   Average educational level of the workforce in Germany for each
level of required skills, 1984–2000*

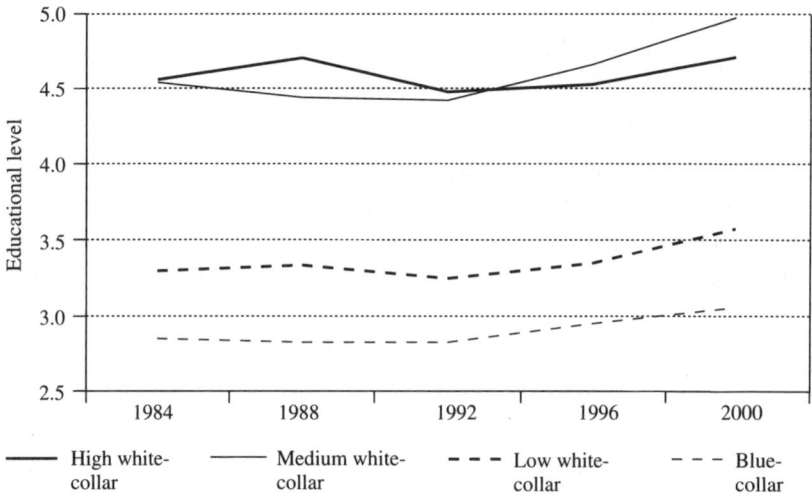

latter phenomenon indicates that next to general upskilling, also bumping down
has occurred.[6]

The above findings suggest that in explaining the development of wages, we
should also take into account the job characteristics of the workforce, next to
personal characteristics. Section 2 shows that this notion is already well established in the literature and presents a wage equation that takes this feature into
account. Section 3 describes the data for which this equation will be estimated.
The new element in our results, compared to earlier studies, is that we track the
development of wages over a longer period, 1984–2000, and show that returns
to education, experience and required skills are rather stable over time (cf. Section 4).

An interesting aspect of our approach is that we are able to analyse the impact of including job characteristics in the wage equation on unobserved heterogeneity. Section 5 takes a first step in that direction and shows how personal
characteristics and job characteristics each influence the mean wage and the
variation in the wage in a different way. It turns out that personal characteristics
like education and experience explain about half of the variation in wages. At
least 20 per cent is explained by variation in job characteristics.

Finally, since similar analyses exist for the Netherlands and the US, we can
compare the results for all three countries. Section 6 shows that the returns to
experience are very close to each other in all countries, while the premiums on
education are much higher in the US compared to Germany and the Nether-

lands. However, the premium on required skills in Germany is similar to that in the US and much higher than in the Netherlands. Section 7 concludes our analysis.

6.2 THE WAGE EQUATION USED

Our approach suggests that in explaining the development of wages, we should take job characteristics into account, next to personal characteristics of the workforce. A specification of the wage equation which neatly allows for both types of characteristics, since it explicitly allows for both overeducation (O) and undereducation (U) next to required education (R), is what Hartog (2000a) calls the ORU-specification:

$$w_i = \alpha\, r_i + \beta.max\{0,(a_i - r_i)\} - \gamma.max\{0,(r_i - a_i)\} + \delta z_i + \varepsilon_i \qquad (6.1)$$

where w_i is the log of wage of individual i, a_i the actual years of schooling and r_i the years of schooling required for the job on which the individual is working—z_i represents the other relevant characteristics. In this equation α represents the premium on required education, β the premium for overeducation and γ the premium for undereducation.

Hartog (2000a, 2000b) surveyed various studies in which this relationship has been estimated. He consistently finds with respect to the premiums that $\alpha > \beta > \gamma > 0$. That is, when a person is working on a job where the required education equals their actual education, they earn more than when they are undereducated for that job. When they are overeducated for that job, they would earn more if they would find a job that required their actual level of education. A consequence of Hartog's finding also is that the ORU-specification performs better than the Mincerian wage equation ($\alpha = \beta = \gamma$) or the Thurow (1975) model of job competition ($\beta = \gamma = 0$).

Groot and Maassen van den Brink (2000) found in their survey that $\alpha > \gamma > \beta > 0$ prevails. The only difference with respect to Hartog's conclusion is the ranking of the premiums for over- and undereducation. We use the ambiguity with respect to this ranking to motivate the restriction $\beta = \gamma$. In that case, we can separate the required skills and actual schooling in the wage equation, which leads to the following specification:

$$w_i = \theta\, r_i + \beta\, a_i + \delta z_i + \varepsilon_i \qquad (6.2)$$

Compared to equation (6.1) this implies that we assume $\beta = \gamma$ and $\theta = \alpha - \beta$ should be positive. The advantage of equation (6.2) is that the specification does not require a direct comparison of actual and required education in terms of years of schooling. Our data do not allow such a comparison: Both actual and required skills are not defined in years of schooling, but in discrete educational and skill levels, respectively. We therefore prefer to impose the restriction that the premiums on under- and overeducation are equal. Moreover, the discrete nature of our measures implies that we estimate the equation in the following form:

$$w_i = \Sigma_{j\,=\,1...S}\,\theta_j\,r_{ij} + \Sigma_{j\,=\,1...E}\,\beta_j\,a_{ij} + \delta z_i + \varepsilon_i \qquad (6.3)$$

where E is the number of educational levels we distinguish and S is the number of skill levels. The parameters θ_j and β_j are the premiums for educational level and skill level j, respectively, and both should be increasing in j, since we expect a higher level to earn a higher premium.

We will estimate equation (6.3) using data for Germany, 1984–2000. The difference with the studies reviewed in Hartog (2000a, 2000b) and Groot and Maassen van den Brink (2000) is that our study systematically covers a longer period. Moreover, we differentiate between different levels of education and different skill levels, although we then have to impose equal returns to under- and overeducation. Section 4 presents the estimation results.

By explicitly observing job characteristics, our analysis also allows us to observe part of the otherwise 'unobserved skills.' Thus we can further analyse the question of unobserved heterogeneity. This is measured by Acemoglu (2002) from the properties of the estimated values of ε in equation (6.3), when this equation is estimated ignoring job characteristics, for example, under the restriction $\theta = 0$. We can compare these with the properties of the residual when equation (6.3) is estimated without this restriction.

Bauer (2002) tackled the problem of unobserved heterogeneity by using the panel structure of the data. He does not discuss the variance of residuals, but shows that a fixed effects model explains the data better than a random effects model which, in turn, is superior to the pooled OLS model. He suggests that this shows that 'the probability of educational mismatch is correlated with innate ability' (p. 222). However, he emphasises that his results should be interpreted with some care because of the low within-sample variation of the schooling variables. In terms of equation (6.1), his finding is that the differences in return to education for over- and undereducation become smaller or disappear altogether when compared to those of adequate education.

Bauer's finding can be partly explained by the way he measures job characteristics, or more precisely required schooling: He uses the mean or modal values of observed schooling within occupational groups. To the extent that over- and undereducation occurs systematically, these observed values do not reflect required education well. Moreover, this method also explains Bauer's finding of low within-schooling variance. On the other hand, his pooled OLS results show much larger differences in returns to over- and undereducation than his fixed-effect estimates. The interpretation that the latter result is due to unobserved innate abilities should be qualified, however, because the fixed effects are also due to large tenure effects in jobs. Muysken (2002) elaborates this point by showing that for many firm- or job-related variables one should realise that average tenure in Germany is in the range six to nine years of current employment. Thus, not only unobserved personal characteristics are incorporated in the fixed effects, but also unobserved job characteristics. The fixed effects method then ignores any tendency for systematic mismatch over the period under study. Amongst others for those reasons, Section 5 takes a different approach to determine the impact of job characteristics on wage differentials.

6.3 THE DATA USED

We have used survey data obtained by the GSOEP for the years 1984–2000 (even years only). These data are a representative sample of the workforce. We eliminated those cases from the survey data for which either some observations were missing (in most cases) or some reported data seemed totally unreliable (in some cases only). Moreover, we selected only persons who received their education and training in West Germany.[7] We used these data to estimate wage equations with explanatory variables that can be attributed either to the personal characteristics of the worker or the job they perform.

Personal characteristics of the worker are first, of course, gender and age. However, since age correlates strongly with total experience, we only allow for an age dummy which indicates whether the worker is younger than 20 years of age or not. The motivation is to allow for the impact of the low wages of trainees and apprentices. The second personal characteristic, then, is working experience. Moreover, in order to allow for decreasing returns to learning on-the-job total experience squared is added. The third personal characteristic is education received. Here, we distinguish between the educational level, on the one hand, and the type of educational instruction, on the other. Finally, we have included number of hours worked as a personal characteristic, although this is already on the borderline with job characteristics.

The characteristics of the job occupied by the worker are, first, the size of the firm in which this job is located and, second, the level of skills required on the job. The latter will be explained in the intermezzo.

6.3.1 Intermezzo: The Measurement of Required Skills

We actually use three measures of required skills next to each other. The first measure is somewhat similar to that used in Daly, Büchel and Duncan (2000) and asks whether the person is working in the occupation for which they are trained.[8] If the respondent answers yes, our dummy variable *trocc* equals unity.

The question used in Daly, Büchel and Duncan (2000) is also used in Büchel and Mertens (in press). However, they complement that question with another question relating to the occupational position of the job holder. The latter question is also used by us to construct the variable *collar,* which we use in Figure 6.2. While Büchel and Mertens (in press) combine both variables in a complex scheme to indicate mismatch status, we use both variables separately.

Finally, we also use a measure which is derived using the Ganzeboom scale, leading to a division into high-, medium- and low-skilled jobs (see Gangl, 2001). This constitutes our variable *funlev.*

We use all three variables independently as indicators of required skills. One of the advantages of using the specification of equation (6.3) is that we do not have to combine them a priori in one indicator.

Actually, in the case of the Netherlands we used a different measure of required skills, which was based on a very detailed classification of various jobs according to required skills (cf. Muysken and Ruholl, 2001). The data are transformed with the so-called ARBI scale, which starts from the detailed occupational classification and divides occupations into seven required skill levels, coded one to seven from low to high. The classification uses the complexity of occupations as a criterion and takes into account, amongst others, the job content, the required knowledge and mental ability.[9] We have used the same transformation for the US data in Muysken, von Restorff and Weissbrich (2002).

An alternative method, which we did not use, can be found in Bauer (2002) for Germany. He employs realised job matches to infer required education either by the mean level of schooling within a certain occupation (Verdugo and Verdugo, 1989), or the modal value (Kiker, Santos and de Oliveira 1997). In both cases a one-standard-deviation range around mean or mode is taken. The outcomes of the three German studies are summarised in Table 6.1.

Turning back to the data we use in this study, information on the means characteristics is summarised for each year in the Appendix together with the natural log of the hourly net wage, which is the dependent variable.

The reason for using net wages is in line with the human capital theory, since it reflects the wage the individual labour supplier will perceive. From the perspective of the assignment theory, the wage should be a mixture of wage costs, reflecting the employers perspective, and net wages. It is obvious that the reported estimation results may reflect taxes and transfer influences.

The data show, not surprisingly, an increasing share of women in the workforce (cf. the gender dummy).[10] Moreover, there has been a slight increase in the number of hours worked (Mhours). Also, the share of young workers under 20 years of age has almost halved, which fits the picture of an increase in higher education. The average experience of the workers remained constant over time. The share of lower educational levels decreases modestly over time, that is, persons who only possess a high school degree, which is compensated by an increase of the share above that level. Thus, the average educational level of the workforce increases over time (cf. also Figure 6.1). The share of persons occupying jobs with higher required skill levels (funlevhi) also increases, whereas the share with medium skill levels (funlevme) decreases. The share of low skilled stayed constant over time. However, the share of blue-collar workers and civil servants clearly fell, while the overall share of white-collar workers rose. The share of people working in management tripled over the time period, while the share of workers in production dropped by almost a third. The share of scientists also rose. The shares or means of the other variables show no clear development over time.

6.4 THE ESTIMATION RESULTS

We used the data presented above to estimate the wage equation in the ORU-specification (cf. equation (6.3)). Since the ordinary least squares estimation results suffer from heteroskedasticity,[11] we re-estimated the equations with the HCCM (Heteroskedasticity Consistent Covariance Matrix) method offered by EViews (White, 1980). This method automatically computes the heteroskedasticity-robust standard errors, hence the t-statistics are also meaningful.

One should realise that when educational attainment as well as job characteristics are endogenous for wages, then the coefficients of OLS wage equations can be biased. Since endogeneity is not an issue in the paper, correlations or partial correlations between education, job characteristics and wages are investigated. Therefore, our findings should not necessarily imply causal effects, and when we use notion of 'impact'—as we admittedly do frequently—this should be interpreted with some reservation from an empirical point of view.

Table 6A.2 in the Appendix shows that the estimated parameter values for most variables are remarkably constant over time—that is, the parameter values lie within a relatively narrow range. This is definitely the case for those variables that have a large impact (cf. Figures 6.4 to 6.7).

The estimation results indicate that almost all variables attributed to personal characteristics are highly significant for all years. As might be expected, being female or young has a negative impact on hourly wages, as does overtime. Both current and previous experiences have a positive impact, although with decreasing returns. Also, the returns to education are positive.

Most of the variables attributed to job characteristics are significant too for all years; and when the job requires a higher level of skills, this generally also yields a higher wage.

Figure 6.4 Premium on 21 years of experience, 1984–2000

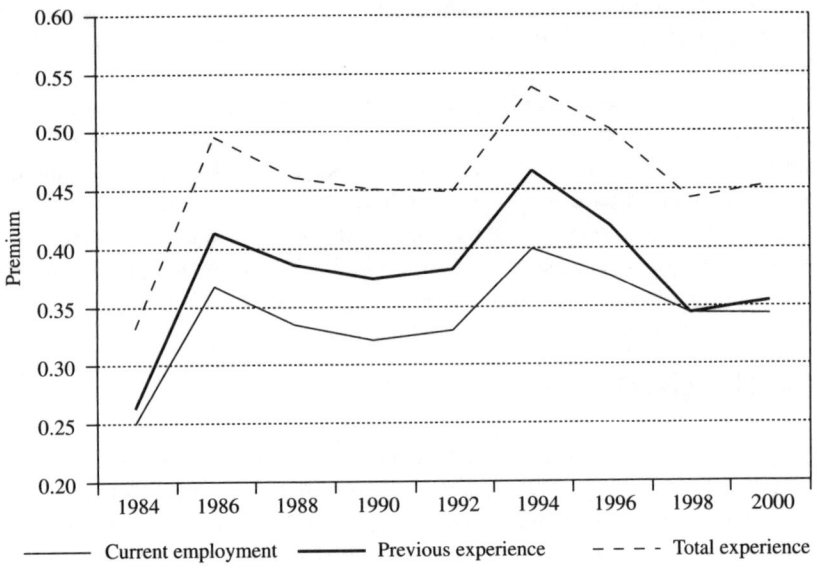

Current employment ——— Previous experience ——— – – – Total experience

Figure 6.5 Premium on education, 1984–2000

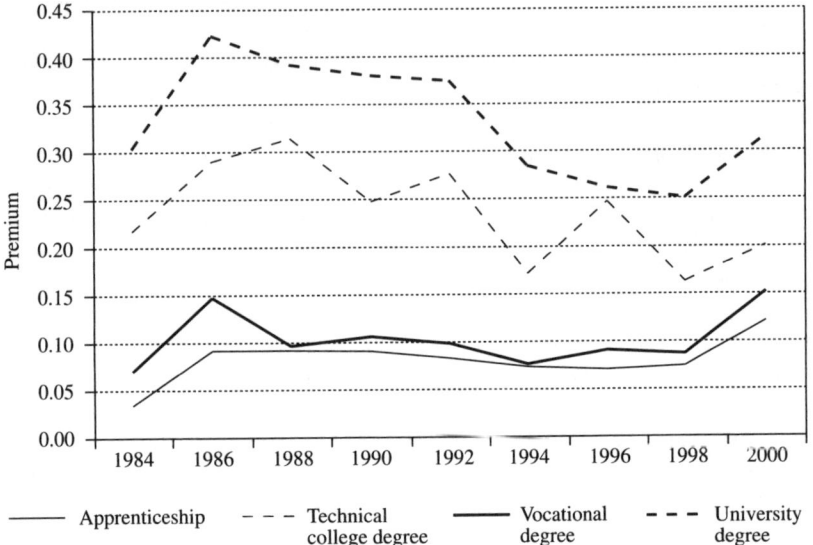

——— Apprenticeship   – – – Technical college degree   ——— Vocational degree   – – – University degree

Since both the direction of educational instruction and the sector in which the person is working are very broad aggregates and the pattern in the estimation results is not very clear, we will not elaborate the results for these two variables. All other results are discussed below.

6.4.1 Age, Gender and Hours Worked

From the estimation results it can easily be inferred that being female implies that one would earn about 25 per cent less of the mean wage, when compared to males with similar characteristics, although this percentage fluctuates over the years. It can also be inferred that for part-time work, decreasing returns to hours worked prevail.[12] The large negative impact of the age dummy is due to the impact of the low wages of trainees and apprentices.

6.4.2 Experience and Education

We look at the returns to experience and education in more detail, since they are crucial elements of a skill variable. Figure 6.4 shows the estimated premium on total experience after 21 years as well as the returns to current employment (9 years on average) and previous employment (12 years on average) for each year in our sample. One can see that this estimated premium is quite stable over the sample period. Moreover, due to the property of diminishing returns, the maximum premium on experience is obtained after around 30 years.

Figure 6.5 depicts the estimated premium on the various forms of education. As one might expect, this premium increases with the level of education. Moreover, the estimated premium for higher levels of education slightly falls over time.

6.4.3 Job Skills Required

An interesting set of variables for our analysis are the skill indicators for the job. Figures 6.6 and 6.7 present the impact of various levels of required skills, one in the form of the collar variable,[13] and one in the form of the required skill level. One can see that the impact generally increases with higher requirements.[14]

Interestingly, the premiums to the collar variable seem to be weakly negatively correlated to the premiums to the functional level variable, that is, the impact of the collar variables has weakened over time and the impact of the functional level has increased, with a drop in 1998.

Figure 6.6   Premium on job levels, 1984–2000

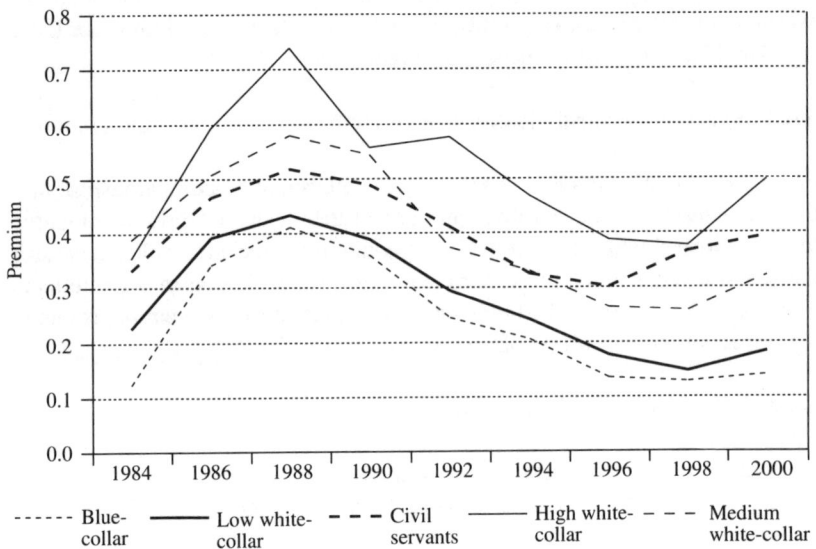

Figure 6.7   Premium on functional levels, 1984–2000

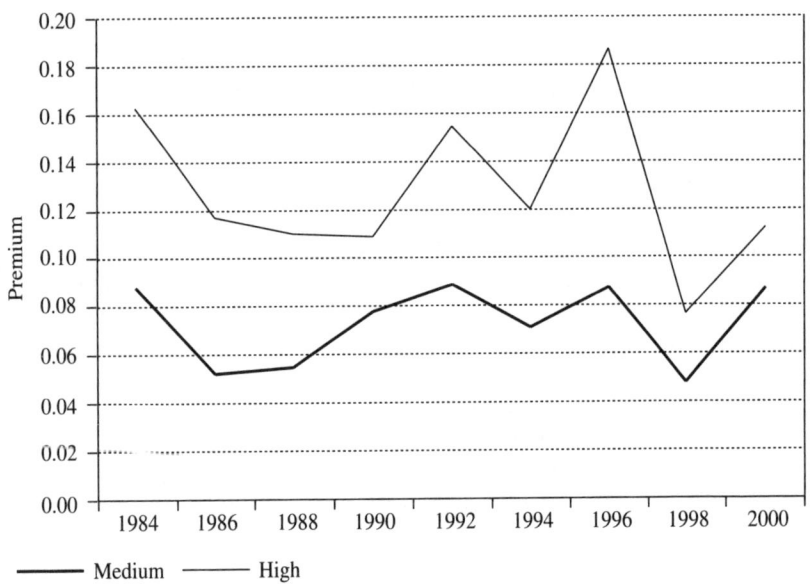

6.4.4 Intermezzo: Interaction Effects

We also tested for interaction effects between personal and job characteristics—in particular between education obtained and job requirements measured by the variable *collar*. According to the assignment approach such interaction would indicate a comparative advantage for certain job education combinations. Almost all combinations turned out to be significant for Germany.

Figure 6.8 illustrates that all educational levels have a 'comparative advantage' with respect to the equivalent collar level. Being a blue-collar worker, the wage is highest with educational level 3, while the same educational level in a high-skilled white-collar position (collar 4) pays a lot less than a higher educational level. These findings suggests that comparative advantages are present in these matches (for a further elaboration see Kiiver, 2003).

Figure 6.8   Interaction effects between education and skills, 2000

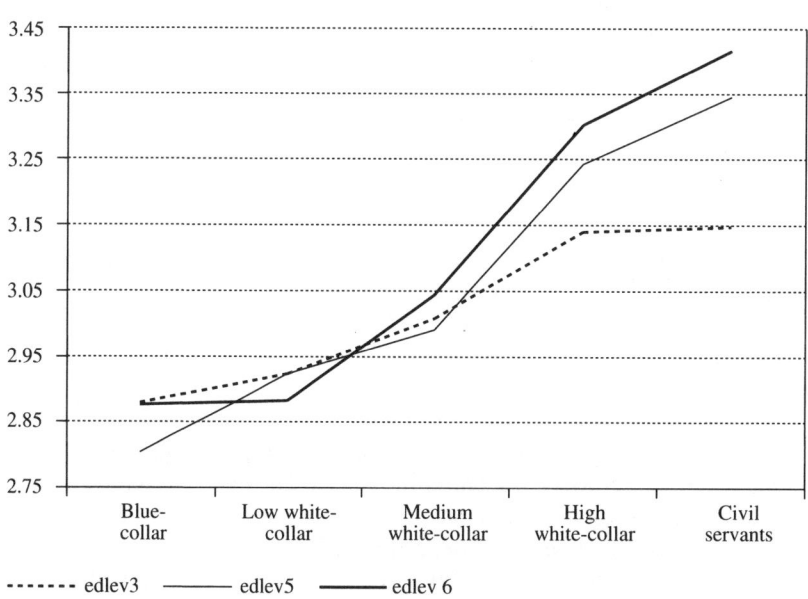

6.5 WAGE DIFFERENCES DUE TO PERSONAL AND JOB CHARACTERISTICS

We found strong heteroskedasticity in our estimated wage equations. This implies directly that increased overall inequality and unobserved heterogeneity will be observed simultaneously. Acemoglu (2002) found a strong increase in unobserved heterogeneity since the early 1970s for the US. He attributes this to an increased return to unobserved skills, assuming no change in the composition of unobserved skills. We have included job levels as an additional characteristic in the wage equation, which enables us to analyse the mpact of this thus far unobserved component on wage heterogeneity. Table 6.2 shows that indeed unobserved heterogeneity measured by the variance of residuals declines somewhat due to the inclusion of job characteristics.

Table 6.2   Variance of residuals before and after including job characteristics as an additional variable in the wage equation, Germany and US

| | Germany | | US | |
	1984	2000	1986	1996
After	0.373	0.345	0.404	0.432
Before	0.379	0.357	0.428	0.452

However, the measures used by Acemoglu are inequality measures on the residuals. Hence, the inequality in the residuals measured in this way is not related to the overall inequality, although this relationship is a prominent feature of Acemoglu's analysis. To develop such a relationship falls outside the scope of the present analysis. We therefore leave a full analysis of unobserved heterogeneity for further research and proceed in a different way here.

Figure 6.9 presents various manipulations with the wage equation of 1992—the results are very similar for the other years. First, we compare the fit of the equation to the observed data for various educational levels. One sees that the wage is slightly under-estimated for all levels.

The 'corrected hourly wage I' indicates the correction for job characteristics—that is, we used the default value of the job characteristics and used the estimated values of the coeffcients to calculate the corresponding wage for each individual. It is interesting to observe that this affects the mean wage of all workers, in particular the mean wage of workers with educational levels 5 and 6. In the latter case these characteristics account for almost 50 per cent of the mean hourly wage. Figure 6.10 shows that the distribution of the wages is also affected by the correction.[15] Whereas the estimated distribution is

Figure 6.9   The mean hourly wage rate for 1992

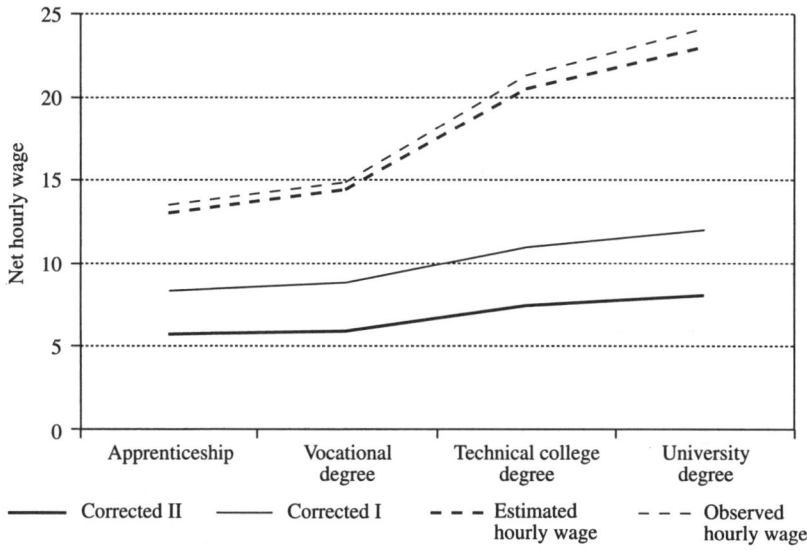

Figure 6.10   The mean hourly wage rate for educational level 3 in various years

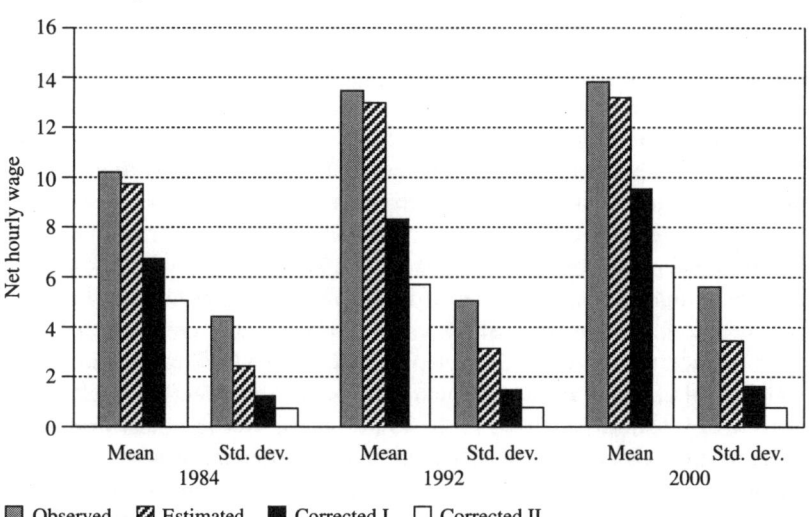

skewed to the right, although mean and mode more or less coincide, the corrected distribution is skewed to the left and the mode exceeds the mean. Thus, wage differences become smaller when corrected for job characteristics. The latter is, in particular, due to the differences in skill levels occupied by workers.

The 'corrected hourly wage II' in Figure 6.9 is corrected for the impact of experience—starting from the corrected hourly wage I, we used the estimated values of the coeffcients to calculate for each individual the corresponding wage in the absence of any experience. One sees that this correction uniformly lowers the mean wage for all educational levels. Figure 6.10 shows that correction for experience also leads to a further reduction in wage dispersion. It shows that most of the dispersion per educational level observed is due to job characteristics and experience. The remaining factors—gender, hours worked, youth and direction of education—only contribute very little to wage dispersion per educational level.

From these results we conclude that one-third to one-half of the total mean wage is independent of additional educational attainment, experience and job characteristics. For all educational levels job characteristics fill most of the gap. With respect to the variation in wages, job characteristics also play an important role. Together with experience they explain an important part of the wage differences amongst workers per educational category.[16] The remaining part of the wage differences is explained by educational level.

6.6 COMPARISON WITH RESULTS FOR THE NETHERLANDS AND THE US

It is interesting to compare the results presented above with those found in Muysken and Ruholl (2001) for the Netherlands and in Muysken, von Restorff and Weissbrich (2002) for the United States—for all three countries we use systematically net wages. The composition of the labour force with respect to skills and required education in the three countries is quite similar. As a consequence the process of upgrading observed in Figure 6.3 for Germany is quite similar to that for the Netherlands and the US. However, Table 6.3 shows that the wage differentials are much larger in the US. The observed wage differentials between highest and lowest education is a factor 2.85. The corresponding factor for Germany is 2.21 (cf. Figure 6.9) and 1.79 for the Netherlands.

Table 6.4 summarises the estimated impact of some personal characteristics for Germany, the Netherlands and the US, averaged over 1994 and 1996. The impact of the gender, age and racial dummies is different, whereas part-time working also has a different impact on hourly wages—all this reflects institutional differences. However, we saw above that experience has a very strong

Table 6.3 Wage differentials highest and lowest education for the Netherlands and the US, 1994, and 1992 for Germany[1]

	Observed	Corrected for job characteristics	Also corrected for experience
US	2.85	2.25	2.11
Netherlands	1.79	1.62	1.35
Germany	2.21	1.73	1.64

Note:

[1] The 1994 results for Germany are influenced too much by the reunification.

Table 6.4 The impact of personal characteristics, the Netherlands, Germany and the US, 1994–1996

	Gender	Age dummy	Black	Man hours	Full-time	Total experience	Total exp. squared
US	−0.165	–	−0.096	−0.00076	0.175	0.030	−0.0005
Netherlands	−0.146	−0.435	–	−0.00125	–	0.033	−0.0005
Germany	−0.296	−0.556	–	−0.00097	–	0.040	−0.0007

impact on wage differentials. In this light it is remarkable that the return to experience is very similar in all three countries.

Figure 6.11 shows that the returns to education in the US are consistently higher compared to those in Germany and the Netherlands. The latter two are close for most levels—except for university education. The returns to required skills are rather close for the US and Germany, however.[17] Figure 6.12 reveals that the latter returns are much higher than those for the Netherlands. We therefore conclude that the main determinant of the higher wage differentials for the US observed in Table 6.3 is the much higher returns to education. The differences between Germany and the Netherlands are caused by higher returns to skills in Germany.

Finally, an interesting observation follows from comparing Figures 6.11 and 6.12. Both in the Netherlands and in the US, the impact of a higher required skill level is lower on average than the impact of a higher level of education. Muysken and Ruholl (2001) use this notion to explain the divergence between educational attainment and wage-productivity growth in the Netherlands. Essentially, they argue that part of the increase in educational attainment is absorbed by increased skill requirements, which have a lower wage premium. A similar analysis might be relevant to the discussion of the productivity slowdown in the US. However, a further elaboration of this notion for the case of Germany is outside the scope of the present paper.

Figure 6.11   The impact of education on wages in Germany, the Netherlands and the US, 1994–1996

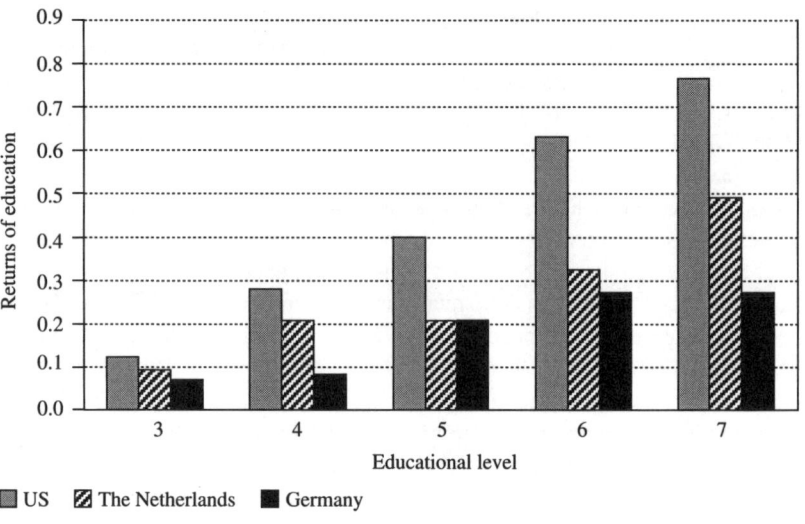

Figure 6.12   The impact of required skills on wages in Germany, the Netherlands and the US, 1994–1996

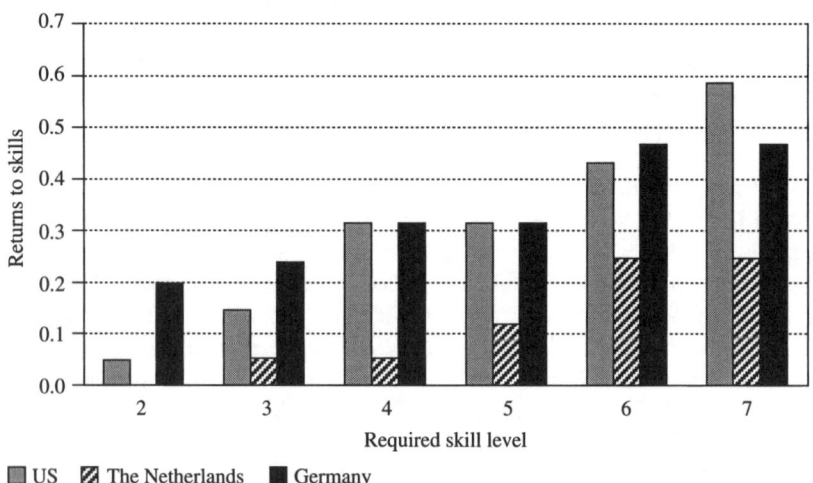

6.7 CONCLUDING REMARKS

In this contribution we estimate wage equations on yearly individual data for Germany, 1984–2000. In the tradition of Hartog's (2000a) ORU-specification, we use job characteristics (e.g., skills required) next to personal characteristics (e.g., schooling and experience) also to explain wages. A new element in our study is that we track the development of wages over a longer period, 1984–2000. We find that returns to education, experience and required skills are rather stable over time (cf. Section 4).

In this context we have emphasized above that when educational attainment as well as job characteristics are endogenous for wages, then the coefficients of OLS wage equations can be biased. Since endogeneity is not an issue in the paper, correlations or partial correlations between education, job characteristics and wages are investigated. Therefore, our findings should not necessarily imply causal effects, and when we use notion of 'impact' this should be interpreted with some reservation from an empirical point of view.

An interesting aspect of our approach is that we are able to analyse the impact of including job characteristics in the wage equation on unobserved heterogeneity. When analysing the impact of both observed and previously unobserved heterogeneity, we find that personal characteristics like education and experience explain about half of the variation in wages. At least 30 per cent is explained by variation in job characteristics.

Finally, since Muysken and Ruholl (2001) and Muysken, von Restorff and Weißbrich (2002) have made a similar analysis for the Netherlands and the US, respectively, we compare the results for these countries. It turns out that the returns to experience are the same in all countries, while the premiums on education are much higher in the US. The premiums on required skills in Germany are in the same range as those in the US, but much higher when compared to the Netherlands. These differences explain the wage differentials between the three countries. This also casts some doubt on the 'universalistic' view on the labour market as expressed in Daly, Büchel and Duncan (2000).

NOTES

1   We would like to thank the unknown referee for their very useful comments.
2   Of course unobserved heterogeneity also plays a role, we elaborate this in Section 5 below.
3   Auerbach and Skott (2000, n. 7) point out rightly that the conclusion of Groot and Maassen van den Brink that the incidence of overeducation has declined is inconsistent with their own regression results.
4   The shares found for female workers are consistently higher for both over- and undereducation.
5   The data for high-skilled jobs from 1992 onwards are affected by the impact of the reunification. We ignore the data for 1994 because definition problems clearly show up here.

6   The exception is high level white-collar workers. However, their share in total employment is very low.
7   The variable 'ost' refers to those persons from the sample who are currently working in the former East Germany.
8   Daly, Büchel and Duncan (2000) use the question 'What sort of training is usually necessary to perform this job?', but the corresponding variable was not significant in our estimations.
9   Some more details are provided in Hartog (1992, pp. 154–155 and Annex 5.2).
10 In most European countries the share of men is larger, although it is decreasing over time. For instance, in the Netherlands the share of men decreased from 64 per cent in 1986 to 56 per cent in 1998.
11 This was obvious from visual inspection of the estimated residuals and confirmed by White's general test.
12 This can be explained since we analyse the impact on net wages, that is, after deduction of taxes and social security premiums. Because these premiums are relatively lower for low incomes, the net hourly wages may be higher when less hours are worked.
13 One should realise that the reference category are persons with information missing on collar. That may induce problems in the interpretation of the coefficients estimated when in the base category, in fact, all types of collar exist and their composition changes over time. However, when we estimated the data with blue-collar as a reference category, the estimation results hardly changed. Also, a further subdivision of blue-collar jobs did not yield significantly different results.
14 An increase of the premium with higher job requirements is also found in Hartog (1992).
15 The figure shows the results for educational level 3, but the results for the other levels are similar.
16 These findings are also consistent with Sels et al. (2000) who found for Belgian white-collar workers in 1998 that wage differences are explained for about 56 per cent by personal characteristics and the remaining part by job and organisation characteristics.
17 We ignore here the skill variables 'trocc' and 'functional levels.' These will add at most 0.2 to the values in Figure 6.12 for Germany.

REFERENCES

Acemoglu, D. (2002). Technical change, inequality, and the labor market. *Journal of Economic Literature*, **XL**, 7–72.
Asselberghs, K., Batenburg, R., Huijgen, F. and De Witte, M. (1998). Bevolking in loondienst naar functieniveau: Ontwikkelingen in de periode 1985–1995. OSA-voorstudie V44 (in dutch).
Auerbach, P., and Skott, P. (2000). *Skill asymmetries, increasing wage inequality and unemployment*. University of Aarhus, Department of Economics (Working Paper 2000/18).
Bauer, T.K. (2002). Educational mismatch and wages: A panel analysis. *Economics of Education Review*, **21**, 221–229.
Blackburn, D., Bloom, D., and Freeman, R. (1992). *Changes in earnings differentials in the 1980s: Concordance, convergence, causes, and consequences*. NBER Working Paper 3901.
Bound, J., and Johnson, G. (1992). Changes in the structures of wages in the 1980s: An evaluation of alternative explanations. *American Economic Review*, **82** (3), 371–392.
Büchel, F., and Mertens, A. (in press). Overeducation, undereducation, and the theory of career mobility. *Applied Economics*.
Daly, M.C., Büchel, F., and Duncan, G.J. (2000). Premiums and penalties for surplus and deficit education: Evidence from the United States and Germany. *Economics of Education Review*, **19** (2), 169–178.

Freeman, R.B. (1976). *The overeducated American.* New York: Academic Press.
Freeman, R.B., and Schettkat, R. (1999). The role of wage and skill differences in US-German employment differences. *Jahrbücher für Nationalökonomie und Statistik,* **219** (1+2), 49–66.
Gangl, M. (2001). *Education and labour market entry across Europe: The impact of institutional arrangements in training systems and labour markets.* University of Mannheim, Center for European Social Research (Working Paper 25).
Groot, W., and Maassen van den Brink, H. (2000). Overeducation in the labor market: A meta-analysis. *Economics of Education Review,* **19** (2), 149–158.
Hartog, J. (1992). *Capabilities, allocation and earnings.* Dordrecht: Kluwer.
Hartog, J. (2000a). On returns to education: Wandering along the hills of Oru Land. In H. Heijke and J. Muysken (Eds.), *Education and training in a knowledge based economy* (pp. 3–45). London: MacMillan.
Hartog, J. (2000b). Over-education and earnings: Where are we, where should we go? *Economics of Education Review,* **19** (2), 131–147.
Juhn, C., Murphy, K.M., and Pierce, B. (1993). Wage inequality and the rise in returns to skill. *Journal of Political Economy,* **101**, 410–442.
Katz, L., and Murphy, K.M. (1992). Changes in relative wages: Supply and demand factors. *Quarterly Journal of Economics,* **CVII**, 35–78.
Kiiver, H. (2003). *Overeducation in Germany—has everything been said?* Unpublished doctoral thesis. Maastricht University.
Kiker, B.F., Santos, M.C., and de Oliveira, M.M. (1997). Overeducation and undereducation: Evidence for Portugal. *Economics of Education Review,* **16** (2), 111–125.
Mincer, J. (1974). *Schooling, experience and earnings.* New York: Columbia University Press.
Muysken J. (2002). *Myths and facts about computer use and wages.* Maastricht University, Mimeo.
Muysken, J., Restorff, C.H. von, and Weißbrich, A. (2002). *The impact of education and mismatch of wages: The USA, 1986–1996.* Maastricht: MERIT Research Memorandum 015.
Muysken, J., and Ruholl, J. (2001). *The impact of education and mismatch of wages: The Netherlands, 1986–1998.* Maastricht: MERIT Research Memorandum 030.
Sattinger, M. (1993). Assignment models of the distribution of earnings. *Journal of Economic Literature,* **31** (2), 831–880.
Sels, L., Overlaet, B., Welkenhuysen-Gybels, J., and Gevers, A. (2000). Wie verdient meer (en waarom)? *Tijdschrift voor arbeidsvraagstukken,* **16** (4), 367–384.
Sicherman, N., and Galor, O. (1990). A theory of career mobility. *Journal of Political Economy,* **98** (1), 169–192.
Thurow, L.C. (1975). *Generating inequality.* New York: Basic Book.
Verdugo, R., and Verdugo, N. (1989). The impact of surplus schooling on earnings: Some additional findings. *Journal of Human Resources,* **24** (4), 629–643.
White, H. (1980), A heteroskedasticity consistent covariance matrix and a direct text for heteroskedasticity. *Econometrica,* **48**, 817–838.
Wolff, E. (2000). Technology and the demand for skills. In L. Borghans and A. de Grip (Eds.), *The overeducated worker? The economics of skill utilization* (pp. 27–56). Cheltenham: Edward Elgar.

APPENDIX

Table 6A.1 The data used

---

diwlnhw: Natural logarithm of hourly net wage, calculated by using the maximum of either actual or agreed upon hours worked per week

gender: Gender dummy is equal to one if person is female

agedummy: Age dummy = 1 if person is younger than 20

cempl: Years a person has worked in the current job
prevexp: Years of experience a person had previously to current job
texpsq: Total years of experience squared

mhours: Number of hours actually worked by a person

edlev2:   Education base level—a person has finished secondary school, but has received no other education
edlev3:   Person has completed apprenticeship
edlev4:   Person has completed vocational training other than apprenticeship
edlev5:   Person has finished technical college (Fachhochschule)
edlev6:   Person has finished university

collar1:   Person has blue-collar job
collar2:   Person has low- or semi-skilled white-collar job or is industrial foreman
collar3:   Person is semi-skilled professional
collar4:   Person has professional or managerial job
collar5:   Person is civil servant
Persons with no information given on collar standing serve as base level

occa: Person is working in business according to one digit isco code (= 4)
occb: Person is working in management according to one digit isco code (= 2)
occc.   Person is working in production according to one digit isco code (= 7)
occd: Person is working as an office worker according to one digit isco code (= 3)
occe: Person is working as a scientist according to one digit isco code (= 1)
Service sector, farming, forestry and fishing serve as base level

funlevlo: Person is working in a low-skilled job according to the classification by Ganzeboom —serves as base level
funlevme: Person is working in a medium-skilled job according to the classification by Ganzeboom
funlevhi: Person is working in a high-skilled job according to the classification by Ganzeboom

trocc: Dummy variable = 1 if person is working in an occupation for whhich they are trained

fsize3:   Size of the firm the person is working in is between 200 and 2,000 employees
fsize4:   Size of the firm the person is working is larger than 2,000 employees
All other firm sizes serve as base level

ost: Dummy variable = 1 if person is working in the former East Germany
The reported descriptives are weighted, reported number of cases are unweighted.

Table 6A.2 *Mean values of the data used*

	1984	1986	1988	1990	1992	1994	1996	1997	1998	1999	2000
GENDER	0.37	0.36	0.38	0.40	0.41	0.41	0.42	0.43	0.44	0.44	0.43
AGEDUMMY	0.06	0.04	0.05	0.04	0.03	0.03	0.03	0.03	0.04	0.03	0.03
CEMPL	8.94	9.47	9.48	9.44	9.67	9.74	8.89	8.12	8.11	8.55	8.05
PREVEXP	12.07	11.64	11.49	11.41	11.75	11.66	11.98	12.92	13.06	13.22	13.26
TEXPSQ	585.36	588.92	587.10	582.46	602.68	600.70	567.95	567.99	574.94	597.39	583.26
MHOURS	168.25	170.09	166.75	166.64	165.76	164.60	163.50	169.89	169.19	168.45	171.53
EDLEV3	0.36	0.36	0.36	0.38	0.38	0.38	0.37	0.42	0.41	0.42	0.44
EDLEV4	0.26	0.24	0.23	0.22	0.23	0.24	0.26	0.20	0.20	0.20	0.20
EDLEV5	0.03	0.03	0.03	0.03	0.04	0.04	0.04	0.09	0.10	0.09	0.10
EDLEV6	0.07	0.07	0.07	0.07	0.07	0.08	0.09	0.10	0.10	0.11	0.11
OCCB	0.01	0.02	0.02	0.02	0.02	0.03	0.03	0.04	0.04	0.04	0.04
OCCC	0.45	0.44	0.44	0.43	0.41	0.39	0.37	0.35	0.33	0.34	0.34
OCCD	0.18	0.19	0.18	0.17	0.18	0.19	0.19	0.18	0.17	0.17	0.16
OCCE	0.15	0.15	0.16	0.16	0.17	0.17	0.19	0.20	0.21	0.22	0.22
COLLAR1	0.48	0.47	0.46	0.46	0.44	0.42	0.40	0.38	0.37	0.37	0.38
COLLAR2	0.26	0.28	0.28	0.29	0.30	0.31	0.32	0.33	0.31	0.32	0.30
COLLAR3	0.06	0.06	0.07	0.07	0.09	0.09	0.11	0.11	0.12	0.13	0.12
COLLAR4	0.01	0.01	0.01	0.01	0.01	0.01	0.01	0.01	0.02	0.01	0.01
COLLAR5	0.07	0.07	0.06	0.06	0.06	0.06	0.06	0.05	0.05	0.05	0.05
FUNLEVME	0.60	0.59	0.59	0.60	0.60	0.59	0.58	0.55	0.54	0.53	0.53
FUNLEVHI	0.14	0.15	0.16	0.16	0.17	0.18	0.19	0.21	0.22	0.23	0.23
TROCC	0.42	0.42	0.42	0.44	0.49	0.50	0.51	0.53	0.54	0.54	0.52
FSIZE3	0.21	0.03	0.23	0.23	0.25	0.23	0.22	0.21	0.21	0.21	0.20
FSIZE4	0.25	0.04	0.25	0.25	0.25	0.24	0.23	0.20	0.19	0.19	0.19
OST	–	–	–	–	–	0.01	0.02	0.26	0.25	0.20	0.12

Table 6A.3 Estimation results for Germany, 1984–2000

	1984	1986	1988	1990	1992	1994	1996	1997	1998	1999	2000
C	1,872	1,515	1,277	1,646	1,975	1,952	2,040	2,024	2,147	2,273	2,091
GENDER	-0.35	-0.30	0.32	-0.28	-0.32	-0.31	-0.29	-0.25	-0.23	-0.28	-0.25
AGEDUMMY	-0.20	-0.44	-0.42	-0.47	-0.46	-0.47	-0.64	-0.44	-0.60	-0.67	-0.53
CEMPL	0.03	0.04	0.04	0.04	0.04	0.04	0.04	0.04	0.04	0.04	0.04
PREVEXP	0.02	0.03	0.03	0.03	0.03	0.04	0.04	0.03	0.03	0.03	0.03
TEXPSQ	-0.0004	-0.0006	-0.0006	-0.0006	-0.0006	-0.0007	-0.0007	-0.0006	-0.0006	-0.0006	-0.0006
MHOURS	-0.001	-0.0008	-0.001	-0.0008	-0.001	-0.0009	-0.001	-0.001	-0.001	-0.002	-0.002
EDLEV3	0.03	0.09	0.09	0.09	0.08	0.07	0.07	0.08	0.07	0.03*	0.12
EDLEV4	0.07	0.15	0.10	0.11	0.10	0.08	0.09	0.09	0.09	0.09	0.15
EDLEV5	0.22	0.29	0.31	0.25	0.28	0.17	0.25	0.19	0.16	0.07	0.20
EDLEV6	0.30	0.42	0.39	0.38	0.37	0.28	0.26	0.28	0.25	0.22	0.32
OCCB	0.29	0.25	0.27	0.24	0.25	0.23	0.25	0.32	0.28	0.24	0.24
OCCC	0.10	0.06	0.03**	0.06	0.08	0.03**	0.08	0.09	0.09	0.09	0.08
OCCD	0.11	0.13	0.11	0.10	0.07	0.10	0.09	0.10	0.11	0.09	0.08
OCCE	0.08	0.12	0.09	0.12	0.11	0.14	0.11	0.18	0.16	0.15	0.13
COLLAR1	0.12	0.34	0.41	0.36	0.24	0.20	0.13	0.20	0.13	0.06*	0.14
COLLAR2	0.23	0.39	0.43	0.39	0.29	0.24	0.17	0.21	0.15	0.13	0.18
COLLAR3	0.39	0.51	0.58	0.54	0.37	0.33	0.26	0.32	0.26	0.24	0.32
COLLAR4	0.35	0.59	0.74	0.56	0.57	0.47	0.39	0.43	0.38	0.39	0.50
COLLAR5	0.33	0.47	0.52	0.49	0.41	0.33	0.30	0.37	0.36	0.33	0.39
FUNLEVME	0.09	0.05	0.05	0.08	0.09	0.07	0.09	0.05	0.05	0.04	0.09
FUNLEVHI	0.16	0.12	0.11	0.11	0.15	0.12	0.19	0.07	0.08	0.09	0.11
TROCC	0.06	0.08	0.08	0.09	0.07	0.08	0.07	0.10	0.09	0.09	0.08
FSIZE3	0.06	0.01**	0.06	0.07	0.06	0.09	0.07	0.12	0.10	0.13	0.13
FSIZE4	0.08	0.10	0.11	0.12	0.12	0.14	0.12	0.16	0.14	0.18	0.17
OST	–	–	–	–	–	0.16	-0.04**	-0.26	-0.20	-0.01**	-0.20
R²	0.49	0.60	0.63	0.61	0.59	0.57	0.56	0.57	0.56	0.52	0.53
Adjusted R²	0.49	0.60	0.63	0.61	0.59	0.57	0.56	0.56	0.55	0.52	0.52
n	3,484	3,214	3,413	3,425	3,281	3,235	3,419	4,857	4,630	4,831	5,267

* Not significant at 5%; ** not significant at 10%.

132

7. Overeducation and Individual Heterogeneity[1]

Michael Maier, Friedhelm Pfeiffer and Winfried Pohlmeier

7.1 INTRODUCTION

For societies, where a large proportion of education is controlled and financed by the public sector without a pricing mechanism, the optimal match between the supply of educational programmes and their efficient use is of fundamental importance. In addition to unemployment caused by a mismatch of qualifications, overeducation can be regarded as another symptom for inefficient use of qualified labour.[2] In order to assess the market value of overeducation, empirical studies distinguish between the returns to required schooling and the returns to overschooling. However, they usually treat returns to education as being homogeneous across individuals and ignore that educational choices are endogenous outcomes of observable and unobservable determinants. In this paper, we stress this issue by analysing the heterogeneous returns to overeducation within the potential outcome approach known from the econometric evaluation literature.

Since there is no clear-cut definition of overeducation, there is an extensive methodological debate on the appropriate measurement for overschooling and whether objective or subjective measures are more adequate.[3] Based on the assumption of homogeneous returns to overeducation, Groot and van den Brink (2000) find in their meta-analysis of 25 econometric studies on overqualification that the estimated returns to overeducation lack robustness concerning the measurement of overeducation. Moreover, the returns to overeducation are significantly lower than the returns to required education only for an objective measure that depends on some difference measures between actual and required years of schooling in a job. The incidence and the earnings consequences of overschooling vary to a considerable degree between studies. Countries, gender, other socio-demographic factors and the definition of the overeducation measurement account for these differences. According to their meta-analysis, the returns to required education are roughly 8 per cent in the US and Europe.

The returns to overeducation are 2.1 per cent in Europe and 3.9 per cent in the US. Groot and van den Brink (2000, p. 153) report that the percentage of the labour force that can be classified as overqualified amounts to 26.3 per cent in the US and 21.5 per cent in Europe and that there is no incidence of a rise in overeducation in the last two decades. Hartog (2000) also reports differences in overeducation between European countries. In this study measurement issues do not alter the general conclusion that the returns to overeducation are lower than the returns to required education. A more critical view of the framework of homogenous returns stems from Bauer (2002), who argues that most of the results for overeducation are based on cross-sectional evidence. According to his findings for Germany based on the German Socio-Economic Panel (GSOEP), the difference between returns to required education and overeducation vanishes when individual heterogeneity is controlled in the framework of a panel fixed effects estimator.

Based on a comparison of educational attainment and job level requirement in Germany, Velling and Pfeiffer (1997) found that the incidence of overeducation is inversely related to the level of educational attainment. Among university graduates, 11 per cent were found to be overqualified. This is compared to 23 per cent of graduates from dual vocational training. Moreover, they show that overeducation varies between academic fields and that the incidence of overeducation is higher among students from social sciences than it is for students from natural sciences and economics. Women and workers with less experience have a higher incidence of overeducation, which seems to be in line with the international evidence (Büchel, 2001; Groot and van den Brink, 2000). Blechinger and Pfeiffer (2000) found that skill obsolescence had risen significantly among German apprentices between 1979 and 1992. According to their analysis, this is due to rapid technical and organisational changes in this period and, correspondingly, a slow response from the officials responsible for the curricula. In addition, the study by Groot and van den Brink (2000) indicated a concentration of overeducation among low-ability workers for whom the returns to overeducation are low.

The literature notes similarities between overeducation and unemployment in the sense of underutilisation of skills acquired in the educational system (see Büchel, 2001; Groot and van den Brink, 2000; Velling and Pfeiffer, 1997). Büchel (2001) observed that overeducation exceeds unemployment rates in each industrialised country. Velling and Pfeiffer's (1997) findings suggest a positive correlation between the incidence of overeducation and unemployment. Groot and van den Brink (2000) reported from OLS estimates that unemployment lowers the returns to required schooling, but has no effect on the returns to overschooling. The causality issues between rising unemployment and prolonged education due to inflexible labour markets has, to the best of our knowledge, not been addressed in the literature so far.

Two major issues that have been raised in the recent empirical literature on human capital investment have been neglected in the context of overeducation. First, education, as well as overeducation, as the individual's choice parameter are endogenous regressors in the standard earnings function. Since coefficient estimates on schooling variables can only be interpreted as causal effects of schooling on earnings if individuals had been randomly assigned to different schooling levels, standard least squares estimates are of a purely explorative nature. Therefore, their usefulness with respect to policy recommendations is limited. In order to assess the causal effect of (over-)education on earnings we, therefore, adopt the concept of the Average Treatment Effect (ATE) of the earnings function developed in the econometric evaluation literature. This is used to quantify the expected earnings difference between two otherwise identical individuals if they had been assigned randomly to S and $S + 1$ years of schooling, respectively. Contrary to previous studies on the ATE in standard earnings functions, which rest on a control function approach, we apply the Conditional Mean Independence (CMI) approach to identify the ATE of schooling and overeducation.

Second, as a choice parameter the individual's schooling level is determined by the individual's observed and unobserved marginal benefits and costs of schooling. Thus, the return of an additional year of schooling presumably varies across individuals. The same argument also holds for the case of overeducation. In fact, one could argue that selection issues are particularly severe for overeducation, since the population of the overeducated is not likely to be a randomly selected subgroup of the total population.

Our paper is organised as follows: In Section 2, we develop the idea of random returns to education based on Card's schooling model (Card, 1999). Following Wooldridge (2002), we identify the ATE via conditional mean independence assumptions and show that the ATE for the continuous treatment variable schooling can be estimated by means of auxiliary regressions. Section 3 describes the data and provides information on the institutional settings in Germany. Our empirical findings are presented in Section 4, while Section 5 concludes and gives an outlook on future research.

7.2 THE CMI APPROACH

Numerous studies on the returns to education emphasise that schooling is a choice variable depending on observable and unobservable factors that determine the individual's marginal costs and benefits of schooling. For the econometrician, this implies that returns to schooling is a random variable correlated with the determinants; that is, the returns to schooling vary across individuals. These basic features are captured in Card's (1999, 2001) model of schooling and earnings which we will use in the sequel as a specification device.

The individual is assumed to choose the optimal amount of schooling, S, and earnings, Y, that maximise their lifetime utility depending on earnings and the disutility of schooling, $\varphi(S)$:

$$\max_{S,\,Y} U(S, Y) = \ln Y - \varphi(S) \text{ with } \varphi'(S) > 0 \text{ and } \varphi''(S) > 0. \qquad (7.1)$$

Let the benefits of schooling (schooling earnings relationship) be $Y = Y(S)$ with $Y'(S) > 0$. This yields the first order conditions:

$$\frac{Y'(S)}{Y(S)} = \varphi'(S). \qquad (7.2)$$

A linear log earnings function for schooling arises if marginal benefits are constant:[4]

$$MB \equiv \frac{Y'(S)}{Y(S)} = \beta. \qquad (7.3)$$

If marginal costs are linear in schooling, then:

$$MC \equiv \varphi'(S) = \gamma + \kappa S, \qquad \kappa > 0. \qquad (7.4)$$

Optimal schooling is given by:

$$S = \frac{\beta - \gamma}{\kappa}. \qquad (7.5)$$

Integration of the marginal benefit function (7.3) yields a log linear earnings function with random coefficients, an individual specific intercept and an individual specific slope coefficient:

$$\ln Y = \alpha + \beta S. \qquad (7.6)$$

Intercept coefficient α captures the absolute productivity (ability) advantages of the agent. Observable factors and unobserved heterogeneity in the absolute and marginal benefits of schooling, as well as factors driving the marginal costs of schooling, enter the earnings function through the coefficients α, β and γ, respectively. Let α be presented by the linear predictor function:

$$\alpha = \alpha_0 + X_1'\alpha_1 + \eta_\alpha, \qquad (7.7)$$

where X_1 is a vector of observables and the random variate η_α captures unobserved heterogeneity in the absolute productivity term. Likewise, marginal productivity may depend on the same set of factors:

$$\beta = \beta_0 + X_1'\beta_1 + \eta_\beta, \qquad (7.8)$$

while marginal cost depends on the X_1 variables as well as on additional cost driving factors X_2:

$$\gamma = \gamma_0 + X_1'\gamma_1 + X_2'\gamma_2 + \eta_\gamma. \qquad (7.9)$$

Inserting equations (7.7) to (7.9) in the schooling equation (7.5) yields a reduced form of the schooling equation:

$$S = \frac{1}{\kappa}[(\beta_0 - \gamma_0) + X_1'(\beta_1 - \gamma_1) - X_2'\gamma_2 + \eta_\beta - \eta_\gamma] = \pi_0 + X_1'\pi_1 + X_2'\pi_2 + \xi \quad (7.10)$$

Note that the returns of an additional year of schooling is now a random variable depending on the level of schooling and the marginal costs of schooling; that is, the returns to schooling vary across the population. The ATE of an additional year of schooling is the mean across all individual returns of an additional year of schooling:

$$ATE = E[E[\ln Y \,|\, S = s + 1, \alpha, \beta] - E[\ln Y \,|\, S = s, \alpha, \beta]] = E[\beta]. \quad (7.11)$$

For example, in the context of the German debate on the effects of shorter secondary schooling, it is interesting to know how much a reduction of schooling changes earnings for those with a given schooling level $S = s$. This effect is the average treatment on the treated effect (ATET) in the continuous treatment effect framework:

$$ATET = E[\beta \,|\, \beta = \kappa \cdot s + \gamma] = \frac{\int_{\beta \geq \gamma} \beta f\beta, \gamma(\beta, \beta - \kappa \cdot s)\, d\beta}{f_{\beta - \gamma}(\kappa \cdot s)}, \quad (7.12)$$

which evaluates the expected returns across all the combinations of marginal benefits and costs of schooling that imply the same optimal schooling level $S = s$.

Similar to the binary treatment effect literature for the case of a continuous treatment, one can distinguish between two approaches to the evaluation problem. Garen (1984), Heckman and Vytlacil (1998) and Wooldridge (1997) propose an IV or control function approach that makes use of control functions such as equations (7.7) and (7.8) to estimate the ATE from the reduced forms for earnings and schooling. The major drawback of this approach is the limited availability of reasonable exclusion restrictions (instruments) that differentiate the causal treatment effect from the selection effect.

Here, we follow a suggestion found in Wooldridge (2002, Chapter 18.5). We estimate the ATE in a random coefficient framework by assuming conditional mean independence. In this case, treatment can be ignored when conditional on a set of covariates. The ATE can be identified under these ignorability conditions if the following assumptions hold.

Identifying Assumptions for the ATE (Wooldridge, 2002, p. 639):

(i) Equation (7.6) holds.
(ii) For a set of covariates X, the following redundancy assumption holds:
   $E[\ln Y \,|\, S, \alpha, \beta, X] = E[\ln Y \,|\, S, \alpha, \beta]$
(iii) Conditional on X, α and β are redundant in the first two conditional moments of S:
   $E[S \,|\, X, \alpha, \beta] = E[S \,|\, X]$ and $V[S \,|\, X, \alpha, \beta] = V[S \,|\, X] > 0$.

Identification condition (ii) obviously holds, since the control variable X enters
the earnings function through α, β and S only. The linear predictor specification
used for illustrative purposes in equations (7.7) and (7.8) is not required to
identify the ATE. In fact, the conditional mean independence approach uses
identification conditions different from the control function approaches in
correlated random coefficient models. Identification condition (iii) denotes that
conditional on the controls, expected schooling is mean independent of α and
β. Thus, no new information is gained in projecting schooling if there are
sufficient controls. This is the crucial identification condition (ignorability condition) needed to identify the ATE.

Proposition 2.1 (ATE)

*Under the identifying assumptions, the average treatment effect for all X in the
relevant population is given by:*

$$E\,[\beta] = E\left[\frac{\text{Cov}[S,\,\ln Y\,|\,X]}{V[S\,|\,X]}\right].\tag{7.13}$$

In the following analysis, we estimate $V[S|X]$ and $\text{Cov}[S, \ln Y|X]$ by means of
linear regression. Replacing the population parameters with the regression estimates yields a consistent estimate of the ATE under the assumption of i.i.d.
observations:

$$\hat{E}\,[\beta] = \frac{1}{n}\sum_{i=1}^{n}\frac{\hat{\text{Cov}}[S_i,\,\ln Y_i\,|\,X_i]}{\hat{V}[S_i\,|\,X_i]}.\tag{7.14}$$

Note that contrary to the IV or control function approach, the CMI approach
does not require exclusion restrictions for instrumental variables in such a way
that the instruments drive the selection process (choice of the optimal years of
schooling). Rather, they are uncorrelated with the error term of the structural
equation. Since the ATE is nothing but the mean of the ratio of second moments
and cross-moments of schooling and earnings conditional on X, more insights
into the causal effects of schooling can be obtained by analysing other distributional properties of this ratio rather than the mean.

7.3 DATA

Our empirical study is based on a sample of full-time employed male workers
from the so-called BIBB/IAB survey on educational and vocational attainment and career (BIBB/IAB, 1999).[5] The BIBB/IAB survey is a 0.1 per cent
representative survey of German workers, which has been conducted every
five to six years since 1979. The last survey dates from 1998/99. The objec-

tive of the survey is to supply 'differentiated, actual data on workers in Germany, their qualifications and working conditions' (Jansen and Stooss, 1993).

For our analysis, we select a sample of German male workers from the most recent survey. One advantage of the most current survey is that it contains comprehensive information on the number of years spent in the educational and vocational education system in Germany. In particular, our data contain extensive information on the successful completion of schooling levels (basic schooling, vocational and university education) and the actual years spent in the educational system to obtain the degree. Hence, our definition of the schooling variable is more closely related to the definition of an input variable than the standard definitions, using either the minimum years required by the individual to receive their highest educational attainment or the average years of schooling necessary to attain a degree. In Germany, three major types of education systems have to be recognised: (1) The general schooling system with compulsory school attendance until the age of 18. This means that youths who do not find a job in the German apprenticeship system (dual vocational training system, DVTS) have to stay in the general schooling system until age 18. (2) The second system, the DVTS, provides apprentices with a mixture of theoretical schooling and practical skill-specific training (see Blechinger and Pfeiffer, 2000). (3) The university system.

As of 1995, about 70 per cent of all German workers had been trained in the DVTS. Although the number of young people entering vocational training is declining, the DVTS remains quantitatively the most important form of training system. Note that despite considerable compulsory school attendance, 10 per cent of the workers have not received a formal vocational degree.

We concentrate on full-time male workers (i.e., we exclude women, self-employed and part-time employed men) because we assume that men by and large have an inelastic labour supply. With this assumption, we can disregard selection into the labour force. Furthermore, we select only workers born after 1945 who were living in West Germany at the time of the survey and had no more than two degrees from either the compulsory educational or the vocational systems. The latter selection criterion excludes roughly 5 per cent of the workers from our analysis. In addition, we trimmed the number of schooling years variable in order to exclude the 1 per cent of observations with the lowest and the 1 per cent with the highest number of years spent in the compulsory educational and vocational systems.

Our earnings variable refers to the natural logarithm of monthly earnings before taxes. In the BIBB/IAB surveys, earnings is devided into 18 categories. We use the mean of each of the categories (e.g., one category is from DM 3,000 to 3,500 and we use the mean value—ln [3,250]). After a listwise deletion of incomplete observations in the explanatory variables, the sample consists of

Table 7.1   Summary statistics of schooling and earnings by skill group

Sample	Observations		Earnings (DM)		Schooling (years)	
	Frequency	Per cent	Mean	Std. dev.	Mean	Std. dev.
Overall sample	7,722	100.0	4,697	1,986.4	14.3	3.5
Unskilled	762	9.9	3,689	1,667.7	10.6	2.4
Vocational training	4,988	64.6	4,302	1,572.0	13.7	2.5
Foreman, senior craftsman	1,330	17.2	5,627	2,017.5	16.5	3.6
University graduate	642	8.3	7,028	2,628.3	19.7	2.7

7,722 observations. Tables 7.1 and 7A.1 present the summary statistics on earnings by skill group and the covariates, respectively.

In order to account for the institutional structure of the German educational and occupational system, we construct four groups of workers (see Table 7.1): workers without any formal occupational degree, workers with an apprenticeship degree (Geselle), workers with senior craftsman qualifications (Meister) or a degree from a university of applied sciences (Fachhochschule) and workers with at least a university degree. As a standard, the years of occupational schooling for the four groups are zero, three, four and five. The overall years of standard schooling for these groups are 10, 13, 15 to 16 and 18.

7.4 EMPIRICAL FINDINGS

As a benchmark for our estimates of the ATE, based on the earnings function with correlated random coefficients, we first present two-stage least squares estimates of the earnings function with homogenous returns to schooling. The instruments used are the unemployment rate at graduation and its interaction terms with age and the squared age variable. This gives us three over-identifying restrictions. The reasoning behind the use of these instruments lies in the specific institutional features of the German vocational system. By opting for the elementary vocational year (Berufsgrundbildungsjahr), youths, especially those without an apprenticeship training position, have the opportunity to prepare for vocational training by attending a full-time school year (optional as part-time school). The preparation year for vocational training (Berufsvorbereitungsjahr) basically serves the same purpose as the elementary vocational year, but in a somewhat broader sense. It prepares youths without an apprenticeship position for vocational training.[6] If unemployment reflects opportunity costs, an individual is more likely to stay in the educational system if employment prospects are low. This argument seems particularly relevant for the case of Germany, where tuition and fees for general schooling and vocational training are rare exceptions or negligible.

Table 7.2 Reduced form estimates of the schooling equation

Variable[1]	β	t-value
Experience	−0.330	−16.65
Experience (squared)	−0.003	−4.96
Handicapped	−0.300	−1.78
Age	0.267	2.43
Age (squared)	0.003	2.12
Unemployment ratio at graduation	−0.331	−1.10
Unemployment ratio at graduation. Age	0.028	1.79
Unemployment ratio at graduation. Age (squared)	0.000	−1.41
Sector (manufacturing)		
Craft	−0.354	−3.45
Trade	−0.136	−1.14
Public Service	0.951	10.62
Agriculture	−0.038	−0.11
Others	0.375	3.32
Firm size (large)		
Small (< 49)	−0.400	−4.28
Medium (50–499)	−0.285	−3.31
City size (large)		
Small (< 20,000)	−0.119	−1.37
Medium (20,000–100,000)	0.083	0.98
Federal state (NRW)		
Schleswig-Holstein and Lower Saxony	0.028	0.27
Hamburg and Bremen	0.290	1.54
Rhineland-Palatinate, Hesse and Saarland	−0.027	−0.26
Baden-Wuerttemberg and Bavaria	−0.047	−0.53
West Berlin	−0.831	−4.45
Constant	6.685	2.94

Notes:
$N = 7,722$; $F(22, 7,699) = 195.84$; $R^2 = 0.36$.

[1] Base categories for the dummy variables in brackets. Dependent variable: years of schooling.

Source: BIBB/IAB survey on educational and vocational attainment and career 1999.

Table 7.2 presents the reduced form estimates for the schooling equation. Given the large value of the F-Test (195.84), we can reject the zero of weak instruments in terms of the relative two-stage least squares (2SLS) bias (> 10%) and the actual size of the 2SLS t-test (> 15%) according to the critical values presented in Stock, Wright and Yogo (2002). The unemployment rate at graduation has a significant impact, which varies across cohorts on the schooling level. Our specification explains 36 per cent of the variation in schooling in the sample. Using the Hausman test (auxiliary regression specification), we have to reject the hypothesis that schooling can be treated as an exogenous explanatory variable.

Table 7.3　2SLS estimates of the earnings equation

Variable[1]	β	t-value
Schooling	0.083	33.57
Experience	0.030	18.09
Experience (squared)	0.000	−9.48
Handicapped	−0.039	−1.88
Sector (manufacturing)		
Craft	−0.050	−3.86
Trade	−0.028	−1.86
Public Service	−0.094	−8.01
Agriculture	−0.244	−5.67
Others	0.012	.85
Firm size (large)		
Small (< 49)	−0.110	−9.49
Medium (50–499)	−0.031	−2.89
City size (large)		
Small (< 20,000)	0.019	1.81
Medium (20,000–100,000)	−0.015	−1.46
Federal state (NRW)		
Schleswig-Holstein and Lower Saxony	−0.049	−3.81
Hamburg and Bremen	−0.095	−4.06
Rhineland-Palatinate, Hesse and Saarland	−0.025	−1.94
Baden-Wuerttemberg and Bavaria	−0.020	−1.80
West Berlin	−0.068	−2.93
Constant	6.92	159.9

Notes:

$N = 7,722$; $F(18, 7,703) = 132.19$; $R^2 = 0.2360$; Hausman test $(N(0,1)) = 20.76$.

[1]　Base categories for the dummy variables in brackets. Dependent variable: logarithm of wage.

Source: BIBB/IAB survey on educational and vocational attainment and career 1999.

The 2SLS estimates of the fixed coefficient earnings function are given in Table 7.3. In addition to the typical covariates schooling, experience and experience squared, we use sectoral dummies, regional dummies, firm size and a dummy variable for handicapped workers as additional controls. The return to an additional school year is 8.3 per cent, which is in line with the international evidence reported by Groot and van den Brink (2000) and Pfeiffer (2000). Ignoring the endogeneity of schooling by estimating the equation using ordinary least squares results in a lower estimate of 4.2 per cent (see Table 7A.2). These differences confirm the international evidence that the return rates obtained from instrumental variable estimators are above the ones from ordinary least squares.[7]

The estimates of the expected rate of return to an additional year of schooling based on the random coefficient model are reported in Table 7.4. In the first line of Table 7.4, we report the ATE using all observations. Outliers turn out to have

Table 7.4 Estimates of the ATE

$\hat{E}[\beta]$	t-value	Quantiles					
		10%	25%	50%	75%	90%	
1.060	1.22	−0.103	0.005	0.076	0.158	0.294	Without trimming
.087	29.94	−0.091	0.007	0.076	0.156	0.283	Trimmed

a strong effect on the estimates of the ATE. Therefore, we also present estimates based on a trimmed sample, where we drop observations below the 1 per cent and above the 99 per cent quantiles of overall samples. Since trimming obviously leads to more plausible estimation results, we discuss the estimation results in the sequel based on the trimmed sample only. The potential outcome approach reveals an ATE of an additional year of schooling at 8.7 per cent, which is significantly different from zero. This estimate does not differ much from the 2SLS results reported above. Angrist and Imbens (1995) show that for models with variable treatment intensity, the 2SLS estimator identifies a weighted average of the treatment effect in the population whose educational attainment was changed by the instrument. Hence, there is no reason to expect *ex ante* quantitatively similar estimates. Using a control function approach, Deschenes (2002) also estimates the ATE within a correlated random coefficient framework for the US. He obtains a value of 16.2 per cent, which is slightly lower than his 2SLS estimate.

The quantiles of the individual return rates reported in Table 7.4 reveal that the impact of educational attainment on earnings is far from being homogeneous. For a quarter of the individuals, the causal return rate is more than 15.6 per cent and for the 90 per cent quantile it is 28.3 per cent. On the other hand, for a quarter of the individuals there are very low or even negative causal return rates. For example, negative return rates may result from a restricted entry into the labour market, in which case education serves as means of bridging over waiting queues in times of unemployment. They can also be the result of a suboptimal matching between heterogenous students and teaching institutions. More descriptive evidence on the distribution of the heterogenous returns is given by the kernel density estimate depicted in Figure 7.1. The estimated distribution of β turns out to be slightly skewed to the right.

In our analysis of the rates of return to overeducation, we assume that the returns to required schooling, that is, the return to the minimum educational attainment legally required to work in the individual's actual profession, may differ from the returns that an individual obtains from educational attainment beyond the required level. Let S denote actual schooling and S_r denote schooling. Then, $S_o = S - S_r \geq 0$ defines overeducation. Distinguishing between the two rates of return yields the following correlated random coefficient earnings function:

Figure 7.1   Kernel density estimates of the random return rate β

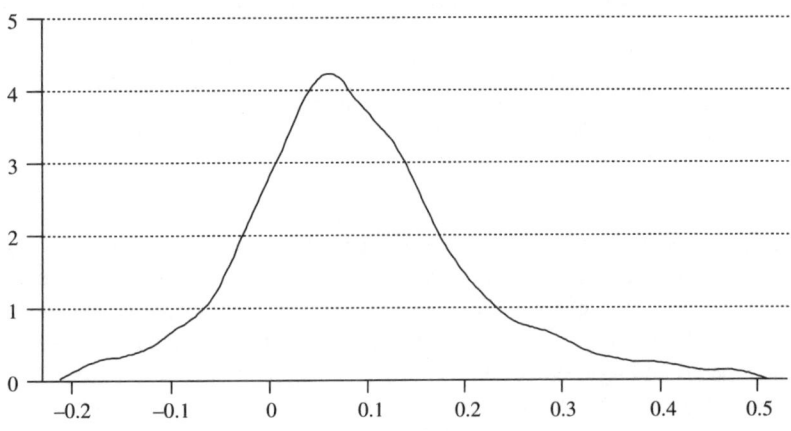

$$E[\ln Y \mid S_r, S, \alpha, \beta_r, \beta_o] = \alpha + \beta_r S_r + \beta_o(S - S_r), \qquad (7.15)$$

where β_r is the return to required schooling and β_o is the rate of return to over-education. Considering equation (7.15) for a given level of required schooling s_r results in a standard correlated random coefficient specification for the sub-group of individuals with schooling level s_r:

$$E[\ln Y \mid S_r = s_r, S, \alpha, \beta_r, \beta_o] = \alpha_o + \beta_o S, \qquad (7.16)$$

where $\alpha_o = \alpha + (\beta_r - \beta_o)s_r$. Hence, $E[\beta_o]$ is the ATE of an additional year of overeducation for individuals with required schooling level s_r. Moreover, our approach does not require an explicit definition of required schooling, which may otherwise be a source of errors in a variables problem. On the other hand, no explicit parameter for the returns of overeducation can be obtained. Since required schooling is treated as given, our approach to estimating the ATE of overeducation neglects the process of selection determining the required schooling level.

Table 7.5   Estimates of the ATE to overeducation

Group	Without trimming		Trimmed	
	$\hat{E}[\beta]$	t-value	$\hat{E}[\beta]$	t-value
Unskilled	0.093	0.83	0.049	1.18
Vocational training	0.069	1.29	0.082	23.25
Foreman, senior craftsman	0.054	2.94	0.061	12.58
University graduates	0.384	2.34	0.237	7.66

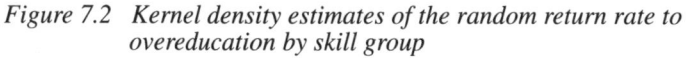

Figure 7.2   Kernel density estimates of the random return rate to overeducation by skill group

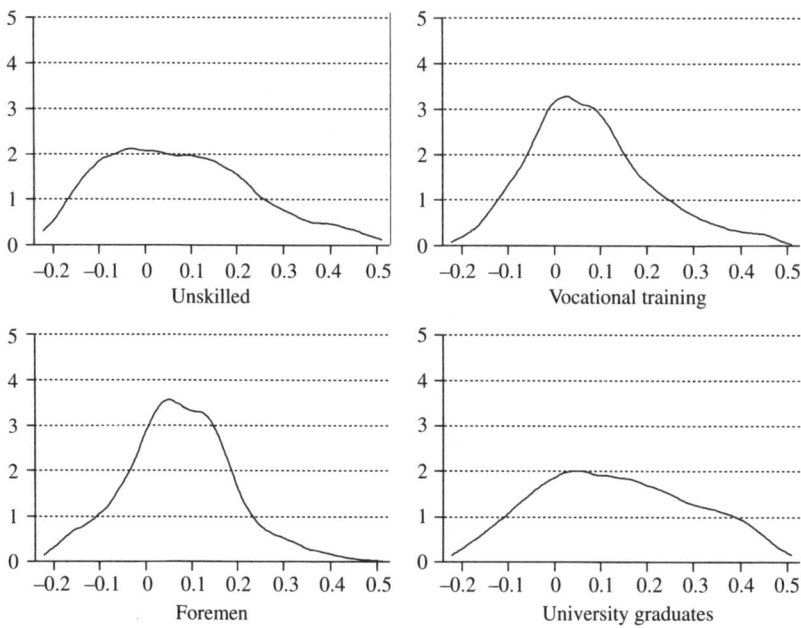

The estimation results for the returns of overeducation for four different employment groups are given in Table 7.5. The estimates of the expected returns to overeducation, by and large, seem to be inversely related to skill level. The higher the educational skills in the employment group under study, the higher the returns to overeducation. The estimates of the expected returns to overeducation are not statistically different from zero for the low-skilled workers. This is in line with findings based on traditional returns estimates (see Groot and van den Brink, 2000). In fact, for the largest group of workers with vocational training, our findings suggest that the average returns to required education and overeducation are rather similar.

There is no evidence that the average returns to overeducation are lower than the returns to required education for university graduates. Since we are not able to control for the required length of academic programmes, the high returns to overeducation for the university graduates pick up fixed effects. Provided that the length of academic programmes is positively related to earnings, our estimates of the return to an additional year of academic education also capture the potential effect of a change of the academic programme rather than the pure effect of extending the study in the same programme.

In summary, our findings for German men suggest that the returns to over-education are similar to returns to required education and, therefore, 'overeducation' seems to be a rational investment strategy used by the skilled. Only in the unskilled group are the returns to overeducation indeed very low on average. Equally important is the finding that there is considerable individual heterogeneity in the returns to education and to overeducation. The assumption on heterogeneous effects of overeducation on earnings provides a richer, more realistic picture than an analysis under the traditional homogeneity assumption. In particular, it provides valuable insights into efficiency aspects of various institutions of the education system. For a considerable share of workers in all skill groups (20%–30%) the expected return to an additional year of overeducation seems to be negative and for a share of 20 per cent or more returns are very high. Additional educational attainment seems to be particularly rewarding in terms of an earnings increase for the university graduates.

Figure 7.2 depicts the distribution of the returns to overeducation for the four skill groups. Visual inspection suggests that the distributions are not that different for the two medium skill groups. In these two groups, skill-specific education dominates with standardised curricula in firms and in school-related education. For the unskilled and the high skilled, however, the distribution is less compressed. That either reflects the higher degree of heterogeneity in the effectiveness of education for these groups or the higher degree of heterogeneity of the education acquired by these groups. Since the data provide no information of institutional diversity, we cannot distinguish these two reasons for heterogeneity empirically.

7.5 CONCLUSIONS

In this paper, we analysed the efficiency of human capital investments in the light of inadequate educational careers and skill obsolescence based on the potential outcome for continuous treatments. Empirical studies on the returns to overeducation usually treat schooling and overeducation as exogenously given rather than as the outcome of an individual's investment decision. Moreover, the return of an additional year of schooling is taken to be the same across individuals. This neglects the fact that unobserved heterogeneity in the benefits and the costs of schooling may generate individually different return rates. Here, we analyse the causal effect of schooling on earnings taking into account the heterogeneity of individual returns using a correlated random coefficient earnings function. Our estimate of the average causal effect of an additional year of schooling is 8.7 per cent, which is close to the two-stage least squares estimate of the rate of return in a traditionally fixed coefficient earnings function, but considerably higher than the least squares estimate.

We find that heterogeneity in the returns does matter and that the monetary benefits of an additional year of schooling vary largely across the population. For 20 to 30 per cent of the male workers in our sample, an additional year of schooling yields negative returns. For more than 25 per cent, the returns are above 15 per cent. For example, negative return rates may result from restricted entry into the labour market in which case education is a means of bridging overwaiting queues in times of unemployment. The large positive returns may result from individual differences in learning abilities, educational costs and educational quality. More research is needed to disentangle the sources of individual heterogeneity.

From our samples of skilled and high-skilled German male workers, there is no evidence that the average returns to overeducation are lower than the average returns to required education. As summarised in the introduction, this seems to differ from the evidence found in most traditional studies. 'Overeducation' should be viewed as a rational investment strategy, especially by a large part of the group of skilled workers. Only in the group of the unskilled are the average returns to overeducation very low indeed. This seems to confirm international findings. However, there is evidence for considerable heterogeneity in the expected returns to overeducation as well as to required education. For 20 to 30 per cent of the workers, returns seem to be negative and investments seem to be wasted.

Since there is little practical experience with the CMI approach applied to correlated random coefficient models, our results, although plausible, should be treated with caution. More evidence based on other data is clearly needed to evaluate the robustness of the results and the virtues of the new econometric technique. Our findings should also be confronted with results obtained by alternative estimation approaches (e.g., control function approaches to the correlated random coefficient model). For policy analysis, other treatment effects such as the effect of treatment on the treated, the treatment on the non-treated and the local average treatment effect should also be evaluated.

NOTES

1 Financial support by the DFG through the research group 'Heterogenous Labor' at the University of Konstanz and the Zentrum für Europäische Wirtschaftsforschung (ZEW), Mannheim, is gratefully acknowledged.
2 See Freeman (1976). Recent comprehensive reviews by Büchel (2001), Hartog (2000), Groot and van den Brink (2000) summarise the debate.
3 Groot and van den Brink (2000) count two different definitions for each: The so-called subjective measures rely either on a self-reported assessment of overqualification or on a comparison between a self-reported assessment of minimum educational requirements for the job and the educational attainment of the worker. The so-called objective measures rely either on the difference between average or modal educational attainment in an occupation and individual educational attain-

148   *Wages*

ment or on a comparison between the actual educational attainment and job level requirements. Büchel and Weißhuhn (1997) develop a subjective indicator validated with objective information from occupational status and educational attainment. For more details and a comprehensive discussion of pros and cons, also compare Büchel (2001), Hartog (2000) and Sicherman (1991).

4 Assuming a linear marginal benefit function results in a log earnings function that contains an additional quadratic schooling term.

5 BIBB: Federal Institute for Vocational Training, or Bundesinstitut für Berufsbildung; IAB: Institute for Labor Market and Occupational Research of the Federal Labour Office, or Institut für Arbeitsmarkt- und Berufsforschung der Bundesanstalt für Arbeit. Data collection is organised jointly by the two organisations: BIBB and IAB. The data are processed and documented by the Central Archive for Empirical Social Research, or Zentralarchiv für empirische Sozialforschung (ZA), Cologne. The BIBB, the IAB nor the ZA take any responsibility for the analysis or the interpretation of the data presented here. For more details, aims and descriptions of the four available surveys, see Dostal and Jansen (2002).

6 Also see Franz et al. (2000) for a study on the impact of vocational training on youth unemployment duration.

7 See Card (2001) for a comparison of recent empirical studies.

REFERENCES

Angrist, J.D., and Imbens, G.W. (1995). Two-stage least squares estimation of average causal effects in models with variable treatment intensity. *Journal of the American Statistical Association,* **90**, 431–442.

Bauer, T. (2002). Educational mismatch and wages: A panel analysis. *Economics of Education Review,* **21**, 221–229.

BIBB/IAB. (1999). *Erwerb und Verwertung beruflicher Qualifikationen von Erwerbstätigen. BIBB/IAB Strukturerhebung 1998/99. Erhebungsmaterialien zur Hauptstudie.* Berlin: Bundesinstitut für Berufsbildung.

Blechinger, D., and Pfeiffer, F. (2000). Technological change and skill obsolescence: The case of German apprenticeship training. In H. Heijke and J. Muysken (Eds.), *Education and training in a knowledge-based economy* (pp. 243–276). New York: St. Martin's Press.

Büchel, F. (2001). Overqualification: Reasons, measurement issues, and typographical affinity to unemployment. In P. Descy and M. Tessaring (Eds.), *Training in Europe: Second report on vocational training research in Europe 2000* (Vol. 2, pp. 453–560). Luxembourg: Office for Official Publications of the European Communities.

Büchel, F., and Weißhuhn, G. (1997). *Ausbildungsinadäquate Beschäftigung der Absolventen des Bildungssystems. Berichterstattung zu Struktur und Entwicklung unterwertiger Beschäftigung in West- und Ostdeutschland.* Berlin: Duncker & Humblot (Volkswirtschaftliche Schriftenreihe, 471).

Card, D. (1999). The causal effect of education and earnings. *Handbook of Labour Economics,* **3**, 1801–1863.

Card, D. (2001). Estimating the returns to schooling: Progress on some persistent econometric problems. *Econometrica,* **69** (5), 1127–1160.

Deschenes, O. (2002). *Estimating the effects of family background on the return to schooling.* Paper presented at the Econometric Society European Meeting (ESEM), Venice.

Dostal, W., and Jansen, R. (2002). Qualifikation und Erwerbssituation in Deutschland. 20 Jahre BIBB/IAB-Erhebungen. *Mitteilungen aus der Arbeitsmarkt- und Berufsforschung (MittAB),* **35** (2), 232–253.

Franz, W., Inkmann, J., Pohlmeier, W., and Zimmermann, V. (2000). Young and out in Germany: On youths' chances of labor market entrance in Germany. In D.G. Blanchflower and R.B. Freeman (Eds.), *Youth employment and joblessness in advanced countries* (pp. 381–425). Chicago: The University of Chicago Press.

Freeman, R. (1976). *The overeducated American.* New York: Academic Press.

Garen, J. (1984). The returns to schooling: A selectivity bias approach with a continuous choice variable. *Econometrica, 52,* 1199–1218.

Groot, W., and van den Brink, H.M. (2000). Overeducation in the labor market: A meta-analysis. *Economics of Education Review, 19* (2), 149–158.

Hartog, J. (2000). Over-education and earnings: Where are we, where should we go? *Economics of Education Review, 19* (2), 131–147.

Heckman, J.J., and Vytlacil, E. (1998). Instrumental variables methods for the correlated random coefficient model: Estimating the rate of return to schooling when the return is corelated with schooling. *Journal of Human Resources, 23,* 974–987.

Jansen, R., and Stooss, F. (1993). *Qualifikation und Erwerbssituation im geeinten Deutschland. BIBB/IAB-Erhebung 1991/92.* Berlin. Bundesinstitut für Berufsbildung.

Pfeiffer, F. (2000). Aufwand und Ertrag. Daten und Fakten zur Bildung in Deutschland und in Europa. In K. Morath (Ed.), *Rohstoff Bildung* (pp. 11–26). Frankfurt a.M.: Frankfurter Institut—Stiftung Marktwirtschaft und Politik.

Sicherman, N. (1991). Overeducation in the labor market. *Journal of Labor Economics, 9,* 101–122.

Stock, J.H., Wright, J.H., and Yogo, M. (2002). A survey of weak instruments and weak identification in generalized method of moments. *Journal of Business and Economic Statistics, 20,* 518–529.

Velling, J., and Pfeiffer, F. (1997). *Arbeitslosigkeit, inadäquate Beschäftigung, Berufswechsel und Erwerbsbeteiligung.* Mannheim: Zentrum für Europäische Wirtschaftsforschung (ZEW Dokumentation 97–02).

Wooldridge, J.M. (1997). On two stage least squares estimation of the average treatment effect in a random coefficient model. *Economics Letters, 56,* 129–133.

Wooldridge, J.M. (2002). *Econometric analysis of cross section and panel data.* Cambridge, MA: MIT Press.

Table 7A.1 Summary statistics of the covariates

Variable	Sample									
	Overall		Unskilled		Vocational training		Foreman		Univers. Grad.	
	Mean	Std. dev.	Mean	Std. dev.	Mean	Std. dev.	Mean	Std. dev.	Mean	Std. dev.
Age	37.47	8.352	36.72	9.017	36.72	8.438	39.762	7.565	39.422	7.168
Age (squared)	1,474	629.5	1,430	662.0	1,420	629.1	1,638	600.4	1,605	573
Experience	18.68	9.46	18.55	10.16	19.00	9.38	20.32	8.93	12.94	8.09
Experience (squared)	438.4	374.0	447.2	395.0	449.1	377.4	492.7	369.5	232.7	242.5
Handicapped	0.038	0.191	0.050	0.218	0.038	0.192	0.038	0.192	0.017	0.130
Sector										
Manufacturing	0.318	0.466	0.357	0.479	0.333	0.471	0.283	0.450	0.226	0.418
Craft	0.213	0.409	0.234	0.423	0.265	0.441	0.103	0.304	0.009	0.096
Trade	0.103	0.303	0.115	0.320	0.121	0.327	0.045	0.208	0.059	0.236
Public Service	0.232	0.422	0.126	0.332	0.160	0.363	0.450	0.498	0.494	0.500
Agriculture	0.009	0.094	0.022	0.148	0.008	0.090	0.006	0.077	0.005	0.068
Others	0.120	0.325	0.134	0.341	0.110	0.313	0.110	0.313	0.201	0.401
Firm size										
Small	0.414	0.493	0.460	0.499	0.450	0.498	0.298	0.457	0.321	0.467
Medium	0.341	0.474	0.331	0.471	0.318	0.466	0.409	0.492	0.399	0.490
Large	0.229	0.420	0.188	0.391	0.216	0.411	0.285	0.452	0.271	0.445
City size										
Small	0.360	0.480	0.297	0.457	0.383	0.486	0.334	0.472	0.305	0.461
Medium	0.276	0.447	0.280	0.449	0.275	0.447	0.295	0.456	0.234	0.423
Large	0.365	0.481	0.424	0.494	0.341	0.474	0.371	0.483	0.461	0.499

Table 7A.1 Summary statistics of the covariates continued

Variable	Overall		Unskilled		Sample Vocational training		Foreman		Univers. grad.	
	Mean	Std. dev.	Mean	Std. dev.	Mean	Std. dev.	Mean	Std. dev.	Mean	Std. dev.
Federal state										
Schleswig-Holstein and Lower Saxony	0.160	0.367	0.150	0.357	0.170	0.375	0.130	0.337	0.162	0.369
Hamburg and Bremen	0.033	0.180	0.034	0.182	0.032	0.178	0.032	0.177	0.040	0.197
North-Rhine Westphalia	0.286	0.452	0.311	0.463	0.276	0.447	0.308	0.462	0.293	0.455
Rhineland-Palatinate, Hesse and Saarland	0.166	0.372	0.138	0.345	0.161	0.367	0.189	0.391	0.190	0.393
Baden-Wuerttemberg and Bavaria	0.320	0.467	0.302	0.459	0.326	0.469	0.320	0.467	0.294	0.456
West Berlin	0.340	0.182	0.066	0.248	0.035	0.184	0.210	0.144	0.020	0.141
Unemployment ratio	4.16	2.83	4.26	2.97	4.24	2.83	3.76	2.76	4.28	2.71
Number of observations	7,722		762		4,988		1,33		642	

Table 7.A2 LSE of the earnings function: Fixed coefficient model

Variable[1]	β	t-value
Schooling	0.042	34.32
Experience	0.028	17.05
Experience (squared)	0.000	−10.83
Handicapped	−0.054	−2.60
Sector (manufacturing)		
Craft	−0.085	−6.73
Trade	−0.036	−2.43
Public Service	−0.025	−2.25
Agriculture	−0.248	−5.79
Others	0.053	3.76
Firm size (large)		
Small	−0.124	−10.71
Medium	−0.039	−3.65
City size (large)		
Small	0.004	0.40
Medium	−0.020	−1.91
Federal state (NRW)		
Schleswig Holstein and Lower Saxony	−0.046	−3.55
Hamburg and Bremen	−0.086	−3.66
Rhineland-Palatinate, Hesse and Saarland	−0.023	−1.81
Baden Wuerttemberg and Bavaria	−0.028	−2.52
West Berlin	−0.110	−4.77
Constant	7.57	284.60

Notes:
N = 7,722; F(18, 7,703) = 135.44; R^2 = 0.24.

[1] Base categories for the dummy variables in brackets. Dependent variable: logarithm of wage.

Source: BIBB/IAB survey on educational and vocational attainment and career 1999.

PART THREE

Measurement

8. Measuring Overeducation with Earnings Frontiers and Panel Data

Uwe Jensen

8.1 INTRODUCTION

Employees are called *overeducated* if the knowledge they have acquired in the education process cannot be fully applied in their present jobs. The overeducation problem is important because it stands for inefficient use of individual and social resources, that is, for superfluous individual and social costs. Many studies show that the amount of overeducation is considerable in many OECD countries (see the contribution by Sloane, Chapter 2 in this volume).

In the analysis of overeducation, many papers concentrate on the economical understanding of the problem and on its descriptive analysis. But another unsolved problem is how to measure overeducation (see Büchel, 2001, pp. 482ff.). The so-called objective, subjective or empirical measures dominating the literature have certain drawbacks and limitations. That is why, in this paper, the income ratio measure is proposed as an addition to the previous measures covering income aspects of overeducation with econometric methods. The cross-section techniques and results of Jensen (2000, 2001a, 2001b) are expanded and improved.

The reminder of this article is as follows: Section 2 discusses the overeducation measures and their limitations. The income ratio measure for overeducation is based on estimating individual potential income with stochastic earnings frontiers. Therefore, Section 3 summarises the necessary details on earnings frontiers and their econometric origin, that is, production frontiers. After an overview on the panel data from the GSOEP in Section 4, the subsequent section presents and discusses the estimation results in detail. Some conclusions close the paper.

8.2 MEASURING OVEREDUCATION

How should overeducation be measured? Three main alternatives are known (Borghans and de Grip, 2000a, pp. 13f.):

(1) The *objective* measure: Professional job analysts try to specify the required level and type of education in particular occupations and, by this
means, provide a classification of occupations into a requirement ranking.
For example, the US Employment Service compiles the Dictionary of
Occupational Titles (DOT) where six components of worker traits are
assessed. The ARBI code, developed by the Dutch Department of Social
Affairs, classifies occupations into seven classes ranging from very simple
work with a training time of a few days to scientific work. These classifications are then converted to years of requested schooling or schooling
dummies which can be compared with the acquired schooling of the individuals in the study.
(2) The *subjective* measure: This approach is based on worker's self-assessment.
For example, the Michigan Panel Study of Income Dynamics asks them:
'How much formal education is required to get a job like yours?' Once
again, this (classified) information can be compared with the actual schooling of the individual.
(3) The *empirical* measure: This approach uses the distribution of schooling
years in a given occupation or a group of occupations. Most commonly, individuals are defined to be overeducated if their schooling level is more
than one standard deviation above the mean of all individuals in that occupation.

Of course, different overeducation measures can lead to different results for the
same individual. Also, of course, all measures can be criticized:

(1) The objective measure, for example, ignores within-occupation variation in
job-specific schooling requirements and it ignores individual trade-offs between education and ability. Furthermore, providing objective measures
with a sufficiently detailed partition into different occupations and accounting for occupational requirement changes over time is extremely expensive
(Borghans and de Grip, 2000a, p. 15). From a statistical view, one should
add that converting metric information (on schooling requirements) into a
few classes involves the danger of loosing much information.
(2) Employees may be inclined to over- or understate the educational requirements of their job leading to biased subjective measures (Borghans and de
Grip, 2000a, p. 16). Furthermore, we should repeat the statistical argument
from the previous item emphasising the danger of loosing much information by classifying metric information into a few classes.
(3) The empirical measure produces results which depend heavily and arbi-
trarily on the choice of the cut-off point (Borghans and de Grip, 2000a,
p. 16). Small groups may raise additional problems. Furthermore, this
method will always identify overeducation even if it does not exist. This
phenomenon is well-known from corresponding poverty measures.

Not unexpected after the previous discussion, the subjective approach seems to have many adherents. Nevertheless, using classified information destroys information. Also, all overeducation measures ignore the income aspect of overeducation. That is why, in this paper, following Jensen (2001a), a fourth way of measuring overeducation will be pursued.

(4) The *income ratio* measure: The individual potential income is estimated with a stochastic earnings frontier. Then, overeducation is measured as the income ratio between potential income and actual income.

Applying individual income as overeducation criterion is criticised because, for example, a Bachelor of Science working as a car dealer, with a considerable income will not be identified as overeducated (Büchel, 2001). The counter-argument is: From an individual and from a social perspective, it is at least questionable if a Bachelor of Science is more adequately employed if they work at a university in a part-time job limited in time and with a minor income. Following the human capital theory, income maximisation *is* an important goal of investments in schooling.

I do not intend to show that the income ratio measure is better than the subjective measure. The income ratio measure is rather intended to be a complement to the latter accounting for important aspects ignored by the subjective (and any other) measure. It could, therefore, be of substantial value for tests of robustness in empirical analyses of overeducation.

8.3 STOCHASTIC EARNINGS FRONTIERS

This section summarises the theory on stochastic earnings frontiers necessary in the following.

8.3.1 Production Frontiers

Frontier functions have been developed for the estimation of economic production functions which provide maximum possible output for given inputs (in line with the microeconomic theory) of the firms in the sample. The econometric task is to estimate a function lying on top of the data cloud.

Aigner and Chu (1968) developed the first parametric frontier model for the estimation of a Cobb/Douglas production function with output y_i and inputs x_{ij} (both in logs):

$$y_i = \alpha + \sum_{j=1}^{k} \beta_j x_{ij} - u_i, \quad u_i \geq 0, \quad i = 1, \ldots, n. \tag{8.1}$$

Then, $\hat{y}_i$ is the estimated maximum possible output for given inputs of the i-th firm. The log output difference $u_i \geq 0$ is interpreted as the technical inefficiency (in logs) of the i-th firm. The untransformed individual efficiency is:

$$\text{EFF}_i = \exp(-u_i) \quad \text{with} \quad 0 \leq \text{EFF}_i \leq 1. \tag{8.2}$$

Model (8.1) lacks an error term. This was the motivation for the following further development to the *stochastic* production frontier introduced by Aigner, Lovell and Schmidt (1977) and Meeusen and van den Broeck (1977). In:

$$y_i = \alpha + \sum_{j=1}^{k} \beta_j x_{ij} + e_i, \quad e_i = v_i - u_i, \quad u_i \geq 0, \quad i = 1, \ldots, n. \tag{8.3}$$

the composed error term e_i consists of the symmetric part v_i representing statistical noise and of the one-sided inefficiency term u_i. v_i and u_i are assumed to be independent.

The advantages (and disadvantages) of working with panel data are well-known in econometrics (see Baltagi, 1995, pp. 3f.). Therefore, stochastic *panel* frontiers have been developed as well. A relatively general model is due to Battese and Coelli (1992). The time-variant inefficiency terms u_{it} are modelled as *random effects* with:

$$u_{it} = \eta_{it} u_i = \exp(-\eta(t-T))u_i, \quad i = 1, \ldots, n, \quad t = 1, \ldots, T. \tag{8.4}$$

The model equation is:

$$y_{it} = \alpha + \sum_{j=1}^{k} \beta_j x_{ijt} + e_{it}, \quad e_{it} = v_{it} - u_{it}, \quad i = 1, \ldots, n, \quad t = 1, \ldots, T, \tag{8.5}$$

with T periods.

v_{it}, u_i and x_{ijt} are assumed to be pairwise independent with the distributional assumptions:

$$v_{it} \sim N(0, \sigma_v^2) \quad \text{and} \quad u_i \sim \text{trunc}_0 N(\mu, \sigma_u^2) \tag{8.6}$$

where $\text{trunc}_0 N(\cdot, \cdot)$ stands for a normal distribution truncated at $u = 0$. Following Battese and Corra (1977), the variances are parametrised as:

$$\sigma^2 = \sigma_v^2 + \sigma_u^2 \quad \text{and} \quad \gamma = \frac{\sigma_u^2}{\sigma^2}, \tag{8.7}$$

with $0 \leq \gamma \leq 1$. Because of:

$$\text{sign}(\eta) = -\text{sign}\left(\frac{d}{dt} u_{it}\right) \tag{8.8}$$

η indicates if the inefficiency of *all* firms increases, decreases or remains constant. See Battese and Coelli (1992) for the log-likelihood function $l(\alpha, \beta, \sigma^2, \gamma, \mu, \eta)$. The ML estimates for model (8.5) with standard asymptotic properties are provided by the non-commercial programme FRONTIER 4.1 (see Coelli,

1996). Using OLS starting values, FRONTIER 4.1 combines a grid search and a Quasi-Newton method.

How can the inefficiency terms be estimated? Since in every stochastic frontier model, the estimation residuals only estimate the composed error e and not u, the inefficiencies must be estimated indirectly with the help of the consistent and minimum mean-squared error predictor for the untransformed individual inefficiency EFF:

$$E(\text{EFF}_{it} \mid e_{it}) = \frac{1 - \Phi \left(\eta_{it}\sigma_i^* - (\mu_i^*/\sigma_i^*) \right)}{1 - \Phi \left(-\mu_i^*/\sigma_i^* \right)} \exp\left(-\eta_{it}\mu_i^* + \frac{1}{2} \eta_{it}^2 \sigma_i^{*2} \right) \quad (8.9)$$

with the standard normal distribution function $\Phi(\cdot)$,

$$\mu_i^* = \frac{\mu \sigma_v^2 - \eta_i^T e_i \sigma_u^2}{\sigma_v^2 + \eta_i^T \eta_i \sigma_u^2} \quad \text{and} \quad \sigma_i^{*2} = \frac{\sigma_v^2 \, \sigma_u^2}{\sigma_v^2 + \eta_i^T \eta_i \sigma_u^2}. \quad (8.10)$$

A second stochastic panel frontier that will be of interest in the following is also based on model (8.5) and was introduced by Battese and Coelli (1995). Now, the time-variant inefficiency terms u_{it} (see model (8.4)) are allowed to depend on some explanatory variables z_{ijt} which may be partly identical with variables x_{ijt}:

$$u_{it} = \delta_0 + \sum_{j=1}^{m} \delta_j z_{ijt} + w_{it} = \hat{u}_{it} + w_{it}, \quad i = 1,\ldots, n, \quad t = 1,\ldots, T \quad (8.11)$$

(*inefficiency effects* specification). The independence assumptions apply likewise. The distributional assumptions are:

$$v_{it} \sim N(0, \sigma_v^2), \quad u_{it} \sim \text{trunco} N(\hat{u}_{it}, \sigma_u^2) \quad \text{and} \quad w_{it} \sim \text{trunc}_{-\hat{u}_{it}} N(0, \sigma_w^2). \quad (8.12)$$

This model can also be estimated by the programme FRONTIER 4.1. The (in)efficiency terms u_{it} or EFF_{it} have to be estimated indirectly again as in the previous case.

See the surveys in Coelli, Rao and Battese (1998), Greene (1997) or Jensen (2001a) for more details on frontiers.

8.3.2 Earnings Frontiers

The ideas and models presented in the previous subsection now are transferred to the estimation of an earnings frontier in a rather straightforward way: Transforming schooling investments (input) to earnings (output) is also a production process which should be performed as efficient as possible.

The earnings frontier model is based on the very popular human capital model by Mincer (1974) for explaining individual income. But, for good reasons, the rigid assumptions of the basic human capital model have often been criticised. In contrast to these assumptions:

- Labour markets and education markets are far from perfect.
- Higher education is not identical to higher productivity, and the latter does not automatically imply higher wages: Much knowledge learned at school or at the university does not come into adequate use in jobs. Applicants with identical human capital stock may have substantial productivity differences in a given job. Also, apparently identical occupations can differ considerably regarding their productivity requirements and wages.
- Employees and employers are not perfectly informed about all labour market aspects relevant to them: Partly considerable information deficits exist on both sides instead. Employers often are not sufficiently informed about the productivity of their employees. Also, if they were, they would very often not be able to allocate the abilities of their employees to the jobs available in the firm. For employees, an efficient job search leads to direct and indirect costs. That is why it is rational to stop the search if a wage offer exceeds a certain reservation wage.

These and many other restrictions to the basic human capital model have led to many extensions like the screening theory and the search theory, etc. The earnings frontier approach accounts for these restrictions by transferring the inefficiency aspect from production frontiers to earnings frontiers.

Extending the cross-section models in Daneshvary et al. (1992) and Jensen (2000, 2001a, 2001b), individual wages *LINC* (in logs) are assumed to depend upon personal characteristics H augmenting human capital stock, job characteristics C and information I on labour market conditions, the wage distribution and job search methods. Individuals stop their search when a wage offer exceeds the reservation wage $LINC_r$. For any set of H and C and perfect information I^*, a potential maximum attainable wage $LINC^*$ exists. Then, $LINC = LINC(H, C, I)$ is estimated as stochastic earnings frontier (see the production frontier model (8.5)):

$$LINC_{it} = \alpha + \sum_{j=1}^{k} \beta_j x_{ijt} + e_{it}, \quad e_{it} = v_{it} - u_{it}, \quad u_{it} \geq 0 \qquad (8.13)$$

for panel data. The explanatory variables x will be introduced in the following section.

Then,

$$\widehat{LINC}_{it} = LINC_{it}^* \qquad (8.14)$$

is estimated maximum possible *(potential) income*. The inefficiency terms:

$$u_{it} = \widehat{LINC}_{it} = LINC_{it} \qquad (8.15)$$

or—with untransformed individual income INC_{it}—better:

$$OVER_{it} = 1 - \exp(-u_{it}) = 1 - \frac{INC_{it}}{\widehat{INC}_{it}} \qquad (8.16)$$

(see equation (8.2)) are interpreted as the cost of imperfect information measuring the *overeducation* of individual number i as the income ratio. This overeducation measure can be derived with the *random effects* specification (8.4) or with the *overeducation effects* specification model (8.11). Note that parametrization (8.16) is different from equation (8.2). v_{it} represents statistical noise as in the previous subsection.

For interpreting parameter values, the untransformed stochastic earnings frontier (see model (8.13)):

$$INC_{it} = \exp(\alpha) \cdot \prod_{j=1}^{k} \exp(\beta_j x_{ijt}) \cdot \exp(v_{it}) \cdot (1 - OVER_{it}) \qquad (8.17)$$

is preferred. All further remarks of the previous subsection concerning modelling and estimation of u, model assumptions, etc. apply likewise.

Jensen (2000, 2001a, 2001b) discussed the advantages of the earnings frontier over the 'average earnings function.' The frontier model includes the important but hardly measurable human capital investment 'search for information.' An average human capital model only explains potential income sufficiently, but individuals do not obtain their maximum possible income because of imperfect information described above. The OLS approach does not take into account the considerable amount of individual inefficiency in finding the suitable jobs and, therefore, falsely interprets inefficiency (overeducation) as misspecification.

8.4 DATA

The data are from waves 12 to 16 (corresponding to the years 1994 to 1998) from the GSOEP provided by the German Institute for Economic Research (DIW) in Berlin (for further information on this database see SOEP Group, 2001). The individuals in the dataset were reduced to those 335 meeting the following requirements:

- only German men,
- only full-time employees or workers in all periods,
- no public service,
- age between 18 (in 1994) and 55 (in 1998),
- providing information to all required variables in all periods.

A reduction to only 335 individuals may seem excessive. But, it can by motivated as follows:

- Most researchers would agree that including women, public servants and self-employed in an earnings function requires a substantial model extension because the determinants of individual income differ considerably in these groups. I have decided to avoid this unnecessary extension because it is the aim of this paper to introduce measuring overeducation via income ratios, not to measure German overeducation as complete as possible.

- The decision for avoiding missing variable problems (the last item) was met for the same reasons.
- Leaving out employees older than 55 years is standard and tries to avoid flexible retirement effects in the sample.

The endogenous variable *LINC* in the earnings frontier (8.13) is the natural logarithm of gross yearly wage income including all extra payments. The exogenous variables in the final estimation presented in the next section are:

1. *AGE:*   age in years divided by 10,
2. *QUUN:* dummy: 1 for qualification for university entrance ('Abitur')— 0 for lower education,
3. *STTC:* dummy: 1 for study at technical college—0 else,
4. *STUN:* dummy: 1 for study at university—0 else,
5. *SENI:* seniority: years of firm tenure divided by 100,
6. *STAT:* job status: Wegener prestige score divided by 1,000,
7. *HOUR:* weekly working hours including overtime divided by 10,
8. *JSAT:* job satisfaction: integer scale ranging from 0 (no) to 10 (yes),
9. *EMPL:* dummy: 1 for employees—0 for workers,
10. *SIZS:* dummy for small firms (less than 20 employees)—0 else,
11. *SIZB:* dummy for large firms (more than 2,000 employees)—0 else.

Several further variables (property, a dummy for being married, health, etc.) have been checked and eliminated because they remained highly insignificant, as could be expected in a panel data model.

Modelling individual inefficiency u by further explanatory variables z following equation (8.11) involves including the following variables in the estimation model. Several metric and dummy variables have been checked, but only the given dummy variables stayed significant. The first four dummies are defined to be 1 roughly for the top 25 per cent of the individuals, respectively. The final two dummies are taken from the International Standard Classification of Occupations (ISCO) main classification provided by GSOEP.

a. *DAGE:* dummy: 1 if AGE ≥ 4.5—0 else,
b. *DSEN:* dummy: 1 if SENI ≥ 0.177—0 else,
c. *DSTA:* dummy: 1 if STAT ≥ 0.737—0 else,
d. *DSAT:* dummy: 1 if JSAT ≥ 9—0 else,
e. *LEAD:* dummy: 1 for executives—0 else,
f. *SCIE:* dummy: 1 for scientists—0 else.

8.5 ESTIMATION RESULTS

The stochastic earnings frontier model (8.13) with (income ratio) overeducation measure OVER$_{it}$ in equation (8.16) derived from inefficiency terms u_{it} modelled as random effects specification (8.4) or as overeducation effects specification (8.11) has been estimated with the data described in the previous section and with the programme FRONTIER 4.1 mentioned in subsection 3.1. The estimation results are shown in Table 8.1.

Table 8.1 Parameter estimates

| Variable | OLS starting values | | Stochastic earnings frontier (13) | | | |
| | | | Random effects (4) | | Overed. effects (11) | |
	Coeff.	t-value	Coeff.	t-value	Coeff.	t-value
Constant	9.2034	58.79	10.0490	64.00	9.3788	56.19
AGE	0.4730	6.07	0.4810	6.17	0.3719	4.53
AGE (SQUARED)	–0.0519	–5.28	–0.0367	–3.74	–0.0366	–3.40
QUUN	0.1093	5.12	0.1700	5.18	0.1134	5.26
STTC	0.2113	6.39	0.1210	2.86	0.1929	5.82
STUN	0.2059	7.06	0.2954	7.37	0.1831	6.25
SENI	0.3236	3.68	0.2286	2.20	0.5237	4.74
STAT	2.4780	8.79	0.6192	3.04	1.8434	5.49
HOUR	0.1079	12.02	0.0414	5.42	0.1162	12.77
JSAT	0.0116	3.56	0.0057	2.39	0.0168	4.54
EMPL	0.1048	6.84	0.0865	6.22	0.0927	6.06
SIZS	–0.1559	–9.15	–0.0333	–2.11	–0.1507	–8.64
SIZB	0.1100	8.00	0.0282	2.16	0.1060	7.73
Constant	–	–	–	–	0.0316	0.84
DAGE	–	–	–	–	0.0686	2.25
DSEN	–	–	–	–	0.0694	1.98
DSTA	–	–	–	–	0.1019	2.55
DSAT	–	–	–	–	0.0595	1.83
LEAD	–	–	–	–	–0.3971	–3.87
SCIE	–	–	–	–	–0.4245	–5.61
σ^2	0.0590	–	0.0949	13.24	0.0575	14.16
γ	–	–	0.8991	155.06	–	–
μ	–	–	0.5843	23.28	–	–
η	–	–	0.0150	4.53	–	–
				χ^2_{mix} (3)		χ^2_{mix} (8)
LR test	–	–	–	1740.04	–	40.97

Source: Own calculations, based on GSOEP data.

All parameter estimates show the expected signs. With the untransformed earnings frontier model (8.17), their interpretation is straightforward. For example, in the random effects specification, studying successfully at a university means multiplying potential income without a study by the factor:

$$\exp(0.2954 \bullet 1) = 1.34, \tag{8.18}$$

ceteris paribus and on average.

8.5.1 Random Effects Specification

We will deal with the interpretation of the results on overeducation now, and we will restrict our attention to the random effects specification, first. FRONTIER 4.1 provides overeducation estimates for every individual in every year. But of course, we will not go into that detail but analyse overeducation on an aggregated level.

A significant $\mu = 0.5843$ means that, for the distribution of the inefficiency terms u_{it}, the more general truncated normal distribution given in model (8.6) is preferred over the half-normal distribution $|N(0, \sigma_u^2)|$ which would result if $\mu = 0$ The highly significant $\gamma = 0.8991$ —see equation (8.7)—means that roughly 90 per cent of total residual variance σ^2 is attributed to inefficiency. This is in line with the LR test statistic clearly rejecting:

$$H_0 : \sigma_u^2 = 0 \quad \text{vs.} \quad H_1 : \sigma_u^2 > 0 \tag{8.19}$$

or equivalently:

$$H_0 : \gamma = 0 \quad \text{vs.} \quad H_1 : \gamma > 0. \tag{8.20}$$

In this respect, see Coelli (1995) for LR tests in frontier models and mixtures of χ^2-distributions.

The result concerning η is somewhat more surprising. In the literature on overeducation, it comes out that overeducation measured in the subjective or objective way—summarised in Section 2—should be increasing over time. But, with the income ratio measure for overeducation used in this paper, the opposite results: As shown in equation (8.8), a significantly positive η means that inefficiency (overeducation) decreases over time. This becomes also evident in Table 8.2 showing the average overeducation for all individuals in the sample. The 1998 result, for example, means that the individuals in the sample waste 45.68 per cent of their potential income, that is, they only receive 54.32 per cent of their potential income—see equation (8.16). Also, we see that overeducation has roughly decreased by 0.5 per cent per year.

The fact that the income ratio measure gives results contrary to subjective or objective measures could easily be explained: Individuals are interested more in sufficient income than in some objective or subjective matching aspects; therefore, they have increased their utility in the sample period. Nevertheless, several aspects of this result are noteworthy.

First, an average overeducation of 46 per cent is different from the cross-section results in Jensen (2000, 2001a, 2001b) providing average overeducation of 22 per cent in 1992. Of course, this could be due to the panel model in

Table 8.2 Mean overeducation

	1994	1995	1996	1997	1998
Stochastic earnings frontier (13) *with random effects (4)* Mean overeducation	0.4758	0.4710	0.4662	0.4615	0.4568
Stochastic earnings frontier (13) *with overeducation effects (11)* Mean overeducation	0.0684	0.0689	0.0691	0.0703	0.0733

Source: Own calculations, based on GSOEP data.

this paper: For the data, it is more difficult to fit one model in five years than one model in only one year. Therefore, the deviations from the model will increase leading directly to increasing inefficiency; but, the increase in overeducation is impressive.

Secondly, the parameter estimates change distinctly from the OLS starting values to the ML random effects results. The changes are not dramatic, but distinct. For example, Jensen (2001a) discussed in detail why this is not very likely to occur if all ideal model assumptions are sufficiently fulfilled. Distinct differences between OLS estimates and ML estimates can indicate unmodelled heteroscedasticity, unsuitable functional form and some influential observations, etc. A detailed data analysis has been performed with the following results: The functional form seems to be correct, and highly influential observations were not found; but, the assumption of having homoscedastic residuals could not be maintained. Also, heteroscedastic residuals lead to biased parameter estimates (in a frontier model), biased variance estimates and biased inefficiency (overeducation) estimates. Therefore, it is now time to analyse the results of the overeducation effects specification equation (8.11).

8.5.2 Overeducation Effects Specification

One comment is due to the procedure in Jensen (2000, 2001a, 2001b). In these works, stochastic cross-section earnings frontiers (using model (8.3)) are estimated first. Then, the transformed overeducation measures u_{it} are analysed for various sample subgroups, that is, means and variances for those subgroups are calculated and tested for being different. There are reasons for proceeding this way, but one ought to mention that this procedure has been criticised in the (production) frontier literature, for example, by Reifschneider and Stevenson (1991). The problem is that in the first (estimation) step, it is assumed that the

u_i or u_{it} are independent and identically distributed (iid) whereas, in the second step (the subgroup analysis), it is assumed that there *is* structure in the u_i or u_{it}. Hence, we will try the theoretically better way in this paper.

The variables z used for modelling individual inefficiency have also been presented in the previous section. Their selection has been somewhat difficult. Various combinations of metric and dummy variables have been checked, but only the given set of dummy variables lead to a significant and relatively stable solution. Nevertheless, the question for the most suitable overeducation speci-fication in the stochastic earnings frontier is certainly not answered completely by this paper.

The estimation results for the stochastic earnings frontier (8.13) with the overeducation effects specification (8.11) can be found in the last two columns of Table 8.1. The parameter estimates for model (8.13) are interpreted as in the previous model. It can be seen that—except age and seniority—the frontier parameter estimates are closer to the OLS estimates than with the previous model. The parameters γ, μ and η are no longer available, but the drastically reduced LR test statistic (but still significant) and the σ^2 estimate indicate that the residuals—and, therefore, inefficiency/overeducation—have reduced con-siderably. The aim of removing heteroscedasticity, therefore, seems to have been fulfilled.

Table 8.2 shows the average overeducation over all individuals for the years in the sample. It can be seen that—in the overeducation effects specification, compared to the random effects specification—these numbers have reduced drastically. Whereas the random effects estimates are probably too high (be-cause of heteroscedasticity), the overeducation effects results may be too small (because $\hat{u}_{it}$ in equation (8.11) has less variation than u_{it}, especially when deter-mined only by six dummy variables). If the aim is to get 'exact' overeducation estimates for individuals, this fact is somewhat unsatisfactory, of course, and requires improvement, for example, by providing a more suitable overeduca-tion effects specification in equation (8.11).

It can also be concluded from Table 8.2 that average overeducation no longer decreases over time. If anything, there is a (certainly insignificant) slight increase of 0.1 per cent per year. Therefore, the phenomenon occurring with the random effects specification should be due to unmodelled heteroscedasticity, as supposed above.

The signs of the parameter estimates in the overeducation effects part (8.11) show that inefficiency and, therefore, overeducation is higher:

- with higher age,
- with higher seniority,
- with higher job status,
- with higher job satisfaction,

- for non-executives,
- for non-scientists.

The results for executives and scientists are in line with previous results from the literature on overeducation, whereas the results for age, seniority, job status and job satisfaction are opposite to those obtained with subjective or objective measures. But, one has to keep in mind that when using the income ratio measure instead, the focus is shifted from some subjective or objective matching aspects to income efficiency. As explained in Section 2, the income ratio measure is intended to be a complement to the subjective or objective measures accounting for important (income and efficiency) aspects ignored by the traditional measures.

The results on the positive influence of job status and job satisfaction are in line with Jensen (2001a). A possible explanation given there is: High status and high satisfaction correlate with high income. Also, if income is sufficiently high, there is the possibility for choosing between (substituting) high income, high status and high satisfaction, to some extent. In this respect, Büchel (2001) asked if increasing overeducation leads to decreasing or to increasing job satisfaction. Jensen (2003) gave the astonishing answer: On average, increasing overeducation (measured with income ratios) leads to increasing job satisfaction. On average, laziness (avoiding high-pressure jobs) seems to be preferred to jealousy (striving for optimal income with maximum effort).

8.6 CONCLUSIONS

In this paper, the income ratio measure for measuring overeducation has been introduced and applied to a panel dataset for the years 1994 to 1998 from the GSOEP. Based on an estimation of individual potential income with a stochastic earnings panel frontier, overeducation is measured as the income ratio between potential income and actual income. It seems to be rewarding to apply the income ratio measure in empirical analyses of overeducation because it allows the inclusion of the (metric) income and efficiency aspects of overeducation, ignored by the well-established objective or subjective measures focusing on some (ordinal) matching aspects.

REFERENCES

Aigner, D.J., and Chu, S.-F. (1968). On estimating the industry production function. *American Economic Review,* **58**, 826–839.

Aigner, D.J., Lovell, C.A.K., and Schmidt, P. (1977). Formulation and estimation of stochastic frontier production function models. *Journal of Econometrics*, **6**, 21–37.

Baltagi, B.H. (1995). *Econometric analysis of panel data*. Chichester: Wiley.

Battese, G.E., and Coelli, T.J. (1992). Frontier production functions, technical efficiency and panel data: With application to paddy farmers in India. *Journal of Productivity Analysis*, **3**, 153–169.

Battese, G.E., and Coelli, T.J. (1995). A model for technical inefficiency effects in a stochastic frontier production function for panel data. *Empirical Economics*, **20**, 325–332.

Battese, G.E., and Corra, G.S. (1977). Estimation of a production frontier model: With application to the pastoral zone of eastern Australia. *Australian Journal of Agricultural Economics*, **21**, 169–179.

Borghans, L., and de Grip, A. (2000a). The debate in economics about skill utilization. In L. Borghans and A. de Grip (Eds.), *The overeducated worker? The economics of skill utilization* (pp. 3–23). Cheltenham: Edward Elgar.

Borghans, L., and de Grip, A. (2000b). *The overeducated worker? The economics of skill utilization*. Cheltenham: Edward Elgar.

Büchel, F. (2001). Overqualification: Reasons, measurement issues, and typographical affinity to unemployment. In P. Descy and M. Tessaring (Eds.), *Training in Europe: Second report on vocational training research in Europe 2000* (Vol. 2, pp. 453–560). Luxembourg: Office for Official Publications of the European Communities.

Coelli, T. (1995). Estimators and hypothesis tests for a stochastic frontier function: A Monte Carlo analysis. *Journal of Productivity Analysis*, **6**, 247–268.

Coelli, T. (1996). *A guide to FRONTIER 4.1: A computer program for stochastic frontier production and cost function estimation*. Armidale, Australia: University of New England (CEPA Working Paper 96/07).

Coelli, T., Rao, D.S.P., and Battese, G.E. (1998). *An introduction to efficiency and productivity analysis*. Boston: Kluwer.

Daneshvary, N., Herzog, H.W., Jr., Hofler, R.A., and Schlottmann, A.M. (1992). Job search and immigrant assimilation: An earnings frontier approach. *Review of Economics and Statistics*, **74**, 482–492.

Greene, W.H. (1997). Frontier production functions. In M.H. Pesaran and P. Schmidt, *Handbook of applied econometrics* (pp. 81–166). Oxford: Blackwell.

Jensen, U. (2000). Measuring earnings differentials with frontier functions and Rao distances. In P. Marriott and M. Salmon (Eds.), *Applications of differential geometry to econometrics* (pp. 184–213). Cambridge: Cambridge University Press.

Jensen, U. (2001a). Robuste Frontierfunktionen, methodologische Anmerkungen und Ausbildungsadäquanzmessung. Frankfurt a.M.: Lang.

Jensen, U. (2001b). The simplicity of an earnings frontier. In A. Zellner, H.A. Keuzenkamp and M. McAleer (Eds.), *Simplicity, inference and modelling* (pp. 277–291). Cambridge: Cambridge University Press.

Jensen, U. (2003). Which feeling is stronger: Jealousy or laziness? In S. Mittnik and I. Klein (Eds.), *Contributions to modern econometrics* (pp. 105–118). Dordrecht: Kluwer.

Meeusen, W., and van den Broeck, J. (1977). Efficiency estimation from Cobb/Douglas production functions with composed error. *International Economic Review*, **18**, 435–444.

Mincer, J. (1974). *Schooling, experience and earnings.* New York: National Bureau of Economic Research.

Reifschneider, D., and Stevenson, R. (1991). Systematic departures from the frontier: A framework for the analysis of firm inefficiency. *International Economic Review, 32,* 715–723.

SOEP Group. (2001). The German Socio-Economic Panel (GSOEP) after more than 15 years—Overview. *DIW-Vierteljahresheft (Applied Economics Quarterly),* **70/1,** 7–14.

PART FOUR

Special groups

9. Credentialism by Members of Licensed Professions[1]

Joan Muysken and Thomas Zwick

9.1 INTRODUCTION

Upskilling is a well-documented phenomenon on the labour markets in all developed countries. Many commentators in the economic profession claim that upskilling may mainly be explained by skill-biased technological change that increases the skill levels required to perform a given job, see Acemoglu (2002) for a survey. Evidence for this conjecture is found in the empirical fact that the shifts in qualification requirements are mainly within narrowly defined jobs, functions and professional groups, instead of shifts between business sectors or industries—see Berman, Bound and Griliches (1994), Falk and Seim (2001) or Zwick (2001).

Rising skill requirements in jobs may also be interpreted as credentialism, however, which is defined as a rising qualification demand that is not matched by rising skill levels needed in production. Green, Felstead and Gallie (2000) and de Witte and Steijn (2000) show that credentialism is widely observed in reality. The credentialism they observe induces overqualification because the tasks could also be executed to the same extent by people with lower qualifications than required. This is evident either from a comparison between firms that apply credentialism and those that do not, or from a comparison between the skills required and the skills needed during the course of time. An example of the latter is that exam failure rates for accountants (CPA's) in the US increased with downturns in economic activity when the exams were graded by the individual states (Young, 1988).[2]

There may be several reasons for credentialism. On the one hand, it may be supply driven. Employers increase their qualification requirements in the wake of the increased skill supply although their skill requirements do not change (Muysken and ter Weel, 2000; Robinson and Manacorda, 1997). Here, credentialism is attributed to strategic employer behaviour: The signalling value of qualifications decreases and employers wishing to recruit employees with the same level of skills as in the past have to ask for higher qualifications. The same phenomenon occurs when there are job queues with increasingly skilled applicants and qualification is used as a low-cost way of allocating places (Green et al., 2000).

On the other hand, next to a product of opportunistic employer behaviour, credentialism may be also a consequence of rent seeking behaviour of employees. In the sociological literature, credentialism by employees is well known, see for example the book edited by Hafferty and McKinley (1993), Freidson (1994) or Franz (1998). This literature focuses on autonomy, control and social status as explanations for credentialism. It is, for example, argued that interest groups that have the right to autonomously set the entry requirements for their profession increase those requirements in order to protect themselves against potential competitors, or these groups increase their own social prestige by requiring the next generation of professionals to pass, for example, university exams instead of polytechnic exams. Economic motivations for credentialism are rarely analysed in the sociological literature, however.

An additional observation in the sociological literature, which is relevant for our purpose, is that only specific groups have the right to set qualification requirements autonomously. The main group seems to be licensed professions and their interest bodies. Professional groups for licensed occupations encompass 'old' professions like medical, pharmaceutical and care professions, 'academic' professions like scientists, engineers and professors and 'guild type' professions like accountants, notaries, lawyers, organised real-estate agents, hairdressers and clergy (see Freidson, 1993; Kleiner, 2000).

This contribution argues that it might be in the economic interest of members of licensed professions to increase qualification demand in the wake of a demand shock, while firms would not increase the skill requirements under the same circumstances. Our argument is based on two important characteristics of licensed professional groups.

First, there exists professional specific human capital that has to be acquired with high training costs. The latter can be in monetary terms but also in time and effort. This specific professional knowledge is frequently useless in other professions.

Second, licensed professions are autonomous in their control over the entrance criteria for new entrants, the training content and level and codes of conduct for professionals (Freidson, 1993; Kleiner, 2000; Wolinsky, 1993). In addition, licensed occupations can effectively monopolise the supply of practitioners because—in contrast to certified occupations—it is legally forbidden to practice this occupation without a license (Kleiner, 2000). In most professions, entrance is regulated via qualification requirements and licensing exams open for everybody and not by a fixed number of entrants. Members of the profession dominate the licensing boards that determine entrance criteria and control entry even when nominally state entities grant permission to practice a licensed occupation. Descriptive analysis of this behaviour can be found in the book edited by Hafferty and McKinlay (1993) and in Spieß and Tietze (2001).

Kleiner (2000) shows that, in general, the requirements for entry into licensed occupations are increasing. Because occupational licensing directly affects approximately 18 per cent of the US workers, for example, its impact on qualification requirements is high. Since the demand for regulated services is growing and more occupations become regulated, professionals contribute increasingly to upskilling. Perloff (1980) argues that licensing laws prevent low-skilled workers from entering licensed professions during periods of peak demand, while unions or employers often relax entry qualifications for non-licensed professionals in similar circumstances. This creates economic rents for members of the licensed occupations. Therefore, occupation associations always have an incentive to restrict entrance by increasing the qualification requirements even when there is no technological need for higher skills. Muzando and Pazderka (1980) and Kleiner (2000) provided empirical evidence that members of licensed professions are able to skim rents by restricting the number of practitioners.

This paper combines the mainly sociological notion of professional autonomy in determining the entry requirements with the economic explanation of upskilling by credentialism. Hereby, the new argument is introduced that credentialism may stem from the strategic behaviour of members of a licensed profession and not—as usually found in the economic literature—of employers. We, hereby try to enhance the understanding of skill inflation and overqualification from an economic point of view and point out its impact on economic variables, such as employment and economic rents from education for various professional groups.

The paper is organised as follows. First, a benchmark model is developed with given skill requirements and an equilibrium with perfect skill match and full employment. Then it is analysed how a demand shock that increases skilled labour demand affects the labour market equilibrium when qualification requirements for skilled labour are exogeneously given. In a next step, it is shown that if the firm was allowed to set the qualification requirements, it would not increase the qualification level after this demand shock. The situation is different, however, if the skilled workers are members of a licensed profession and, therefore, can set the qualification requirements. It can be shown that under general and plausible conditions the professionals can increase their surplus by raising the qualification requirements. This increase in qualification requirements induces overqualification because it is not induced by technological change but by rent maximisation of professionals. The final section derives some conclusions from our analysis.

9.2 THE BENCHMARK MARKET EQUILIBRIUM WITH GIVEN SKILL REQUIREMENTS

The relevant production factors are the number of employed skilled workers l and their specific human capital per worker c. The amount of specific skills required for the job is initially given exogeneously by technology. The base wage rate for unskilled work is given for all participants on the labour market. Firms cannot substitute skilled workers by unskilled ones or workers with another specialisation. Demand for skilled labour by the firm is decreasing in the skill mark-up.[3] Each skilled worker earns a skill mark-up on the base wage rate. Since individuals differ in their costs of acquiring skills, endogenous skilled labour supply is increasing in the skill mark-up. Free formation of the skill mark-up at a given base wage rate then leads to market clearing.

9.2.1 The Behaviour of the Firm

We assume that the representative firm is confronted with an inelastic demand for its good y and a given price p. This can be either a situation of perfect competition, where no individual supplier can influence the price, or a situation where the price is fixed externally—by the government, as is the case for many medical services, or by a professional body, as, for instance, for notary services in some countries.[4] The firm employs l workers who all have the same skills level c. This level is measured by a professional license that is only granted when the candidate can prove certain specific skills. We therefore assume that skills and qualifications are identical and there is no asymmetric information on the actual skill level between employees and the firm. The production function of the firm $f(l,c)$ is in labour and skills only and f is well behaved and has the property $lf_l > cf_c$, or, in other words, an increase in the number of employees has a stronger effect on productivity than an increase in human capital. This property is needed to allow the firm to set skill requirements (cf. Section 3).

The wage rate per worker consists of two components: First, there is a base wage rate w per worker, independent of the level of skills. Second, there is also a skill mark-up $\delta > 0$ per unit of human capital, proportional to the wage rate. Hence, the firm pays each employed worker a wage $w(1+\delta c)$. This specification reflects that at a zero skill level the base wage w paid on the unskilled labour market is earned. The base wage rate is set outside the firm at $\underline{w}$, and for the benchmark scenario we assume that the amount of skills required for the job $\underline{c}$ is given by the technology used. The firm sets demand for labour, l, such that its profits π are maximised for each mark-up δ. The profits are given by:

$$\pi = pf(l, \underline{c}) - w(1 + \delta\underline{c})l. \tag{9.1}$$

Maximisation of equation (9.1) with respect to l then yields the first order condition:

$$pf_l = \underline{w}[1 + \delta\underline{c}]. \tag{9.2}$$

Equation (9.2) shows that demand for labour is set such that the value marginal product of labour equals marginal labour costs. This implies that for a given base wage rate and skill level, demand for labour l is decreasing in the skill premium δ. Figure 9.1 represents this by the downward sloping demand curve L^D.

When a positive demand shock occurs, which manifests itself by an exogenous price increase for the goods produced, the demand curve shifts to the right, for example to $L^{D'}$, since it then becomes more profitable to produce goods y.

If we use a Cobb/Douglas production function as an example:

$$f(c,l) = c^\alpha l^\beta \quad \text{with } 0 < \alpha < \beta < 1, \tag{9.3}$$

demand for labour is:

$$l = \underline{c}^{\alpha/(1-\beta)}[\beta p/\underline{w}(1+\delta\underline{c})]^{1/(1-\beta)}. \tag{9.4}$$

9.2.2 The Behaviour of the Workers

Let in every period an identical generation of potential entrants leave school and decide whether to invest in skills or not. We assume that skilled job entrants find a suitable job with certainty when they invest in skills. The risk to fail the licensing exam, being forced to take another job than that one is educated for and unemployment are, of course, important empirical phenomena and agents may voluntarily take the risk not to find an adequate job after training (see Kleiner, 2000; Maurizi, 1974; Zwick, 2000).[5] The introduction of the risk not to find an adequate job after training would complicate our model. These complications generate little new insights, however, because the main mechanisms that drive our results remain unchanged. The mechanisms are the positive impact of the bonus on the attractiveness of the profession and the negative impact of the required qualification level on the eagerness of potential entrants to qualify for the profession. Intuitively, we therefore assume that the number of people interested in a licensed profession does not surpass demand by much and the skilled labour market is in equilibrium before the demand shock. This means that there are as many skilled entrants as there are insiders retiring from skilled jobs. Let each year j' workers retire while there are n incumbent workers.

The new entrant workers are heterogeneous in their abilities to acquire knowledge. When we rank the workers from 1 to z, individual 1 has the lowest

Figure 9.1   Demand and supply of labour (at given skills $\underline{c}$)

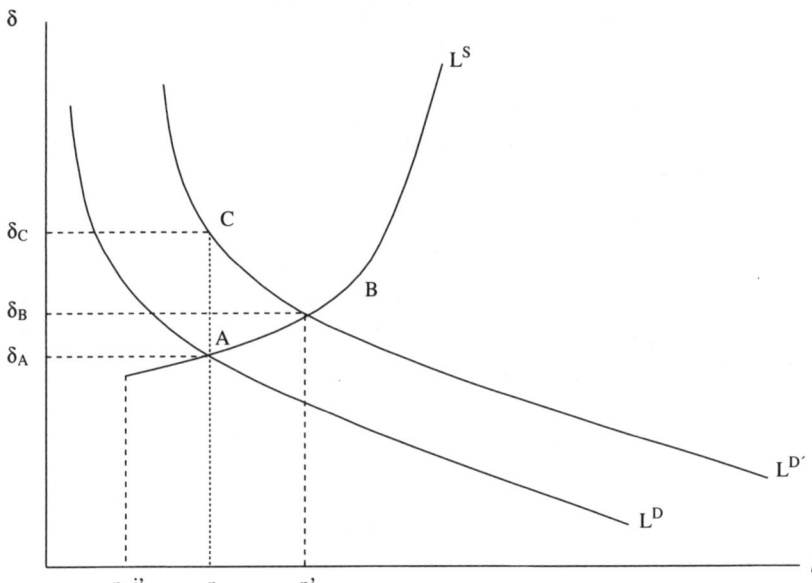

costs in obtaining a certain skill level c, whereas individual z has the highest
costs. As a consequence, we can represent the costs for individual j to obtain
the necessary skill level c by $K(c, j)$, where K is increasing in both c and j. When
we assume that the workers only take the contemporary situation in wages and
training necessities into account, we find for worker j the following surplus s_j
when they invest in skill level $\underline{c}$:

$$s_j = \underline{w}(1+\delta\underline{c}) - K(c, j) \qquad K_{\underline{c}}, K_j, K_{\underline{c}\underline{c}}, K_{jj}, K_{\underline{c}j} > 0. \qquad (9.5)$$

The outside option for worker j is to earn the unskilled base wage $\underline{w}$ instead of
investing in skills and earn this surplus. We therefore assume that there is only
one representative skilled type of job relevant or interesting for the potential entrants into the skilled labour market who have the option either to invest in skills
$\underline{c}$ or not to train at all and work in the unskilled labour market. Potential entrants
train if their surplus exceeds the base wage $\underline{w}$ paid on the unskilled labour market. There are no barriers to obtain skills and the number of entrants in the skill
group is not regulated by restrictions in numbers but by economic incentives.

The marginal worker j_m who invests in $\underline{c}$ for a given skill premium δ then is
determined from:

$$\delta\underline{c}\underline{w} = K(\underline{c}, j_m). \qquad (9.6)$$

Since the costs of acquiring $\underline{c}$ are increasing with the ranking of the worker, equation (6) implies that the supply of skilled labour given the skill level $\underline{c}$ is increasing in the skill premium δ. Figure 9.1 represents this by the upward sloping supply curve L^S, which starts at the remaining number of incumbent workers $n - j'$. This is the number of employees in equilibrium minus the exogenous number of retired workers.

An example is the simple cost function:

$$K(\underline{c}, j) = c^\xi j^\phi, \qquad \xi, \phi > 1 \tag{9.7}$$

which yields the following supply function of new workers:

$$e = (\delta \underline{c}^{1-\xi} \underline{w})^{1/\phi}. \tag{9.8}$$

9.2.3 The Market Equilibrium

The behaviour of the representative firm and of the entrants implies that the market equilibrium can be represented by point A in Figure 9.1. That is, for the level of required skills $\underline{c}$, the firm employs n workers who earn a skill premium δ_A while $j_m = j'$ entrants train themselves in order to obtain the necessary skill and replace the j' insiders who retire from the labour market in the same period.

When a positive demand shock occurs, which manifests itself by an exogenous price increase, the demand curve for skilled labour shifts outwards to $L^{D'}$. The skill premium increases to δ_B and this attracts $e = n'-n$ additional entrants to supply labour in every period when the level of skills $\underline{c}$ remains unchanged. When nothing else changes, the equilibrium in the next period is at point B in Figure 9.1 with n' skilled workers.

9.3. THE FIRM SETS SKILL REQUIREMENTS

Let the skill requirements $\underline{c}$ be optimal before the demand shock. The question then is whether it is profitable for the firm to change its qualification requirements after the demand shock.

When the firm determines skill requirements, it maximises profits with respect to skills, taking into account the labour supply function (9.6). Moreover, since demand for skills is set before employment, the demand function for labour implied by equation (9.2) also holds. Substitution of $l = n - j' + e(c; \delta)$, where $e(c; \delta)$ is the labour supply function (9.8), in the profit function and maximising with respect to c yields:

$$[pf_l - w(1 + \delta c)]e'(c; \delta) = -[pf_c - w\delta l]. \tag{9.9}$$

Since equation (9.2) holds, the left hand side of equation (9.9) equals zero and, hence, the right hand side should also equal zero. Therefore equation (9) boils down to a maximisation of the profit function (9.1) with respect to c and l:

$$pf_c = \underline{w}\delta l, \qquad (9.9a)$$
$$pf_l = \underline{w}[1 + \delta c]. \qquad (9.9b)$$

Dividing these equations gives:

$$\delta c = 1/[\phi(l,\,c) - 1], \qquad (9.10)$$

with $\phi(l,\,c) = lf_l/cf_c > 1$, remember we assume $lf_l < cf_c$ in Section 2.1.

In the case of the Cobb/Douglas production function (9.3), $\phi(l,\,c)$ is a constant. Since in that case, δc is also a constant, the firm wants to impose higher skills only when it can pay a lower skill premium. The latter would also imply a higher demand for labour, since labour demand is decreasing in the skill premium (see equation (9.4)).[6] However, after the demand shock less than the required $n'-n$ additional entrants are willing to supply labour for a lower premium than δ_B (cf. Figure 9.1) and this, therefore, cannot be an equilibrium.[7] Hence, it is not profitable for the firm to increase the skill premium, since this decreases profits. Therefore, the skill requirements $\underline{c}$ remain profit optimal in the new equilibrium point B.

It is a question for future research to what extent this result can be generalised beyond the Cobb/Douglas production function. Actually, it seems quite reasonable that a lower skill premium leads to higher profits together with an increase in demand for both skills and labour. In order to obtain the result that the firm never changes its optimal skill requirement $\underline{c}$ after a positive demand shock, more general production functions have to satisfy $dc/d\delta < 0$ and, hence, using equation (9.10): $1 < \phi < cf_c/(f_c + cf_{cc})$.

4.   THE MEMBERS OF THE PROFESSION SET SKILL
REQUIREMENTS

An alternative to the assumption that the firm sets the skill requirements is to assume that the employees are members of a professional group and they are able to set the qualification requirements for entrants into the profession. The members of the profession have to take into account that an increase in the skill premium after the positive demand shock induces more entrants. An increase in the skill premium such that the demand for skilled labour would still be n after the positive demand shock (see δ_C in Figure 9.1) would attract more than j' entrants to supply skills and an excess supply of skilled workers would occur (see point C in Figure 9.1). This would introduce competition on the skilled labour market and a risk of skill mismatch and unemployment for all skilled workers. We assume that this is not in the interest of the members of the profession. The skilled professionals want to be sure to keep the adequate jobs for their education, instead.[8]

A typical way to keep the number of entrants low, when an oversupply of skilled professionals threatens, is to increase the required skills to join the licensed profession (see Kleiner, 2000; Maurizi, 1974).[9] This is, however, not free of costs for the members of the profession because they have to invest in the new skills required as well in order to form a homogeneous professional group. When a professional group requires entrants to be able, for example, to handle a new specific software, this group usually also carries out training for incumbent professionals in this software obligatory. Kleiner (2000) reports that professional associations usually require license holders to attend continuous training seminars. The following extension of the model demonstrates that if the members of the profession increase the required qualification level in the wake of a demand increase, they obtain a higher surplus under very general circumstances: It only has to be assumed that both, demand for labour and its supply, shift inwards at increasing skills. One sees directly from Figure 9.1 that members of the profession increase the required skills level at least as long as the supply curve shifts inwards faster than the demand curve.

9.4.1 The Impact of Skill Requirements on Demand for Labour

For simplicity we confine the analysis to the case of the Cobb/Douglas production function. From equation (9.2) one finds that the labour demand curve shifts

to the left with an increase in required skills c when $\delta > \delta^* = \frac{1}{c} \cdot \frac{\alpha}{1-\alpha}$ When we denote the demand curve for labour by L^D, we find:

$$l = L^D(\delta, c) \quad L^D_\delta < 0; L^D c < 0 \text{ for } \delta > \delta^* \qquad (9.11)$$

We assume that δ^* is relatively low, such that with higher required skills the demand curve for labour shifts inwards over the relevant range. Figure 9.2 shows this as the new demand curve for labour $L^{D''}$.

9.4.2 Reaction of Members of the Profession to the Demand Shock

The n members of the profession in the firm are able to control the number of entrants to the firm after the demand shock by setting the skill requirements c. We assume that the members of the profession determine these requirements, such that their surplus s_i is maximised, without risking loosing their job. Since the initial skills of the members of the profession are $\underline{c}$, the additionally required skills are Δc when the increase in demanded skills for entrants are also applied to the members. We find the following surplus:

Figure 9.2   Demand and supply of labour (at increased skill requirements)

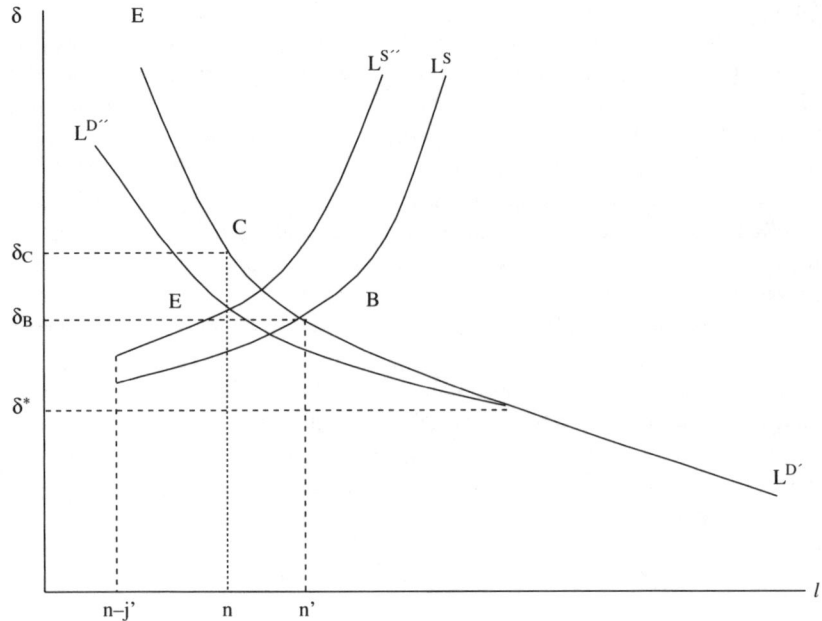

$$s_i = \underline{w}(1+\delta[\underline{c} + \Delta c]) - C(\Delta c), \tag{9.12}$$

where $C(\Delta c)$ are the costs for an increase in the qualification requirements. We assume that these incremental costs are the same for all members of the profession and $C'(\Delta c)>0$.

As before, we assume that there are j' members of the profession who quit their job. Since the members of the profession do not want to risk their jobs, they accept e additional entrants to the extent that:

$$n - j' + e(\delta,c) = L^D(\delta,c) \tag{9.13}$$

does hold.[10] Equation (9.6) above shows that the number of entrants is increasing in the skill premium and decreasing in skill requirements, that is, $e = e(\delta,c)$—hence, we have here $e_\delta > 0$ and $e_c < 0$. The latter condition follows from total differentiation of equation (9.6), which shows that the labour supply curve shifts to the left, that is, $de/dc < 0$, as long as the investment costs in human capital for new entrants are elastic with respect to skills, that is $\Xi^K_c > 1$, where Ξ^K_c represents the elasticity of K with respect to c. Since this is a plausible assumption—compare for instance equation (9.7), which yields an elasticity $\xi > 1$—we assume that the labour supply curve shifts to the left over its whole range with increased skill requirements set by the professional interest groups. Figure 9.2 depicts this by the labour supply curve $L^{S''}$.

The members of the profession maximise their surplus (9.12) with respect to Δc subject to condition (9.13) with $c = \underline{c} + \Delta c$ and $e \geq 0$. This yields the first-order condition:

$$\underline{w}\delta\{\Xi^{\delta}_{c} + 1\} = C'(\Delta c), \tag{9.14}$$

where Ξ^{δ}_{c} represents the elasticity of δ with respect to c resulting from equation (9.13). From equation (9.14) it follows that whenever $\Xi^{\delta}_{c} > -1$, we find $\Delta c > 0$. Equation (9.13) shows that the latter holds when:

$$[L^{D}_{c} - e_{c}] > -[e_{\delta} - L^{D}_{\delta}]c/\delta. \tag{9.15}$$

The members of the profession, therefore, increase their surplus by raising the skill requirements if the difference between the negative reaction of labour demand on an increase in the skill requirements and the negative reaction in skill supply on the increase is larger than the right hand side of equation (9.15) which is a negative figure. Therefore, the labour demand reaction should not be too much smaller than the labour supply reaction when c increases. In terms of Figure 9.2, the inward shift of $L^{D''}$ should be large enough relative to the inward shift in $L^{S''}$.

It is not clear, however, whether equation (9.15) implies that the skill mark-up δ has to increase with c. From equation (9.13), we know that $d\delta/dc = [L^{D}_{c} - e_{c}]/[e_{\delta} - L^{D}_{\delta}]$. Since the numerator is positive, we find $d\delta/dc > 0$ only if:

$$-L^{D}_{c} < -e_{c}. \tag{9.16}$$

In terms of Figure 9.2, condition (9.16) implies that in order to find a higher skill premium at increased skill requirements, labour supply $L^{S''}$ should shift faster inwards than labour demand $L^{D''}$ when c increases. Then the new market equilibrium at the intersection of $L^{D''}$ and $L^{S''}$ is at a bonus level higher than δ_{B}, see, for example, the new equilibrium indicated at point E.

A comparison of conditions (9.16) and (9.15) shows that when increased skill requirements lead to an increased skill premium under the given demand and supply conditions, that is, without attracting too many new entrants, it is always surplus maximising for the members of the profession to increase the skill requirements. But also when an increase in requirements does lead to a lower premium, it can be utility enhancing for the members of the profession to increase the qualification requirements—as long as the premium decrease is sufficiently compensated by the additional revenues generated by the increase in skills.

We therefore conclude that members of the profession react to the demand shock by increasing the required level of skills as long as equation (9.15) is sat-

isfied. This leads to an increased premium for the members when equation
(9.16) does hold, while the profit of the firm decreases. Notice that the training
costs of the members of the profession do not play a role in obtaining this
result. Therefore, upskilling may be beneficial even when the members of the
profession are required to invest in training in order to obtain the same higher
qualification level as the entrants. The condition for credentialism of members
of licensed professions is that after a demand shock, labour supply reacts more
elastic than labour demand in response to the increased qualification demand.
This condition seems especially plausible in the case of licensed professions:
While increased qualification requirements deter many potential job applicants, the substitution possibilities between labour and qualification for professional work is small when the qualification of the professionals and their wage
demands increase.

The increase in qualification demand leads to a rent shift away from firms
to members of the profession. This is inefficient because the upskilling is not
triggered by technological requirements, but by rent-seeking behaviour of the
skilled employees. In addition, competition on the skilled labour market is
artificially reduced and less potential entrants decide to train for the profession
while the skilled wages are higher if the members of the profession have the
right to set the qualification requirements.

9.5 CONCLUSIONS

This paper demonstrates that upskilling may not only stem from skill biased
technological change but also from credentialism, that is, an increase in the
qualification level demanded to perform a job that is not matched by an increased skill demand. The new aspect is that credentialism is not a result of
strategic behaviour of employers, but a consequence of rent-seeking behaviour of members of licensed professions in the wake of positive demand
shocks.

In our model, after a positive demand shock it is not optimal for the firm to
change its initially optimal skill requirements. When the members of the profession have the possibility to set the qualification requirements—because the
profession is licensed, for example—they inflate these although the new technology does not demand higher skills. The only condition for credentialism is
that the potential job entrants react stronger on the qualification increase than
the employers. The higher skill demand increases the rent share of the members
of the profession and forces the firms to pay a higher wage. The consequence
of this rent seeking behaviour of the members of a licensed profession is that
employment in the profession is lower than it would be when the firm would
set the skill requirements.

Another consequence of credentialism is overqualification. Overqualification can be measured by subjective assessment, job descriptions or by broader measures taking specific tasks, qualification levels and skills required in comparable jobs into account (Büchel, 1998; Zwick, 2001). All measurement variants listed above would lead to an increase in measured overqualification. When job entrants and qualified professionals would compare their qualification level with the job contents demanded in jobs not covered by licensed professions or the development of the qualification demand of the firms, they would realise that their qualification increased more than necessary and they would classify themselves as overqualified. When the professionals would compare the increase in qualification requirements during the course of time with the technological development and the qualification demand implied by it, they also would come to the conclusion that their qualification level increased stronger than necessary by technological change.

In order to reduce credentialism and the other negative consequences of rent seeking behaviour of members of licensed professions, additional competition on the market for skills may be achieved by switching from licensing to certification. With certification, services may also be offered by those who do not have a license, while the consumers or the employing firms decide whose services to buy (see also Kleiner, 2000). Those who offer services or products although they are not certified, act as a natural increase of competition in a market with entry barriers. In our model, this would imply that firms could employ differently skilled employees (those with traditional licenses and those with new certificates) who would earn different wages and substitute between those when wage demands and qualification requirements for certain professional groups would reach a critical level in comparison to the technically required skills.

NOTES

1   We thank Peter Dolton, Bruno Decreuse, Bettina Müller and the participants of the Association Française de Sciences Economiques conference 2002 in Lyon for their stimulating comments on an earlier version.
2   This is consistent with Kleiner's observation that 'when there is perceived to be an oversupply in the occupation, the regulatory board can raise the test scores required to pass the exam.' (2000, p. 197).
3   We assume that when individuals hire a professional, their behaviour is similar to firm behaviour, that is, individuals are price inelastic and substitute between qualification and labour.
4   We have also developed a model with monopolistic competition, but a feasible solution of this model requires elastic demand for goods and services (e.g., Acemoglu, 2002). Since we think this is highly implausible for the goods and services we are discussing, we use inelastic demand at a given price.
5   Maurizi (1974) finds that pass rates are used as a 'fine tuning' mechanism of licensing boards to keep the rents of practitioners high. But, he also observes a long-run secular trend in increases in entrance requirements.

6   This does not only hold for given skills. From the Cobb/Douglas function we find $\phi(l, c) = \beta/\alpha$. Equation (9.10) yields $c = [\alpha/(\beta-\alpha)]/\delta$ as demand for skills. When substituted in equation (9.4) this implies the following labour demand function: $l = k\delta^{-\alpha/(1-\beta)}$, where k is a constant. Hence, demand for labour is also declining in the skill premium with endogenous skills.
7   Figure 9.1 explains the situation for a given level of skills. However, it is obvious that when a higher level of skills would be required, even less entrants would supply labour at premium δ_B because L^S shifts to the left when c increases (cf. equation (9.8)).
8   This assumption is frequently made in the insider/outsider literature (see Fiorillo, Santacroce and Staffolani, 1999; Lindbeck and Snower, 1988; Muysken and Zwick, 2000).
9   Another popular reaction of professionals is an artificial reduction in the number of entrants allowed to obtain a license. We assume, however, that everybody is free in the qualificational choice and that the professionals cannot effectively control the number of licenses granted.
10 Notice that a positive demand shock is necessary to leave equilibrium A in Figure 9.1 and induce the possibility to increase the skill requirements and the number of entrants beyond j'.

REFERENCES

Acemoglu, D. (2002). Technical change, inequality, and the labor market. *Journal of Economic Literature,* **40**, 7–72.
Berman, E., Bound, J., and Griliches, Z. (1994). Changes in the demand for skilled labor within U.S. manufacturing: Evidence from the annual survey of manufacturers. *Quarterly Journal of Economics,* **109**, 367–397.
Büchel, F. (1998). *Zuviel gelernt? Ausbildungsinadäquate Erwerbstätigkeit in Deutschland.* Bielefeld: Bertelsmann.
Falk, M., and Seim, K. (2001). The impact of information technology on high-skilled labor in services: Evidence from firm-level panel data. *Economics of Innovation and New Technology,* **10**, 289–323.
Fiorillo, F., Santacroce, S., and Staffolani, S. (1999). An insider-outsider model with non-trivially heterogeneous labour force. In M. Gallegati and A. Kirman (Eds.), *Beyond the representative agent* (pp. 307–322). Cheltenham: Edward Elgar.
Franz, H. (1998). *Zwischen Markt und Profession.* Göttingen: Vandenhoeck & Ruprecht.
Freidson, E. (1993). How dominant are the professions? In F. Hafferty and J. McKinlay (Eds.), *The changing medical profession: An international perspective* (pp. 54–66). Oxford: Oxford University Press.
Freidson, E. (1994). *Professionalism reborn: Theory, prophecy and policy.* Cambridge: Polity Press.
Green, F., Ashton, D., Burchell, B., Davies, B., and Felstead, A. (2000). Are British workers becoming more skilled? In L. Borghans and A. de Grip (Eds.), *The overeducated worker? The economics of skill utilization* (pp. 77–108). Cheltenham: Edward Elgar.
Green, F., Felstead, A., and Gallie, D. (2000). *Computers are even more important than you thought: An analysis of the changing skill-intensity of jobs.* London: Centre for Economic Performance (Discussion Paper 0439).
Hafferty, F., and McKinlay, J. (1993). *The changing medical profession: An international perspective.* Oxford: Oxford University Press.
Kleiner, M. (2000). Occupational licensing. *Journal of Economic Perspectives,* **14**, 189–202.
Lindbeck, A., and Snower, D. (1988). Cooperation, harassment, and involuntary unemployment: An insider-outsider approach. *American Economic Review,* **78**, 167–188.

Maurizi, A. (1974). Occupational licensing and the public interest. *Journal of Political Economy,* **82**, 399–413.

Muysken, J., and ter Weel, B. (2000). Overeducation and crowding out of low-skilled workers. In L. Borghans and A. de Grip (Eds.), *The overeducated worker? The economics of skill utilization* (pp. 109–1323). Cheltenham: Edward Elgar.

Muysken, J., and Zwick, T. (2000). *Wage divergence and unemployment: The impact of insider power and training costs.* Mannheim: Zentrum für Europäische Wirtschaftsforschung (ZEW Discussion Paper 00-3).

Muzando, T., and Pazderka, B. (1980). Occupational licensing and professional incomes in Canada. *Canadian Journal of Economics,* **13**, 659–667.

Perloff, J. (1980). The impact of licensing laws on wage changes in the construction industry. *Journal of Law and Economics,* **23**, 409–428.

Robinson, P., and Manacorda, M. (1997). *Qualifications and the labor market in Britain 1984–1994: Skill biased change in the demand for labor or credentialism.* London: Centre for Economic Performance (Discussion Paper 330).

Spieß, K., and Tietze, W. (2001). *Gütesiegel als neues Instrument der Qualitätssicherung von Humandienstleistungen.* Berlin: Deutsches Institut für Wirtschaftsforschung (DIW Discussion Paper 243).

Witte, M. de, and Steijn, B. (2000). Automation, job content, and underemployment. *Work, Employment and Society,* **14**, 245–264.

Wolinsky, F. (1993). The professional dominance, deprofessionalization, proletarianization, and corporatization perspective: An overview and synthesis. In F. Hafferty and J. McKinlay (Eds.), *The changing medical profession: An international perspective* (pp. 11–24). Oxford: Oxford University Press.

Young, S.D. (1988). The economic theory of regulation: Evidence from the uniform CPA examination. *The Accounting Review,* **63**, 283–291.

Zwick, T. (2000). Overqualification makes low-wage employment attractive. In L. Borghans and A. de Grip (Eds.), *The overeducated worker? The economics of skill utilization* (pp. 133–156). Cheltenham: Edward Elgar.

Zwick, T. (2001). Supply of human capital in times of skill biased technological change. *Jahrbücher für Nationalökonomie und Statistik,* **221**, 322–335.

10. The Determinants and Consequences of Graduate Overeducation

Peter Dolton and Mary Silles

10.1 INTRODUCTION

Over the last 25 years, the rapid expansion of the education system in the UK resulted in large increases in the supply of highly educated workers. Over the same period, we have seen an increase in the rate of return to education and rising wage inequality. However, a growing literature on the economics of education has demonstrated that there have been widespread skill-shortages and deficiencies at the intermediate skill level, pointing to the neglected vocational element of education in the UK (McIntosh and Steedman, 2000; Prais, 2001). In addition, a related literature has suggested that between 30 and 40 per cent of university graduates have jobs that do not require a university degree (Dolton and Vignoles, 2000; Sloane, Battu and Seaman, 1999). The link between these two important findings has generated the literature on 'overeducation' or downward occupational mobility (see Berg, 1970; Freeman, 1976). In this paper using the Newcastle Alumni Survey,[1] which was especially designed to permit new research in this field, we examine how overeducation could arise and attempt to verify whether or not a significant number of graduates are genuinely overeducated. Our focus is on the explanation of overeducation in the first and current job and how this may be endogenously related to wage determination.

The synchronisation between university qualifications and the labour market has an important bearing on the ability of graduates to enter graduate-level occupations. The extent to which learned skills can be transferred to the labour market varies markedly with the type of degree and the specialisation component of qualifications. In recent years, alongside the rapid expansion in higher education, there have been important changes in the types of qualifications being awarded by universities. There has been a substantial growth in the number of students studying degrees in media studies, sport and leisure and similar areas which, at face value, seem to be vocationally orientated. The rationale is that these new qualifications have emerged in response to changing economic needs. Whilst these courses are very popular at the new universities in the UK and enjoy buoyant demand, there is evidence that unemployment of graduates from these courses is high.

Standards in education are also a critical concern to employers. If the quality of qualifications is perceived to have been 'watered down,' firms may upgrade their educational requirements to ensure the recruitment of the most able graduates. This may happen for all jobs in the hierarchy. Thus, overeducated workers could essentially be comprised of those who have non-professional qualifications, a low quality of education or both. As a result of these changes, university graduates may be taking jobs today requiring less than a university degree. This phenomena, labelled 'bumping down' in the literature, is one that would not have occurred (or occurred to a lesser degree) in the past.

Empirical evidence on these trends over time in the UK is scarce, but a brief consideration of the available Department for Education and Skills (DfES) data shows us the rate of increase of qualified school leavers, the growing pool of the qualified and the extent of educational grade inflation. Figure 10.1 shows us the proportion of each school-leaving cohort who qualify as graduates three years later. This trend is steeply upward, showing that less than 3 per cent of school leavers in the UK achieved a degree three years later in 1955, whereas in the 1990s this figure had risen to around 16 per cent.[2] Figure 10.2 provides some limited evidence of qualification inflation. The graph shows that the proportion of school leavers achieving two or more 'A' level passes has risen from 5 per cent in 1955 to around 20 per cent in the last few years. In the same graph it shows that the proportion of graduates attaining an upper secondary degree or above has risen from 27 per cent in 1966 to 63 per cent in 2001.

Although these graphs show how the supply of qualified manpower has been increasing, it does not provide evidence of the presence or scale of the overeducation problem. An informed analysis of this would require clear evidence on the demand for qualified manpower. Sadly, comprehensive data on this does not exist.

One consequence of over-supply of qualified manpower is that there may be a trade-off between schooling and other forms of human capital such as on-the-job training, years of experience and ability (Sicherman, 1991; Sloane, Battu and Seaman, 1999). The discrepancy between required and acquired schooling may only be a short-run phenomenon if graduates temporarily work in jobs that provide them with the skills to be used later in higher-level positions. However, permanent ability differences between similarly educated workers could result in workers with similar levels of schooling having different wage profiles at all stages of the life cycle. Pryor and Schaffer (1999) showed that US workers who experienced downward occupational mobility generally had lower cognitive skills irrespective of educational credentials.

Figure 10.1 Proportion of school leavers achieving a degree three years later

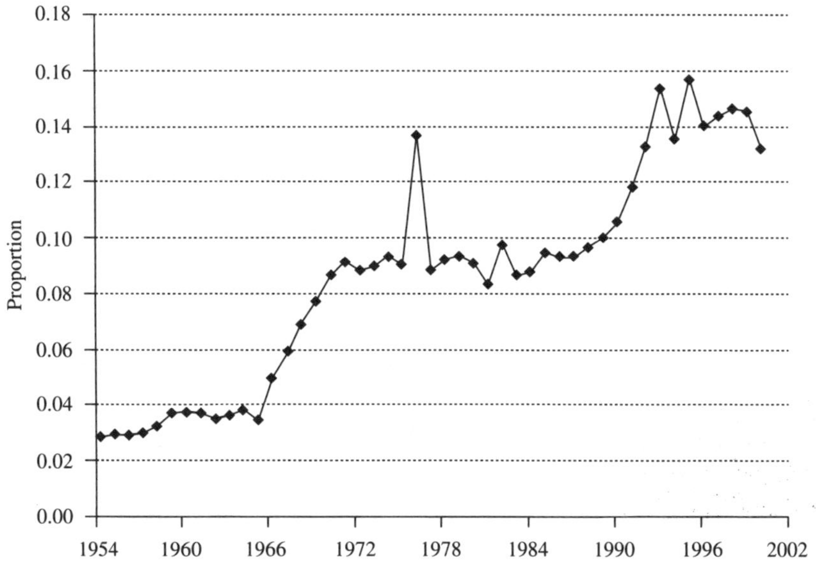

Source: DfES statistics in education.

Several reasons may also be advanced to explain why overeducation in future employment could be intrinsically linked with overeducation on entering the labour market. In the literature to date, observing someone in the 'overeducated' state has usually been viewed as a 'static condition,' which does not change as a person continues to work in the labour market.[3] Clearly this is naïve—some workers may start in a job for which they are overqualified, but quickly progress to something more appropriate to their qualifications. Likewise, other workers returning to the labour market after some time out of employment, or having moved locations, may seek to simply return to the labour market by taking a job beneath their qualifications. Conversely their first job may have been in their chosen graduate profession. These dynamic aspects of the overeducation phenomena—which is the recognition that over the life-course people may shift in and out of overeducation—should be explicitly recognised.

There are other explanations of the dynamic pattern of over education. For instance, a lower-level position in first employment may be difficult to recover from due to the obsolescence of skills that are not being used. Alternatively, once an individual has been in a lower-grade job it may be hard to 'trade-up' to a more demanding job as an employer could take their earlier experience as a

Figure 10.2   The growing pool of the qualified in the UK

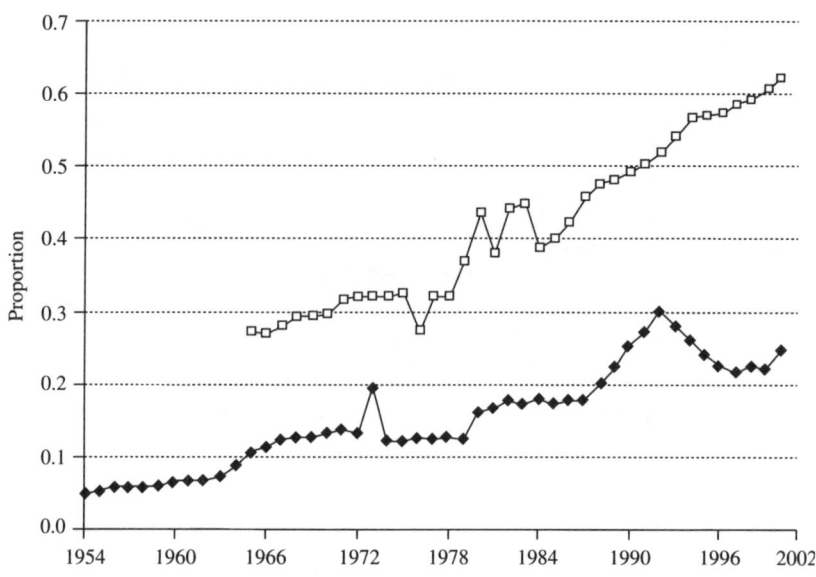

—□— Per cent of graduates with first or upper second degrees
—◆— Per cent of school leavers with two or more A-levels

negative signal of low ability and/or motivation. Such ability differences, the career-orientation of qualifications, and the quality of education could also permanently place graduates in lower-level occupations. These attributes of graduates create an unobservable factor that may have an effect on the probability of being overeducated in both first and later employment. In addition to separately modelling first and current employment, using two separate simple probit equations, one of the most distinguishing features of this research is that overeducation is also modelled using a bivariate probit in order to explicitly take into account the potential dependence between overeducation in first and later employment and its endogeneity with earnings potential.

Beyond all aspects of human capital and job characteristics, several factors may give rise to labour market rigidities that limit the capacity of the market to fully utilise and reward highly-educated workers. Such constraints could arise from family commitments, regional immobility or restrictive work practices. The Newcastle Alumni Survey contains detailed information on individual family circumstances and personal commitments, which we will examine to see how far they may result in some graduates taking jobs that require less than their educational credentials.

A further distinguishing feature of our study is that we have clear information on qualifications necessary to enter the job and those thought necessary to actually perform the job. Most research papers on this topic typically have one or the other of these pieces of information. For example, Duncan and Hoffman (1981) and Sicherman (1991) have data on the qualification necessary acquired the job, but others, for example, Rumberger (1987) and Hartog and Oosterbeek (1988) have information on qualifications necessary to perform the job. None of these studies have both types of information. This feature affords us an opportunity to study the relationship between these two types of questions.

The remainder of this paper is set out as follows. The next section briefly describes the Newcastle Alumni Survey and presents some descriptive statistics highlighting the pattern of initial and current overeducation. Our results largely indicate that previous studies may have overstated the true incidence of overeducation in the labour market. Section 3 considers the econometric estimation problems associated with the modelling of overeducation and puts the present contribution in context. In Section 4, we further the literature by comparing the determinants of overeducation using several estimation techniques. The empirical evidence is largely in line with the conventional wisdom that the career orientation of educational qualifications is highly significant in terms of labour market placement in an appropriate job. Section 5 illustrates how the estimation methods may affect the size and significance of the estimated earnings effect of overeducation. Finally, Section 6 concludes the paper.

10.2 THE NEWCASTLE ALUMNI SURVEY

This study uses data from the Newcastle Alumni Survey, which was collected at the University of Newcastle-upon-Tyne in 1998. The sample for this survey was selected using the Newcastle University Alumni Database of graduates and post-graduates. At the time the survey was carried out, 43,099 alumni were in this database. However, only 3,187 indicated their interest in participating in 'careers research' and were posted the questionnaire. Overall, 2,434 members returned the questionnaire, most of whom had graduated in the 1990s. Although a generally satisfactory response rate (76.37%) had been achieved, anything less than a perfect response raises the question of whether those who replied were representative of the 'statistical universe' of graduates who could have been sampled. Specifically, it is important to note that alumni members are slightly more likely to be female and science and technology graduates with a high degree class—although these differences between graduates who are also alumni, and those that who are not, is not statistically significant. The main causes of non-response are unknown as the survey was posted and no other contact was made.

It should be appreciated that, at the time of the survey, the graduates were of different ages, since they are sampled from the stock of alumni from many previous years. Since the data we use involves graduates from 1970 to 1997, it is not surprising that the later cohorts have higher representation, since alumni associations are a relatively recent phenomena and most recent cohorts are more likely to stay in touch in the short-run and be easier to trace if their contact details change. This composition by graduation year was taken into account in the estimation by the size of the cohort by the year of graduation. The questionnaire information was retrieved by the careful design of our survey, which asked quite clearly and separately about the first job after graduation and their current job.

Since we are only interested in the UK labour market, our sample excludes all individuals living abroad during either their first or current job (i.e., 343 persons). In addition, we drop graduates from the faculty of medicine (i.e., 232 persons) and those who graduated before 1970 (i.e., 220 persons), since these individuals are unlikely to be overeducated. Finally, we only focused on individuals who are currently in employment at the time of the survey. This left us with a final sample of 852 graduates in their first job, of whom we observed 731 in their current job. We lose a significant number of observations due to missing data. To take account of the uneven distribution of responses across years, we generated sample weights based on our samples of 852 and 731 persons. The regression analysis was performed using these yearly weights. All descriptive statistics are reported for the maximum possible sample size. Table 10A.1 provides the summary statistics of the variables used in this study for our samples.

At the outset it should be stressed that overeducation may be lower in this sample of University of Newcastle graduates than a population survey of graduates for several reasons. Firstly, Newcastle University is a 'Russell Group' university with well above average quality students, in terms of the 'A' level university entrance requirements; second, the data was collected over the 1970 to 1997 period and particularly graduates from the earlier years are less likely to be affected than recent graduates. Finally, the balance of subjects studied by the Newcastle graduates is more likely to be Science or Education than Arts and Humanities, which is more commonplace in other universities. The implication of these differences between a sample of Newcastle University graduates and a national sample of graduates is that the levels of overeducation in our sample may be lower than those based on national samples.

The most distinguishing feature of the Newcastle Alumni Survey is that it is the only British dataset that contains two direct questions measuring the extent of education under-utilisation. The first question is: 'What is/was the minimum formal qualification level required for *entering* this job?' and the second question is: 'What do you believe to be the education level required to *actually do* this job?' Answers to both questions are on a four-point scale as follows: post-graduate

*Table 10.1   Distribution of qualifications required to **enter** work*

Levels	Current job		First job	
	N	Per cent	N	Per cent
Post-graduate qualification	172	13	44	5
Degree	380	52	323	27
Sub-degree qualification	82	11	71	8
No qualifications	96	13	503	60
Total	731	100	852	100

Source: Newcastle Alumni Survey.

*Table 10.2   Distribution of qualifications required to **actually perform** work*

Levels	Current job		First job	
	N	Per cent	N	Per cent
Post-graduate qualification	184	25	121	14
Degree	385	53	290	34
Sub-degree qualification	115	16	182	21
No qualifications	47	6	264	31
Total	731	100	852	100

Source: Newcastle Alumni Survey.

qualification, degree, sub-degree qualification and no qualifications required. The first question provides a match between acquired and required qualifications to obtain the job, whereas the second question provides a direct measure of overeducation in terms of job content. We suggest that it is the qualifications required to do the job that are really relevant in determining whether someone is overeducated, rather than the requirements for entering the job. Tables 10.1 and 10.2 allow us to compare these two questions. They show that the level of overeducation is systematically higher if the question posed relates to qualifications for entry into a job, rather than qualifications to actually do the job. Table 10.1 shows that 68 per cent of our sample are overeducated in their first job if qualifications on entry are used as the criterion for the determination of overeducation. In contrast, Table 10.2 suggests that 52 per cent of our sample are overeducated in their first job if the second question relating to performing the job is used. The overeducation variable used throughout the remainder of this analysis is constructed from the second question in the survey. Hence, we define, for the purposes of our statistical analysis, overeducation as a dummy variable, coded 1 if a graduate requires a post-graduate qualification or a degree to actually perform a job and 0 otherwise.

*Table 10.3   Per cent of overeducated workers by different categories of
           graduates*

	First job N = 852	Current job N = 731
Total percentage overeducated	52.00	22.00
Gender		
Male	51.92	24.41
Female	52.66	20.00
Faculty		
Engineering and technology	45.93	15.13
Agriculture, science	56.27	26.61
Administration, business, social science,		
professional, vocational subjects	51.65	16.83
Languages	54.55	30.77
Arts and humanities	59.12	33.61
Education	7.69	4.35
Class of degree		
First class	33.85	18.18
Second upper	51.97	22.58
Second lower	55.88	21.72
Third	61.22	27.27
Qualifications		
Professional qualification	47.22	17.96
No professional qualification	55.30	25.50
Post-graduate degree	45.00	13.75
No post-graduate degree	56.58	27.71
Employment characteristics		
Part-time	66.09	30.56
Full-time	50.07	21.70
Self-employed	57.14	36.36
Employee	52.06	21.20
Sector		
Public administration	45.40	19.83
Education	13.13	8.26
Industry including public utilities	50.25	20.96
Commerce	73.28	32.48
Self-regulating professions	27.40	10.94
Other	75.66	35.66
Firm size		
< 25 employees	68.92	32.37
25–99 employees	45.51	14.86
100–499 employees	49.40	19.66
> 500 employees	41.28	21.76
Occupation		
Manager	52.27	22.43
Professional	24.90	9.56
Associate professional	39.81	23.39
Other occupation	80.00	47.76

Table 10.3 Per cent of overeducated workers by different categories of graduates continued

	First job N = 852	Current job N = 731
Labour market mobility		
Relocate for first/current job	31.14	21.74
Did not relocate for first/current job	59.94	22.90
Family commitments		
Partner	–	20.25
No partner	–	26.85
Child	–	21.65
No child	–	23.06
Partner prior to first job	40.00	–
No partner prior to first job	53.16	–
Child prior to first job	31.79	–
No child prior to first job	57.44	–
Debt commitments		
Debts > 1,000	64.96	–
No large debt	47.41	–

Source: Newcastle Alumni Survey.

One criticism widely levelled at any subjective measure of overeducation based on self-reported questions is that of 'credentialism.' The argument suggests that educational requirements to acquire a job are often judged to exceed those to perform the job, as employers insist on entry barriers to jobs based on higher educational qualifications than are actually necessary. As all previous studies for the UK that we are aware of have relied on questions framed as in the first question, the validity of this argument has beenl impossible to establish. The summary statistics in Tables 10.1 and 10.2 suggest, from the perspective of the individual, that this argument could be flawed, as a higher proportion of people believe a degree was necessary to actually perform their jobs rather than to acquire their jobs. This conclusion is, of course, subject to the usua caveats associated with any subjective self-reported measure of overeducation.

Tables 10.1 and 10.2 demonstrate that between first and current employment, the percentage of workers who are overeducated fell from 52 to 22 per cent. This suggests a considerably lower number of overeducated workers than previous studies on British data (see Dolton and Vignoles, 2000; Sloane, Battu and Belfield, 2000; Sloane, Battu and Seaman, 1999). Table 10.3 provides us with some descriptive statistics, which inform us about the likelihood of being overeducated in first and current jobs by occupation, sector, education, family commitments and other characteristics. Unsurprisingly, the rate of overeducation is lowest in the self-regulating professions and education as these occupations almost universally require a degree to do them. Conversely, the commerce sector has a greater diversity of job openings and many of them may not require a degree to actually perform the work. In addition, those working for large companies are less likely to be overeducated as are those graduates with a higher class of degree and degrees in science and technical subjects. In terms of subject specialism, education graduates are the least likely to be overeducated, since they mainly become teachers, which is a graduate occupation.

Looking more closely at the labour market mobility information it seems that those who were not prepared to relocate for their first job are more likely to be overeducated. Finally, it would seem that those who did not have a child prior to their first job and those with a large debt are more likely to be overeducated. It is possible that this is consistent with the explanation that those people who either have less responsibilities or take them seriously, may be less committed to finding a graduate job. We find that similar proportions of men and women are overeducated in both first and current employment, which is in line with earlier studies, such as Dolton and Vignoles (2000).

Before examining in more detail the possible explanations of why a graduate may accept a job not commensurate with their qualifications, it is instructive to examine movements in and out of various education/employment positions over time. Table 10.4 presents the transition matrix between first and current overeducation using data from the Newcastle Alumni Survey. The main downward diagonal elements of the table show the number of graduates who remain in the same position in both periods. The other positions in the table show the numbers who move into higher- or lower-level positions over time.

In our sample, a graduate has a 62 per cent probability of staying in the same level job and a 38 per cent probability of changing position. There is some evidence of downward occupational mobility with a limited number of graduates moving to lower-level positions over time. Our tabulations suggest that 6 per cent of graduates (17 out of 272) who initially entered degree-level jobs now hold lower-level positions. Moving in this downward direction across the matrix of transitions, that is, from left to right, could be the result of labour market constraints, such as family commitments and regional immobility. By contrast, from 346 graduates who initially held jobs that did not require a degree (i.e., were in either sub-degree or the no qualification category) 225 of them are currently positions which need a degree to perform the job. This implies an upward mobility rate, out of initial graduate overeducation, of around 65 per cent. These figures suggest that the process of finding a suitable job commensurate with one's education may take some time. The longer a person is in the labour market, the more likely they are to be successful in their search and 'trade-up' to a graduate job. This means that surveys relating to overeducation which take place 'too soon' after graduation may overstate the size of the problem as they will report some people in low-level jobs which they will subsequently leave.

Table 10.4   Transition between first and current employment

First job	Current job				
	Post-graduate	Degree	Sub-degree	No qualif.	Total
Post-graduate	112	0	0	1	113
Degree	30	225	11	6	272
Sub-degree	17	53	78	2	150
No qualification	28	87	40	41	196
Total	187	365	129	50	731

Source: Newcastle Alumni Survey.

At the same time, we must also be aware that there are a small proportion of graduates who will move to lower-level jobs possibly due to personal or family reasons. These factors suggest that a study of movements between graduate and non-graduate jobs from first to current jobs is insightful and indeed central to an understanding of the process of overeducation.

To understand the determinants of overeducation and movements along the transition matrix it is important to understand how overeducation could arise and persist. Previous studies have not provided wholly satisfactory or empirically verified explanations of overeducation. In pure human capital theory an individual's earnings are a function of acquired education as job characteristics are assumed to be able to take advantage of the higher level of human capital of graduates (Becker, 1975). Accordingly, one may expect that firms would upgrade their production techniques in order to take advantage of the increased graduate supply.

Conversely, if individuals are in jobs where their education is under-utilised they should receive less than their potential marginal product and, correspondingly, a pay penalty should be associated with education under-utilisation. It is this phenomenon that is termed overeducation. An overeducated worker earns less than a similarly educated worker whose skills are fully utilised. In this context, the crucial questions are: (1) Why would a worker take up such a job? (2) Why would a firm not utilise the entire endowment of its workers' human capital? One answer to the first question is that the individual may face short-run personal, family, location and other constraints that limit their opportunity set. One potential explanation of the second question is that it will take time for employers to verify a worker's marginal product and, hence, most firms may keep open the possibility of moving an individual from a job for which they are overeducated, into one which more closely matches their productive potential, after a suitable period has elapsed in which the firm can verify a workers productive potential for the job. These responses are speculative and we seek evidence to substantiate them from our empirical analysis.

10.3 ESTIMATION METHODS

The overeducation literature to date has assumed that the process by which an individual becomes overeducated is strictly exogenous to the determination of earnings. This means most of the recent research has relied on the following wage function to measure the relationship between overeducation and wages:

$$\ln y_i = \beta_0 + \beta_{1k} X_{ki} + \beta_2 S_i + \mu_i \qquad (10.1)$$

where S is an indicator variable taking the value 1 if the person is in a job (and 0 otherwise), for which they are overeducated, X is a (k dimensional) vector of other characteristics and μ is the error term. More recently, Sloane, Battu and Seaman (1999) modelled overeducation at an initial labour market state ($j = 1$) and at some time afterwards ($j = 2$). These authors, however, continued to assume that the overeducation process is exogenously determined. Following Sloane et al. (1999) a straightforward first wage specification is specified as follows:

$$\ln y_{ji} = \beta_{0j} + \beta_{1kj} X_{kji} + \beta_{2j} S_i^j + \mu_{ji}, \quad j = 1, 2 \qquad (10.2)$$

where S^j for $j = 1,2$ is a measure of skill under-utilization in first and later employment. Henceforth, we will drop the individual i subscript notation.

The explicit assumption in both equations (10.1) and (10.2) is that wage determination and being in a job for which a person is overeducated are not endogenously related. Typically, this rules out the situation in which someone will deliberately compromise and take a less (educationally) demanding job at a lower wage in order to avoid a lengthy and costly job search, as a temporary measure to reduce debt or even as a permanent lifestyle decision. Clearly assuming that wages and job match are exogenous is a simplification of reality. In the model which follows we explore relaxing this assumption. Clearly there are a variety of ways of modelling this kind of selectivity problem. One can use a control function approach and an instrumental variable (IV) approach, a matching function approach or a simulation MCMC approach with Bayesian methods. We explore only the control function and the IV alternative in this paper.

The control function approach allows that the overeducated are likely to be a non-random sample from the population and, therefore, may receive lower wages even if they had found jobs commensurate with their qualifications. A standard solution to the problem of causal inferences is the Treatment Effects technique where we posit the existence of an observed covariate that is a determinant of overeducation, but is uncorrelated with wages. Hence, our alternative model structure involves estimating the following overeducation probit equation:

$$S^j = \delta_j Z_j + \varepsilon_j, \quad j = 1, 2 \qquad (10.3)$$

where S^j is a measure of skill under-utilisation and Z is a vector of characteristics that are thought to determine overeducation. Predicted values of S^j are then used to compute the Heckman (1979, 1990) selection adjustment term, $\hat{\lambda}$, as follows:

$$\hat{\lambda}_j = \frac{\phi(\hat{\delta}Z)}{\Phi(\hat{\delta}Z)} \tag{10.4}$$

where $S = 1$, and:

$$\hat{\lambda}_j = \frac{-\phi(\hat{\delta}Z)}{1 - \Phi(\hat{\delta}Z)} \tag{10.5}$$

where $S = 0$. ϕ is the normal probability distribution function, and Φ is the normal cumulative distribution function. In the control function approach it is crucial that Z includes at least one variable that can be legitimately excluded from X. This exclusion restriction is an important identification condition for this model.[4]

Along with the actual values for overeducation, $\hat{\lambda}$ is entered into the following wage equation, which is our second earnings specification:

$$\ln y_j = \beta_{0j} + \beta_{1kj} X_{kj} + \beta_{2j} S^j + \theta_j \lambda_j + \mu_j, \quad j = 1,2 \tag{10.6}$$

The probit specification assumes independence between overeducation in both periods. However, several reasons may be advanced for a high degree of complementarity between overeducation in both stages including the effects of unobserved characteristics, such as ability, as well as observed attributes, such as faculty of degree. For this reason, overeducation is also modelled using a bivariate probit as follows: $S^j = 1$ if $S^{j*} > 0$, $S^j = 0$ otherwise:

$$S^{j*} = \alpha_j Z_j + \varepsilon_j, \quad j = 1,2 \tag{10.7}$$

$[\varepsilon_1, \varepsilon_2] \sim$ bivariate normal $[0,0,1,1,\rho]$ and $E[S^{1*} \mid S^2, Z_2] = \alpha_1 Z_1 + \rho\lambda_2$

S^{j*} is the latent variable corresponding to S^j. The ρ term measures the correlation between the unobservables in the overeducation equations.

Following an extension of the Heckman procedure outlined in Ham (1982), using the above bivariate model, we can correct for sample selectivity in the form of a second Treatment Effects model, which is our third wage specification, as follows:

$$\ln y_2 = \beta_0 + \beta_1 X + \beta_2 S^1 + \beta_3 S^2 + \theta_1 \lambda_1 + \theta_2 \lambda_2 + \mu \tag{10.8}$$

where y_2 is wages in current employment, λ_1 and λ_2 are generated from the bivariate probit model above. The λ variables in the regression are computed from:

$$\lambda_1 = \phi(w_1)\Phi\big[(w_2 - \rho w_1)/(1 - \rho^2)^{1/2}\big]/\Phi_2$$
$$\lambda_2 = \phi(w_2)\Phi\big[(w_1 - \rho w_2)/(1 - \rho^2)^{1/2}\big]/\Phi_2 \tag{10.9}$$

For the case where $S^1 = S^2 = 1$, $w_1 = -\alpha_1 Z_1$, $w_2 = -\alpha_2 Z_2$. The bivariate normal CDF is: $\Phi_2 = \Phi(w_1, w_2, \rho)$. ϕ denotes the normal probability distribution function and Φ is the normal cumulative distribution function as before. To derive the other cases, we change the sign of w_1 when $S^1 = 0$, w_2 when $S^2 = 0$, and ρ when $S^1 \neq S^2$. In the Treatment Effects models, the standard errors are corrected for heteroscedasticity and the appropriate asymptotic covariance matrices computed as in Pagan (1984).

Notwithstanding the formal econometric model we adopt, it must be stressed that there are various detailed specification issues in this model. First, it is unclear whether: the S_1 should be included in the S_2 equation; secondly, since the data relates to graduates from 1970 to 1997 does this mean that if we include a dummy for the year of graduation that this would be a proxy for the changing level of overeducation across time; and finally, what are valid exclusion restrictions which can be assumed to condition overeducation, but not earnings. As these are empirical matters we will return to them in the following empirical section.

10.4 THE DETERMINANTS OF OVEREDUCATION

Table 10.5 presents the results of a probit model for the determinants of overeducation in first and current employment.[5] One interesting result is that there appears to be no gender difference in overeducation as women are no more likely to be overeducated than men. Our results show that arts and humanities graduates are less likely to find work commensurate with their qualifications than those of other faculties. However, irrespective of subject of the study those who graduate with first-class honours are more likely to find jobs commensurate with their qualifications. Undertaking a post-graduate degree also increases the probability of being in a graduate-level job. One of the results which may, at first sight, seem curious is the nature of the work experience effect. The linear effect is positive and the squared term is negative. This suggests that the probability of being overeducated declines non-linearly with work experience. This is consistent with a statistically insignificant and positive coefficient on the linear experience term.

Not surprisingly, we find that occupation and sector of work are not independent of overeducation. Graduates in professional, associate professional and managerial occupations have a greater propensity to be in graduate-level jobs than those in the base group.[6] Graduates who work in the self-regulating professional or the education sector are less likely to be overeducated than in other sectors. This is, perhaps, because the majority of graduates in education are teachers and those in the self-regulating professional sector usually require a degree, such as in accountancy. Graduates in part-time positions or working

Table 10.5   The determinants of overeducation: Probit model

	5.1 First		5.2 Current		5.3 Current	
	Coef.	Std. Err.	Coef.	Std. Err.	Coef.	Std. Err.
Gender						
Female	0.037	0.151	0.077	0.166	0.077	0.172
Faculty—engineering and technology						
Agric, science	0.197	0.196	0.379*	0.212	0.400*	0.223
Administration, business, social science, professional, vocational subjects	−0.223	0.201	0.035	0.221	0.127	0.245
Languages	−0.438	0.342	0.614*	0.370	0.718*	0.368
Arts and humanities	0.114	0.258	0.594**	0.239	0.706**	0.258
Education	−1.486**	0.404	−0.503	0.458	0.097	0.518
Class of degree—default pass/third						
First class	−0.504*	0.302	−0.614*	0.356	−0.541	0.351
Second upper	−0.008	0.227	−0.393*	0.216	−0.433*	0.228
Second lower	0.055	0.224	−0.516**	0.219	−0.594**	0.225
Qualifications						
Professional qualification	−0.080	0.128	−0.065	0.140	−0.066	0.151
Post-graduate degree	−0.134	0.131	−0.496**	0.203	−0.488**	0.216
Employment characteristics						
Part-time	−0.129	0.165	0.371*	0.207	0.624**	0.210
Self-employed	−0.346	0.257	0.019	0.246	−0.088	0.268
Occupation—default (all the others)						
Manager	−0.334	0.296	−0.536**	0.220	−0.680**	0.238
Professional	−1.178**	0.168	−1.076**	0.204	−1.058**	0.218
Associate professional	−0.783**	0.168	−0.438**	0.175	−0.417**	0.190
Sector—default education						
Public admin.	0.983**	0.256	0.141	0.293	0.129	0.303
Industry incl. public utilities	0.991**	0.266	0.226	0.263	0.147	0.274
Commerce	1.535**	0.281	0.583**	0.275	0.571**	0.280
Self-regulating professionals	0.282	0.319	−0.121	0.365	−0.070	0.370
Other	1.212**	0.266	0.395	0.274	0.253	0.283
Firm size—default < 25						
25–99 employees	−0.426**	0.177	−0.281	0.208	−0.396*	0.224
100–499 employees	−0.381**	0.187	−0.217	0.183	−0.343*	0.198
> 500 employees	−0.553**	0.168	0.120	0.193	−0.001	0.205
On-the-job experience (years)						
Training	–	–	−0.119	0.141	−0.068	0.147
Age	–	–	0.036	0.124	0.069	0.138
Experience	–	–	0.032	0.131	0.028	0.147
Experience squared	–	–	−0.003**	0.001	−0.004**	0.001
Unemployment	–	–	0.000	0.141	−0.064	0.157
Mobility						
Relocate for this job	−0.587**	0.164	0.293*	0.176	0.392**	0.190
Relocate for this job: female	−0.513*	0.308	−1.168**	0.340	−1.265**	0.367

Table 10.5   The determinants of overeducation: Probit model continued

	5.1 First		5.2 Current		5.3 Current	
	Coef.	Std. Err.	Coef.	Std. Err.	Coef.	Std. Err.
Family commitments						
Partner prior to first job	–0.102	0.209	–	–	–	–
Child prior to first job	–0.285*	0.165	–	–	–	–
Partner	–	–	–0.008	0.154	0.045	0.161
Child (0,1)	–	–	–0.107	0.191	0.013	0.198
Debt commitments						
Debts > 1,000	0.356**	0.149	–	–	–	–
Cohort effects						
Participation rate	1.691	4.796	–	–	–	–
Unemployment rate	–0.285	3.379	–	–	–	–
Year of graduation (1, 2 ...)	–0.005	0.021	–	–	–	–
Past overeducation						
Overeducation in first job	–	–	–	–	1.122**	0.160
Constant						
Constant	–0.03	0.93	–1.102	2.708	– 2.747	3.029
N	–	852	–	731	–	731
Log likelihood	–	–389.981	–	–278.829	–	–248.541

*   The coefficient is statistically significant at the 10 per cent level;
** The coefficient is statistically significant at the 5 per cent level.

Source: Newcastle Alumni Survey.

in small firms are more likely to be overeducated than their otherwise similar counterparts. One interpretation of this reduced form specification is that the sector and occupation dummies are proxies for demand side or matching variables and, as such, the significance of the effects is not surprising.

Graduates who are overeducated at the start of their careers find it considerably more difficult to acquire graduate jobs later in comparison with those initially in jobs for which a degree is required. The effect of initial overeducation on the probability of being overeducated in the future is statistically significant with on-the-job training, age making no discernible impact. However, experience has a significant effect with higher levels of job experience decreasing the probability of overeducation.

Relocating to take a first job increases the probability of being well-matched, whereas relocating to take a current job decreases the probability. On interacting mobility with gender, however, we find that women who relocate are more likely to find work commensurate with their qualifications in their current position.

Looking at family commitment variables, having children prior to a first job decreases (at the 10% level of significance) the probability of being

Table 10.6   The determinants of overeducation: Bivariate probit model

	First		Current	
	Coef.	Std. Err.	Coef.	Std. Err.
Gender				
Female	0.076	0.162	0.025	0.179
Faculty—engineering and technology				
Agric, science	0.074	0.189	0.474**	0.228
Administration, business, social science, professional, vocational subjects	−0.380*	0.217	0.120	0.248
Languages	−0.504	0.406	0.734*	0.403
Arts and Humanities	−0.118	0.238	0.708**	0.274
Education	−1.716**	0.830	−0.360	1.067
Class of degree—default pass/third				
First class	−0.301	0.321	−0.601*	0.334
Second upper	0.206	0.228	−0.391*	0.218
Second lower	0.281	0.216	−0.490**	0.217
Qualifications				
Professional qualification	−0.211	0.133	−0.146	0.149
Post-graduate degree	−0.108	0.139	−0.512**	0.211
Employment characteristics				
Part-time	−0.177	0.211	0.477*	0.246
Self-employed	−0.253	0.543	−0.066	0.274
Occupation—default (all the others)				'
Manager	−0.127	0.240	−0.581**	0.225
Professional	−1.054**	0.177	−1.031**	0.201
Associate professional	−0.737**	0.166	−0.421**	0.180
Sector—default education				
Public administration	1.065**	0.296	0.277	0.294
Industry incl. public utilities	0.939**	0.301	0.241	0.301
Commerce	1.458**	0.314	0.705**	0.305
Self-regulating professions	0.135	0.361	0.018	0.411
Other	1.143**	0.300	0.403	0.282
Firm size—default < 25				
25–99 employees	−0.363**	0.181	−0.356*	0.211
100–499 employees	−0.371**	0.186	−0.298	0.211
> 500 employees	−0.679**	0.168	−0.026	0.179
On-the-job experience (years)				
Training	–	–	−0.030	0.145
Age	–	–	0.037	0.101
Experience	–	–	0.032	0.105
Experience squared	–	–	−0.003**	0.001
Unemployment	–	–	−0.049	0.112
Mobility				
Relocate for this job	−0.585**	0.159	0.232	0.162
Relocate for this job: female	−0.419	0.300	−1.090**	0.482

Table 10.6 *The determinants of overeducation: Bivariate probit model*
              continued

	First		Current	
	Coef.	Std. Err.	Coef.	Std. Err.
Family commitments				
Partner prior to first job	−0.007	0.270	–	–
Child prior to first job	−0.279*	0.167	–	–
Partner	–	–	0.045	0.166
Child (0, 1)	–	–	−0.089	0.171
Debt commitments				
Debts > 1,000	0.346**	0.137	–	–
Cohort effects				
Participation rate	4.170	5.014	–	–
Unemployment rate	−2.578	3.639	–	–
Year of grad. (1, 2 ...)	−0.004	0.021	–	–
Constant				
Constant	−0.581	0.967	−1.211	2.173
Disturbance correlation				
ρ	0.666**	0.070	–	–
N	–	731	–	–
Log-likelihood	–	−578.51	–	–

* The coefficient is statistically significant at the 10 per cent level;
** The coefficient is statistically significant at the 5 per cent level.

Source: Newcastle Alumni Survey.

overeducated. This clearly reflects the greater responsibility young parents bear and the greater need to get the highest possible return on their education. In contrast, our results show that children and marital status have no measurable effect on overeducation in current employment. One might expect that this effect is different for women and men. However, our sample is not large enough to meaningfully interact family commitment variables with gender.

High debt commitments (i.e., debts in excess of £1,000 upon leaving the university) raise the probability of being overeducated in the first employment. This could be due to the fact that debt may place pressure on graduates to find some work immediately, thereby, forcing them into jobs for which they are overeducated.

The probit specification assumes independence between unobserved factors that may influence overeducation in both periods. However, several reasons may be advanced for a high degree of complementarity between overeducation in both stages including the effects of unobserved characteristics, such as ability. For this reason, the results of modelling overeducation as a bivariate probit are presented in Table 10.6, where each outcome depends on a list of regressors and is affected through the error structure by the other decision.

The ρ term displayed at the bottom of Table 10.6 measures the correlation between the unobservables in both overeducation states. These results show that there is a significant and positive correlation between the unobservables in the overeducation equations. It could be the case that this unobservable difference is capturing an implicit division between career- and non-career related qualifications and/or some other form of heterogeneity among graduates. The other results from bivariate probit equations are very similar to those in the separately estimated probit models already discussed.

10.5 THE IMPACT OF OVEREDUCATION ON WAGES

One of the key questions of this literature is what are the consequences of being an overeducated worker. Do they earn less than otherwise similarly educated workers whose jobs are commensurate with their educational qualifications? It could be the case that many graduates in non-graduate positions may transform these jobs and earn the same as other workers in graduate-level positions (Mason, 1996). Therefore, if overeducation is really the result of skill underutilisation, a lower quality of education or a lower level of ability it should be reflected in a lower level of wages. This section investigates the relationship between overeducation and wages. The wage data in the Newcastle data is in twenty annual wage intervals ranging from less than £2,000 to £70,000. Our wage measured is the log of mid-point value of the earnings interval deflated at 1995 prices. The question asked the individual to report gross salary in the job (before tax and deductions, including bonuses, overtime and London allowance).

Table 10.7 displays the effect of overeducation and other determinants on wages in first employment. We focus only on the coefficients associated with overeducation and omit the details of coefficients on the controlling regressors.[7] The first column of Table 10.7 reports the simple OLS estimate of the effect of overeducation on wages. The second column presents the results of the Treatment Effects models. Under OLS estimation the estimated pay penalty associated with overeducation is 18 per cent in the first employment. These results can be compared to those of Dolton and Vignoles (2000) and Sloane, Battu and Seaman (1999). The former study estimated a pay penalty within the range of 13 and 18 per cent, whereas the latter estimated a pay differential of 10 per cent for men and 20 per cent for women.[8]

When we correct for endogeneity using the Treatment Effects method, the selectivity term is statistically insignificant as is the overeducation term, which suggests that overeducation in first employment may be a random (or temporary) phenomenon. Furthermore, the Hausman test indicates that there is no statistical difference between the IV and OLS estimates. The exclusion restrictions to identify the system comprised of the relocation and family and debt

Table 10.7   The effect of overeducation on wages in first employment

Model	1		2	
Wage Estimation Method	OLS		Treatment Effects	
Selection Model	None		Probit	
Exclusion Restrictions	None		Relocation/Dept.	
	Coef.	Std. Err.	Coef.	Std. Err.
Overeducation variable				
Overeducation (0,1)	–0.176**	0.061	–0.057	0.220
Selectivity term				
λ			–0.074	0.132
N	852		852	
R^2	0.175		0.175	
F-test on the excluded instruments: F(2, 825)			14.36	
Partial R^2			0.060	
Sargan test			0.170	
Hausman t-test			0.020	

Controls: Gender, faculty—engineering and technology, class of degree, qualifications, employment characteristics, occupation, sector, firm size.

*   The coefficient is statistically significant at the 10 per cent level;
** The coefficient is statistically significant at the 5 per cent level.

Source: Newcastle Alumni Survey.

commitment variables. The a priori justification for the use of the variables as exclusion restrictions are that it can be argued that relocation and the size of one's student debt could determine whether an individual is prepared to accept a job for which are they are overqualified, but that debt and relocation factors themselves should not necessarily directly effect the level of the their wage. In our data the use of these exclusion restrictions is validated by the Sargan (1958) test and Bound, Jaeger and Baker (1995) test. The identification was further assisted by other exogenous variables relating to the year the individual went to university and the participation rate for that year or the graduate unemployment rate prevailing when the person graduated. This result could be very important as it suggests the erroneous use of OLS to gauge the magnitude of the overeducation effect on first earnings and could overstate its importance considerably. This over-estimate of the overeducation effect is relative to a model in which the magnitude earnings and being in the state of overeducation are determining endogenously.

Table 10.8 presents the effects of overeducation and other variables on wages in current employment, where the selection terms are derived from either probit or bivariate probit estimation models. Again, we focus only on the overeducation coefficients and omit the controlling regressors. Column I displays the simple model where an overeducation dummy is included in the

Table 10.8 The effect of overeducation on wages in current employment
a)

Model	I	II	III	IV
Estimation technique	Mid-points	Mid-points	Mid-points	Mid-points
Selection techique/ estimation equation	None	Probit, equation 5.2	Probit, equation 5.3	Bivariate probit, Table 6
Exclusion restrictions	None	Mobility, family commitments	Mobility, family commitments, overeducation in the first job	Mobility, family commitments

b)

	Coef.	Std. Err.	Coef.	Std. Err.	Coef.	Std. Err.	Coef.	Std. Err.
Overeducation variables (0,1)								
Current job	−0.268	0.066	−0.713**	0.217	−0.879**	0.137	−0.802**	0.350
First job							−0.097	0.140
Selectivity term								
λ-current job			0.264**	0.125	0.399**	0.081	0.339*	0.207
λ-first job							0.046	0.116
N	731		731		731		731	
R^2	0.492		0.495		0.510		0.514	
F-test on the excluded instruments:								
$F_{(2, 699)}$			5.55					
Partial R^2			0.008					
Sargan test			0.731					
Hausman t-test			2.077					

Controls: Gender, faculty—engineering and technology, class of degree, qualifications, employment characteristics, occupation, sector, firm size.

* The coefficient is statistically significant at the 10 per cent level;
** The coefficient is statistically significant at the 5 per cent level.

Source: Newcastle Alumni Survey.

wage regression. Column II reports the control Function Treatment Effects model where the selectivity term is derived from the probit model in which no account is taken of overeducation in the first employment. Column III is identical to column II except for the use of an additional exclusion, which enters the selection equation that is overeducation in the first job. Finally, column IV presents an alternative Treatment Effects model in which both first and current employment overeducation terms are included and two associated selection terms calculated from the bivariate probit model (see equation (10.9)) are used to correct for sample selection. In current employment, the effect of overeducation is much more serious than in the first employment. According to the naïve OLS estimate, the pay penalty associated with overeducation stands at 27 per cent.

Using the Heckman sample selection (or control function) estimation approach, the effect of overeducation on earnings rises almost threefold to 71 and 88 per cent in specifications II and III, respectively. Moreover, the selection terms with respect to overeducation in current employment are positive and statistically significant across specifications. Though the estimates in specification III are more precise, there is no statistical difference between the estimates in specifications II and III. A Hausman test shows that the difference between the instrumental variable and OLS is statistically significant. These results indicate that the OLS estimate of the (negative) impact of overeducation is biased downwards. Moreover, the results in specification IV reveal that overeducation in first employment does not determine earnings at a future date, except indirectly through its effect on future overeducation. In this specification, where selection is modelled by a bivariate probit, the estimate on overeducation is 80 per cent, which is not substantially different from that produced in specifications II and III.

How do we reconcile the differences in the wage effect estimates of overeducation in the different econometric models? It is not straightforward to calculate the scale of selectivity effects in these models (see Dolton and Makepeace, 1987), but the simplest calculation is to consider the overeducation effect for someone who is overeducated, but possesses the characteristics which most likely places them in this category. In this case, the limiting value of the λ term in (10.4) is unity. This means we can, in the limit, add the selectivity effect to the treatment effects estimate of overeducation to establish the overall effect of overeducation on earnings. This logic in specification II gives an estimate of 45 per cent and specification III an estimate of 47 per cent. These results are in contrast to those provided by Dolton and Vignoles (2000) and Sloane, Battu and Seaman (1999). These authors reported that the effect of overeducation on earnings fell over the first six years after graduation. Our estimates suggest that the effect of current overeducation on current earnings could be substantial and much higher than those obtained by ignoring the endogeneity of overeducation and earning determination.

The validity of our exclusion restrictions (including the relocation interacted with gender) in current employment was checked using the standard tests. Despite the fact that our mobility instruments pass these tests, these variables are weak instruments. There were no strong instrumental variables available in our data to control for sample selection bias of being overeducated in current employment. Instead, what we found was that there was a strong unobservable dependence between overeducation in the current and first employment. Furthermore, overeducation in the first employment was not a good predictor of current earnings except indirectly through its effect on overeducation in current employment. Accordingly, we checked the sensitivity of our results as reported above using overeducation in first the employment and also re-modelled the first stage equation using a bivariate probit. It remains an open-ended question whether or not overeducation in first the employment can be used to legitimately instrument overeducation in subsequent employment. Our conclusion is that econometric specification and modelling on this topic is difficult and our results suggest that OLS estimates may significantly under-state the true effect of overeducation on earnings.

10.6 CONCLUSION

The first objective of this study was to investigate the incidence of overeduca-tion in the graduate labour market. Empirical work, to date, on overeducation has almost exclusively defined overeducation as a level of educational attain-ment, which is greater than the educational requirements of the job. The edu-cational requirements used in many studies have typically referred to the edu-cation level necessary to qualify for a job rather than to perform a job and have suggested that overeducation is as high as 30 or 40 per cent. Estimates of over-education generated from these statistics may incorporate an element of 'qual-ification inflation' (i.e., where employers upgrade the educational requirements of the job, but do not change its content), which may yield under-estimates of the true incidence of overeducation. In contrast, our research, which relies on data from the Newcastle Alumni Survey, made a clear distinction between edu-cational requirements to enter a job and the education level actually needed to perform the job. Our data is rare in having both types of information, which en-abled us to compare them. A further feature of our data is that it allowed us to explore the relationship between overeducation initially (on entering the labour market after graduation) and overeducation in the current job. Our descriptive statistics revealed that over half of our sample were in overeducation initially, but this had fallen to about one-in-five university graduates not being employed in graduate-level positions after spending some time in the labour force.

The second objective of this study was to model whether someone was in the state of overeducation (both initially and currently) endogenously with the de-termination of earnings. The empirical work relied on bivariate probit modelling techniques as well as simple probit estimations to capture unobserved factors determining overeducation in both initial and later employment. Our findings suggested that being overeducated in the first employment could permanently hold graduates in lower-level occupations throughout their careers. In particular, we demonstrated that graduates of the faculty of arts and humanities are less likely to be in graduate-level jobs than those of the faculty of technology and engineering. Having spent some time in work, there was little evidence that on-the-job training or later relocation improved the prospects of graduates. However, we found that there was a significant dependency between unobserved factors determining overeducation in both initial and later employment. The correlation of unobserved ability differences between similarly educated workers and the quality of education are possible explanations of these findings. However, since the research presented here is based on one large civic university, differences in the quality of education across institutions cannot explain our findings. More needs to be understood about the fundamental factors that switch workers out of lower-level positions and into jobs commensurate with their qualifications. Such an understanding would be central to successfully alleviating the problem of overeducation among existing graduates.

The final contribution of this paper was not only to highlight the potential size of the negative earnings effect of being overeducated, but to warn that such an estimation is highly sensitive to the nature of the model used to capture the endogeneity of overeducation and earnings determination. Erroneous application of OLS estimation relating to overeducation, which ignores this endogeneity, could result in an overestimate of its initial negative earnings effect but an under-estimate of its later earnings effect. These results are, of course, dataset specific and it is a matter of some interest to investigate how other datasets and modelling techniques may adjust our views about the likely consequences of overeducation.

NOTES

1   This survey was funded by the Economics Department and the Alumni Office at the University of Newcastle-upon-Tyne, and the Government Office North-East.
2   Note that this proportion is much lower than the much publicised participation rates, since the numerator records only those getting degrees and does not include lower levels of post-school qualifications. In addition, the figure only includes those who actually pass degrees and, hence, also factors in the drop-out rate and the university exam failure rate.
3   Dekker, de Grip and Heijke (2000) is one exception.
4   Goldberger (1983) has formally shown that a minimum condition for identification in this model can be the functional form assumption relating to the joint distribution of the two stochastic error terms, but that reliance on such a condition can lead to parameter estimates which are unstable with respect to specification changes.
5   A single asterisk means that the coefficient is statistically significant at the 10 per cent level on a two-tailed test (i.e., the t-statistic is greater than 1.64) and two asterisks that the coefficient is significant at the 5 per cent level on a two-tailed test (i.e., the t-statistic is greater than 1.96).
6   The default category is comprised of clerical occupations, manufacturing crafts, personal and protective services, sales, plant and machine operatives and other occupations.
7   The complete tables are reported in a fuller companion paper by Dolton and Silles (2001).
8   Dolton and Vignoles' (2000) results depend on the extent of overeducation, whereas the estimates provided by Sloane, Battu and Seaman (1999) were those of a binary overeducation variable.

REFERENCES

Asplund, R., and Liljia, R. (2000). Has the Finnish labour market bumped the least educated? In L. Borghans and A. de Grip (Eds.), *The overeducated worker? The economics of skill utilization* (pp. 57–77). Cheltenham: Edward Elgar.

Becker, G. (1975). *Human capital.* New York: Basic Books.

Berg, I. (1970). *Education and jobs: The great training robbery.* London: Penguin.

Bound, J., Jaeger, D., and Baker, R. (1995). Problems with instrumental variables estimation when the correlation between the instruments and the endogenous explanatory variable is weak. *Journal of the American Statistical Association,* **90** (430), 443–450.

Bound, J., and Johnson, G. (1992). Changes in the structure of wages in the 1980s: An evaluation of alternative explanations. *American Economic Review,* **82** (3), 371–992.

Dekker, R., de Grip, A., and Heijke, H. (2002). The effects of training and overeducation on career mobility in a segmented labour market. *International Journal of Manpower,* **23** (2), 106–125.

Dolton, P., and Makepeace, G. (1987). Interpreting sample selection effects. *Economic Letters,* **24**, 373–379.

Dolton, P., and Silles, M. (2001). *Overeducation in the graduate labour market: Some evidence from alumni data.* London: Centre for the Economics of Education (CEE Discussion Paper 9).

Dolton, P., and Vignoles, A. (2000). Incidence and effects of overeducation in the UK graduate labour market. *Economics of Education Review,* **19** (2), 179–198.

Duncan, G.J., and Hoffman, S.D. (1981). The incidence and wage effects of overeducation. *Economics of Education Review,* **1** (1), 75–86.

Freeman, R. (1976). *The overeducated American.* New York: Academic Press.

Goldberger, A. (1983). Abnormal selection bias. In S. Karlin, T. Amemiya and L. Goodman (Eds.), *Studies in econometrics, time series and multivariate statistics* (pp. 67–84). Stanford: Academic Press.

Green, F., Ashton, D., Burchell, Davies, B., and Felstead, A. (2000). Are British workers becoming more skilled? In L. Borghans and A. de Grip (Eds.), *The overeducated worker? The economics of skill utilization* (pp. 77–106). Cheltenham: Edward Elgar.

Ham, J. (1982). Estimation of a labour supply model with censoring due to unemployment and underemployment. *Review of Economic Studies,* **49** (3), 335–354.

Hartog, J., and Oosterbeek, H. (1988). Education, allocation and earnings in the Netherlands: Overschooling? *Economics of Education Review,* **7** (2), 185–194.

Heckman, J. (1979). Sample section bias as a specification error. *Econometrica,* **47** (1), 153–161.

Heckman, J. (1990). Varieties of selection bias. *American Economic Review,* **80** (2), 313–318.

McIntosh, S., and Steedman, H. (2000). *Low skills: A problem for Europe. Final report to DGXII of the European Commission on the New Skills Programme of Research.* Brussels: DG Research of the European Commission.

Mason, G. (1996). *Graduate utilisation and the quality of higher education in the UK.* London: National Institute Economic Review (Discussion Paper 158).

Mason, G. (2000). *The mix of graduate and intermediate-level skills in Britain: What should the balance be?* London: National Institute Economic Review (Discussion Paper 161).

Pagan, A. (1984). Econometric issues in the analysis of regressions with generated regressors. *International Economic Review,* **25**, 221–247.

Prais, S. (2001). Developments in education and vocational training in Britain: Background note on recent research. *National Institute Economic Review,* **178**, 73–74.

Pryor, F., and Schaffer, D. (1999). Who's not working and why: Employment, cognitive. In M. Gregory (Ed.), *Skills, wages, and the changing U.S. labor market.* Cambridge: Cambridge University Press.

Rumberger, R.W. (1987). The impact of surplus schooling on productivity and earnings. *Journal of Human Resources,* **22** (1), 24–50.

Sargan, D. (1958). The estimation of economic relationships using instrumental variables. *Econometrica,* **26**, 393–415.

Sicherman, N. (1991). Overeducation in the labour market. *Journal of Labour Economics,* **9** (2), 101–122.

Sloane, P.J., Battu, H., and Belfield, C.R. (2000). How well can we measure graduate over-education and its effects? *National Institute Economic Review,* **171**, 82–93.

Sloane, P.J., Battu, H., and Seaman, P.T. (1999). Overeducation, undereducation and the British labour market. *Applied Economics,* **31** (11), 1437–1453.

Spence, M. (1973). Job market signalling. *Quarterly Journal of Economics,* **87** (3), 355–374.

Stewart, M. (1983). On least squares estimation when the dependent variable is grouped. *Review of Economic Studies,* **50** (4), 737–753.

Verdugo, R., and Verdugo, N. (1989). The impact of surplus schooling on earnings: Some additional findings. *The Journal of Human Resources,* **24** (4), 629–643.

Wolff, E. (2000). Technology and the demand for skills. In L. Borghans and A. de Grip (Eds.), *The overeducated worker? The economics of skill utilization* (pp. 27–56). Cheltenham: Edward Elgar.

APPENDIX

Table 10A.1 Summary statistics

| | N = 852 | | N = 731 | |
	Mean	Std. Dev.	Mean	Std. Dev.
Log of wage variable				
First job	9.646	0.754	9.640	0.753
Current job, mid-points	9.497	0.618	9.503	0.616
Overeducation				
First job	0.520	0.457	0.480	0.459
Current job	0.200	0.405	0.223	0.401
Gender				
Female	0.347	0.476	0.345	0.476
Faculty				
Engineering and technology	0.182	0.386	0.189	0.392
Agriculture, science	0.314	0.464	0.303	0.460
Administration, business, social science,				
professional, vocational subjects	0.284	0.451	0.286	0.452
Languages	0.035	0.184	0.032	0.175
Arts and humanities	0.155	0.362	0.161	0.368
Education	0.030	0.170	0.029	0.168
Class of degree				
First class	0.080	0.272	0.082	0.274
Second upper	0.386	0.487	0.386	0.487
Second lower	0.409	0.492	0.411	0.492
Third	0.057	0.232	0.060	0.238
Pass	0.067	0.250	0.060	0.238
Qualifications				
Professional qualification	0.426	0.495	0.437	0.496
Postgraduate degree	0.420	0.494	0.405	0.491
Employment characteristics				
Part-time	0.122	0.327	0.103	0.304
Self-employed	0.036	0.187	0.110	0.313
Sector				
Public administration	0.202	0.401	0.183	0.387
Education	0.147	0.354	0.176	0.381
Industry incl. public utilities	0.220	0.415	0.222	0.416
Commerce	0.146	0.353	0.154	0.362
Self-regulating professions	0.087	0.282	0.085	0.279
Other	0.198	0.399	0.181	0.385
Firm size				
< 25 employees	0.238	0.426	0.234	0.424
25–99 employees	0.225	0.418	0.209	0.407
100–499 employees	0.189	0.392	0.251	0.434
> 500 employees	0.294	0.456	0.282	0.450

Table 10A.1 Summary statistics continued

	N = 852		N = 731	
	Mean	Std. Dev.	Mean	Std. Dev.
Occupation				
Manager	0.060	0.237	0.178	0.383
Professional	0.350	0.477	0.393	0.489
Associate professions	0.267	0.442	0.292	0.455
Other occupation	0.323	0.468	0.137	0.344
Labour market mobility				
Relocate for job	0.291	0.454	0.268	0.443
Relocate for job: female	0.059	0.235	0.062	0.241
Family commitments				
Partner prior to first job	0.084	0.278	0.089	0.284
Child prior to first job	0.315	0.465	0.304	0.460
Partner	0.728	0.445	0.719	0.450
Child	0.487	0.500	0.479	0.500
Debt commitments				
Debts > 1,000	0.236	0.425	0.231	0.421
On-the-job experience—current job only				
Training	–	–	0.659	0.474
Age (years)	–	–	36.85	7.99
Experience (years)	–	–	14.78	7.85
Unemployment (years)	0.357	1.077	0.379	1.139

11. Educational Mismatch and Ethnic Minorities in England and Wales[1]

Harminder Battu and Peter J. Sloane

11.1 INTRODUCTION

A significant literature exists on the labour market performance of ethnic minorities. In the UK it is well recorded that ethnic groups experience higher unemployment, lower earnings and lower occupational attainment relative to whites (Blackaby et al., 1998, 1999). For the US there are similar findings, albeit with a greater attention to spatial constraints, with the labour market disadvantage of African-Americans reflecting a growing suburbanisation of employment opportunities (Arnott, 1998; Kain, 1968). Essentially, a mismatch between residential location and employment opportunities makes it harder for blacks to commute or gain knowledge about job opportunities.

However, little or no attention has been paid to overeducation amongst ethnic minorities, despite a growing literature examining whether workers, in general, are being fully utilised in the workplace. The general consensus is that significant numbers of workers are either overeducated or undereducated, the former occurring when actual education exceeds that formally required for the job and the latter when educational attainment is below that formally required. In the US, Sicherman (1991) found that around 40 per cent of the workforce were overeducated, while 16 per cent were undereducated. For the UK, Sloane, Battu and Seaman (1999) found that around 31 per cent of the British workers were overeducated, 17 per cent were undereducated and the remainder properly matched.

The concern with mismatch arises because it has a detrimental long-term effect on individual productivity, imposes wage penalties and reduces job satisfaction. Existing empirical studies have found a benefit from surplus education in terms of a positive return to earnings, but also a penalty, since this return is less than the return to a perfectly matched worker (Alba-Ramírez, 1993; Hartog, 2000; Sloane, Battu and Seaman, 1999). With respect to job satisfaction, higher attained education brings with it higher expectations in terms of challenging and interesting work duties. An imbalance between actual and required education generates worker dissatisfaction (Tsang, Rumberger and Levin, 1991). To the extent that higher dissatisfaction generates lower work effort this reduces worker productivity and thus the individual rate of return. Focusing on graduates, Battu, Belfield and Sloane (2000) found that well-matched graduates have higher job satisfaction than those who are in non-graduate jobs.

As far as we are aware, this is the first study to focus explicitly on mismatch amongst ethnic minorities. Other research tends to focus on the population as a whole with a passing attention to ethnic groups. Duncan and Hoffman (1981) found that around 49 per cent of black males in the US have more education than is required in their jobs compared to 42 per cent of the workforce as a whole. For the UK, Alpin, Shackleton and Walsh (1998) found that non-white graduates were more likely to be overeducated (29.9%) compared to whites (26.8%). However, the heterogeneous ethnic profile of the non-white population in terms of ethnic origin is not acknowledged and no distinction is made between ethnic minorities who are native and those who are foreign-born. This is problematic, since it is known that economic deprivation is relatively more acute for certain ethnic groups (in the UK, the Bangladeshis) and these are more often than not also the most recent arrivals (Blackaby et al., 1998, 1999; Leslie, 1998).

But why might non-whites have a higher incidence of overeducation relative to whites? One argument might be that if there is discrimination, non-whites will find it harder to find a job and thus be prepared to make greater compromises; that is, take a job that is not commensurate with their qualifications. Given that educational attainment has risen amongst ethnic groups as a whole and that ethnic students are comparatively well-represented in higher education (Owen et al., 2000), greater overeducation and thus lower earnings may place doubts on the worth of human capital as a mechanism for overcoming disadvantage (Leslie and Drinkwater, 1999).

Another argument revolves around the spatial constraints faced by ethnic groups. Commuting distances for ethnic groups tend to be shorter and this reduces the chances of a better match, thereby increasing the probability of being overeducated. The lack of access to a private vehicle may be the constraining factor here, and there is some evidence that a higher proportion of Bangladeshi and Pakistani individuals are likely to walk to work relative to whites (Blackaby et al., 1999). On the other hand, McCormick (1986) argues that commute times should be higher for non-whites (using the British Household Panel Study [BHPS] we find that non-whites have commute times which are three to four minutes longer); the argument being that those with high unemployment and low earnings in their local labour market may be willing to accept more distant employment simply in order to gain employment or raise earnings. This in turn could improve matches and reduce overeducation amongst non-whites.

This study attempts to fill a gap in the overeducation literature and examine the imbalance between educational and occupational attainment for non-whites in England and Wales. By utilising data from the Fourth National Survey of Ethnic Minorities 1993/94 (FNSEM), we examine three issues. First, what is the incidence of overeducation amongst the ethnic groups in England and Wales? Second, what factors cause any mismatch? Third, what are the consequences of this mismatch in terms of earnings? It needs to be emphasised that our basic premise is that overeducation stems from discrimination, rather than implying that too much education has been provided for ethnic minorities. The positive return to overeducation serves to emphasise this point.

10.2 DATASET

The data are derived from the FNSEM conducted in 1993/94. The dataset includes a standard set of variables capturing individual, demographic and job characteristics (Modood et al., 1997). This has the advantage that it oversamples ethnic minority groups and explicitly acknowledges the heterogeneity within the non-white population. The downside is that we must be cautious in comparing averages across white and non-white groups. The ethnic population is composed of six groups: Caribbean, Indian, Pakistani, African-Asian, Bangladeshi and Chinese. The African-Asians are those of Asian origin who settled or were born in East Africa but later settled in the UK (Modood et al., 1997). Many were expelled from East Africa during the 1970s.

The 1991 Census of Population was used to select the sample of ethnic minorities included in the survey. In particular, all 9,527 electoral wards in England and Wales were divided into three bands according to the proportion of the population who were members of ethnic minorities. Within each band a sample of wards was chosen and within each of these selected wards a sample of addresses was picked. Interviewers then visited 130,000 addresses to identify any members of the target minority groups living there who could then be interviewed. At each household containing adults from ethnic groups, one or two were selected for interview. Two questionnaires were randomly assigned to the two adults selected with the same core set of questions but a different set of secondary questions. A majority of the selected individuals were interviewed by a member of their own ethnic group either in English or in their own language, thereby maximising the response rate and reducing any potential source of bias. Interviews were obtained in 3,291 ethnic households and with 5,196 ethnic individuals. A comparison sample containing white households is also available with 2,867 white interviews.[2] Limiting the analysis to those aged 20 to 64 years inclusive there are 1,764 employed non-whites and 1,154 employed whites.

Table 11.1 Means and standard deviations

Variable	Non-whites			Whites		
	Obs.	Mean	Std.	Obs.	Mean	Std.
Age	1,764	36,761	10,149	1,154	38,146	10,799
Male	1,764	617	486	1,154	441	497
Married	1,764	774	418	1,154	716	451
Indian	1,764	275	447			
Caribbean	1,764	301	459			
African-Asian	1,764	190	392			
Pakistani	1,764	129	335			
Bangladeshi	1,764	53	224			
Chinese	1,764	53	224			
Fluent	1,734	748	434			
Years since migration	1,303	22,220	8,879			
Ward unemployment < 5%	1,764	46	209	1,154	238	426
Ward unemployment 5–10%	1,764	249	432	1,154	550	498
Ward unemployment 10–15%	1,764	284	451	1,154	165	371
Ward unemployment 15–20%	1,764	159	366	1,154	28	164
Ward unemployment > 20%	1,764	262	440	1,154	19	137
Own group concentration < 5%	1,764	334	472	1,154	824	381
White boss	866	764	425	1,138	972	165
Weekly pay	1,408	241,111	159,088	1,072	267,998	181,824
Workplace size 500 plus	1,581	163	370	1,125	170	376
Trade union at work	854	405	491	1,146	337	473
Public sector worker	839	417	493	1,111	332	471
North	1,764	11	106	1,154	117	322
Yorkshire and Humberside	1,764	60	237	1,154	100	300
East Midlands	1,764	43	202	1,154	62	242
South-East	1,764	579	494	1,154	287	452
South-West	1,764	9	92	1,154	143	350
West Midlands	1,764	208	406	1,154	103	304
North-West	1,764	54	227	1,154	70	256
Wales	1,764	15	121	1,154	25	157
East Anglia	1,764	22	145	1,154	93	290
Supervised	1,745	271	445	1,151	407	492
Training	861	396	489	1,147	586	493
Number of cars in household	1,750	1,100	751	1,147	1,308	765

Note:
The smaller observations for white boss, trade union, public sector and training reflect the nature of the dataset. Two questionnaires were randomly assigned to the two adults selected in each household with the same core set of questions, but a different set of secondary questions. Thus, only half the sample answered some of the questions.

Some descriptive statistics for the sample are given in Table 11.1. As is common in previous analyses using this dataset the data throughout is unweighted (Dustmann and Fabbri, 2000; Lindley, 2002). Care thus needs to be taken in interpreting our descriptive statistics especially when comparing whites with non-whites. In general, we find that non-whites tend to be slightly younger and more likely to be married if male, and fewer live in very low unemployment wards or have a white employer. They are more likely to be in a workplace where there is a trade union present and many more work in the public sector. They have lower weekly pay (for males only), and are spatially concentrated in the South-East and West Midlands. Fewer have supervised or received workplace training, and the average number of vehicles in their households is lower.

The dataset also contains detailed information on educational qualifications. Our measure of education is the respondent's highest qualification. A complication arises, since around three-quarters of ethnic minorities are immigrants so that part of their stock of human capital may be accumulated abroad and this may be less highly valued by employers than UK-acquired human capital. Table 11.2 provides a breakdown of the educational profile of our seven ethnic groups. Over three-quarters of whites have only UK qualifications, relative to around a half of non-whites. Within the non-white category the Caribbeans, who arrived the earliest into the UK, are the closest to whites with around 67 per cent having only UK qualifications. In contrast, only a fifth of the Bangladeshi group (the latest arrivals) possess only UK qualifications. A quarter of non-whites possess only foreign qualifications with the highest rates being amongst the four South Asian ethnic groups. Ten per cent of non-whites possess both UK and foreign qualifications with the highest incidence being amongst the Chinese (around 24%). The incidence of no qualifications is highest for the Bangladeshi and Pakistani groups (50.54% and 35.24% respectively).

The fact that non-trivial numbers of ethnic group members hold both foreign and UK qualifications raises the issue of how to treat foreign qualifications in our measure of highest qualification. Shields and Wheatley Price (2002, p. 142), using the same dataset, take the UK qualifications as the highest. Their argument is that, 'any UK education will have been undertaken at an older age and is therefore likely to be of a higher level.'

Our own calculations reveal, however, that around a quarter of the small number who possess both UK and foreign qualifications have lower UK qualifications. In particular, many immigrants who have degree level qualifications from outside the UK have accumulated, at a later stage, a range of commercial, clerical and other sub-degree qualifications within the UK. These qualifications may represent the normal upgrading of skills and/or an attempt to counteract discrimination against foreign qualifications.

Two alternative assumptions are then made about foreign qualifications in our measure of each respondent's highest qualification. In the first case, we treat UK and foreign qualifications as equivalent (highqual) and in the second case and given the small numbers involved we treat UK qualifications as the highest (highqual1), where respondents possessed both types of qualifications. In both cases, we generate six education dummies: no qualifications, commercial and apprenticeship, O-levels, A-levels, vocational degrees (teaching, nursing and other qualifications) and degree (including post-graduate degree).

Table 11.2   The educational profile of ethnic groups (in %)

	Whites	Caribbean	Indian	African-Asian	Pakistani	Bangla-deshi	Chinese
UK only	77.38	67.42	37.94	47.16	32.60	21.51	53.76
Foreign only	1.56	3.95	24.74	20.30	23.79	19.35	7.53
UK and foreign	1.65	5.08	11.13	11.04	7.93	8.60	23.66
No qualifications	19.15	23.54	25.98	21.19	35.24	50.54	15.05
N	1,154	531	485	335	227	93	93

Table 11.3 provides a summary of the educational attainment of various ethnic groups for both measures of highest qualification. The distributions are similar across the two measures albeit for Indians and Bangladeshis there are lower percentages with a degree under highqual1. Across both measures we find that the Chinese community and to a lesser extent Indians and African-Asians are much more likely to have a degree than whites, whilst fewer Caribbeans possess a degree. In line with Table 11.2 the incidence of zero qualifications is highest amongst the Bangladeshi and Pakistanis. These wide differences across ethnic groups are in accordance with other evidence (Cabinet Office, Performance and Innovation Unit, 2002) and suggest that focusing simply on whites and non-whites could be potentially misleading.

Another dimension of ethnic disadvantage is the occupational crowding of ethnic groups into lowly paid and less prestigious jobs. There is evidence (not reported here) that non-white workers have a lower representation in the managerial and professional groups relative to whites and are much more highly represented in the lowest manual occupational groupings. Excluding the white and Chinese groups, over 20 per cent of the remaining groups are in the low-skilled/unskilled categories and for the Indian and Pakistani groups the figures are in excess of 30 per cent. Second, three groups, namely whites, African-Asian and Chinese have relatively high concentrations in the managerial and professional categories. Third, nearly half of Bangladeshi men and well over half of Bangladeshi women are in junior non-manual and personal services, predominantly restaurant work. In summary, the data reveals considerable heterogeneity across the ethnic groups in terms of educational and occupational attainment.

To ascertain the extent of mismatch between educational and occupational attainment we use a variant of a popular measure of educational mismatch. This measure focuses on the distribution of educational qualifications in a given occupation. In particular, a comparison is made between the mean or modal level of education for an occupation and that actually attained. Under a variant of this, overeducation is defined as one standard deviation above the mean qual-

Table 11.3 Respondents highest qualification using highqual (highqual1) (in %)

	Whites	Caribbean	Indian	African-Asian	Pakistani	Bangladeshi	Chinese
Degree	13.86 (13.52)	5.84 (5.65)	26.80 (20.82)	20.90 (19.10)	16.30 (14.10)	17.20 (12.90)	30.11 (27.96)
Vocational	13.08 (13.17)	15.25 (15.25)	7.42 (8.87)	7.16 (7.76)	5.29 (5.29)	0.00 (1.08)	21.51 (21.51)
A-level	16.46 (16.64)	14.31 (14.31)	12.37 (13.20)	18.81 (19.40)	11.89 (13.22)	8.60 (8.60)	15.05 (15.05)
O-level	24.87 (24.87)	28.81 (29.00)	18.56 (19.18)	25.07 (25.07)	23.79 (24.23)	15.05 (15.05)	11.83 (13.98)
Commercial	12.48 (12.56)	11.68 (11.68)	8.04 (11.13)	6.57 (7.16)	4.85 (5.29)	7.53 (10.75)	6.45 (6.45)
None	19.25 (19.24)	24.11 (24.11)	26.80 (26.80)	21.49 (21.49)	37.89 (37.89)	51.61 (51.61)	15.05 (15.05)
N	1,154	531	485	335	227	93	93

Note:
Highqual1 in parentheses treats UK qualifications as the highest attained level of education, whereas highqual treats UK and foreign qualifications as equivalent.

223

ification level for that occupation. The problem with this method is that the choice of one standard deviation seems arbitrary. Furthermore, the use of one standard deviation forces symmetry into the measure, equalising over- and undereducation. There is no reason why this should be the case and other measures routinely find that the proportion of workers who are overeducated is larger than the proportion of undereducated.

Here we make use of the modal rather than a mean approach (Table 11.4). Required education is then equal to the modal level of education for that individual's occupation. Given that highqual and highqual1 have similar distributions we use highqual as our measure of highest qualification. A worker would then be overeducated if their actual education exceeded the modal value of education in their occupation, adequately educated if actual education equalled the modal level of required and undereducated if their actual education was lower than the mode. The modal measure has the advantage of being less sensitive to outliers and to technological and workplace change (Kiker, Santos and de Oliveira, 1997). Given the possibility that we might obtain unreliable estimates where there are few cases in particular occupations we use occupations disaggregated at the 2-digit rather than 3-digit level. Where occupations have less than ten observations the occupation was merged with the adjacent occupation, providing us with 60 occupational groups. For each of these groups we use the modal level of education as the required level of education and calculate mismatch by comparing this with the attained level of education.[3]

Table 11.4 summarises our estimates, and we find that whites are less likely to be overeducated and more likely to be undereducated than any of the ethnic minority groups. Around a third of non-whites are overeducated, with 17 per cent undereducated and the remainder adequately educated. The highest incidence of overeducation is amongst Indians at around 39 per cent, while in contrast the Bangladeshis seem to be well-matched with approximately 61 per cent of them being in jobs where they are fully utilised. Where foreign qualifications are downgraded relative to UK qualifications (highqual1) the incidence of mismatch across our various ethnic groups is largely unchanged, though the

Table 11.4 Degree of educational mismatch (in %)

	Whites	Caribbean	Indian	African-Asian	Pakistani	Bangla-deshi	Chinese
Overeducated	29.38	30.89	39.18	38.21	35.68	33.33	31.18
Adequately educated	41.59	48.40	41.95	44.48	48.90	61.29	58.06
Undereducated	29.03	20.72	15.88	17.31	15.42	5.38	10.75
N	1,154	531	485	335	227	93	93

incidence of overeducation falls slightly for the South-Asian groups (not reported here).

11.3 EMPIRICAL STRATEGY

11.3.1 Determinants of Educational Mismatch

The nature of our dependent variable indicates that the multinomial logit estimation procedure would be appropriate. In particular, we estimate two sets of coefficients, β_1 (overeducated) and β_3 (undereducated). From these two sets of coefficients we can calculate the probability P_{ij} of individual i being overeducated ($j = 1$) or undereducated ($j = 3$), conditional on a vector of personal characteristics x_i.

Separate regressions are run for whites and non-whites with ethnic dummy variables for each ethnic group included in the former. Owing to the problem of too few cases for some ethnic groups the Chinese are excluded from our analysis and the Pakistani and Bangladeshi groups, given their similarities, are combined. The omitted category is Indian. A small number of cases also prohibited us from running separate regressions for each ethnic group. Our specification of x_i includes the standard demographic variables (age, age [squared], gender, marital status), a range of job- and work-related characteristics (shiftwork, workplace size, trade union at the workplace, public sector, training, supervised) and information about the local labour market (unemployment rate at the ward level). In addition, and for non-whites only, we also include dummy variables for individuals who were UK-born, whether they possessed foreign qualifications (both are interacted with ethnic group membership) and language fluency. Fluency is based on interviewers' evaluation of respondents' speaking ability (those considered fluent were coded 1 and those deemed fair, poor or none coded 0).

An important characteristic of ethnic minorities is their concentration within high unemployment ethnic enclaves (Peach, 1996). According to the assimilation theory, interactions between ethnic minorities and the white majority improve ethnic minorities' social capital and job finding networks (Weinberg, 2000). The assimilation process may, however, be hindered by the concentration of individuals from the same ethnic group. To capture the influence of spatial constraints and ethnic enclaves we include a dummy for having a white boss, a banded continuous variable for ethnic concentration at the ward level and the number of cars in the household (Raphael and Stoll, 2000).

11.3.2 Effects on Earnings

The earnings data in the FNSEM are banded. Individuals were asked to indicate
which of 16 weekly income bands best captured their income where this refers
to usual gross pay from their main job including overtime and bonuses before
deductions. The advantage of earnings bands is that individuals may be more
accurate in their answers than where they are asked to give a precise figure. On
the other hand, around 20 per cent of observations on earnings are missing and
although the response rate was good for some groups (whites, Caribbeans,
Bangladeshi and Chinese) it was poor amongst Indians and Pakistanis. Modood
et al. (1997) suggested that the 'missing' observations are likely to fall dispro-
portionately into the high earning groups, so that the mean level of earnings may
be understated. Nevertheless, it is comforting to find that mean earnings using
midpoints are significantly lower for non-whites overall, with Bangladeshis
having the lowest earnings and African-Asians and the Chinese displaying
parity with whites. Rather surprisingly given the formers' job-level distribution,
Indian mean earnings were below those of the Caribbeans. The mean earnings
for Indians may be depressed by their higher refusal rate in the survey.

The banded nature of earnings in the FNSEM leads us to use two estimation
methods. The first method uses midpoints and produces estimates using least
squares (OLS). The dependent variable (the log of weekly earnings) takes the
midpoint of 16 bands with the upper limit of the final band determined by multiplying the lower threshold by 1.5. This procedure has been used by Chiswick
and Miller (1995) and Lindley (2002). However, this is rather *ad hoc* and may
generate inconsistent estimates (Stewart, 1983). Thus, we also employ an interval regression model where the dependant variable (earnings) is categorical and
ordered and the cut-off points are known. This is a maximum likelihood estimator and generates consistent estimates of the parameter values.

Assuming a model structure of the following form for individual i (where i
$= 1, 2, ..., N$):

$$y_i = x_i' \beta + \mu_i \qquad (11.1)$$

where y_i is our unobserved observation i of (continuously distributed) the log
of earnings, x is a vector of regressors, β our unknown parameters and μ_i is the
random error term. Under the assumption of conditional lognormality of earnings,

$$y_i \,|\, x_i \sim N(x_i' \beta, \sigma^2). \qquad (11.2)$$

With K groups (here we have 16 bands), the k-th is given by (A_{k-1}, A_k) and A_0
$= -\infty$, and $A_k = +\infty$.

In practice the OLS and interval regression method produced very similar
results, so that only the results from the latter are reproduced here.

The specification of our earnings equation is grounded in the assignment theory (Sattinger, 1993) where we have a supply side (what workers bring to the labour market in terms of educational qualifications) and a demand side (the requirements of the firm in terms of educational qualifications). Traditional human capital and job competition approaches are seen as special cases where either the supply or demand side is suppressed.

The assignment specification includes a required education variable (S_r) and dummies for over- (S_o) and undereducation (S_u). Other controls (z_i) included are age and its square, dummies for gender, marital status, industry and region of residence. The regressions are run separately for whites and non-whites and to capture the importance of assimilation effects separately for native and non-native non-whites. The earnings function has the form:

$$\ln y_i = \beta_i z_i + \chi_i S_r + \eta_i S_o + \theta_i S_u + \varepsilon_i \qquad (11.3)$$

11.4 EMPIRICAL FINDINGS

The multinomial logit regressions results are given in Tables 11.5 and 11.6 with coefficients and marginal effects reported for whites and non-whites respectively. We find the following. Being overeducated falls with age for non-whites (with more work experience). Gender and marriage have no significant effect on the probability of being matched or otherwise for either group. Being UK-born and being fluent increases the likelihood of mismatch (both over- and undereducation) for non-whites. One explanation might be that being UK-born and fluent increases the spread of educational attainment and thus the probability of mismatch. The foreign-born without language skills then have fewer educational qualifications and are employed in a narrow range of occupations.

Non-white workers with foreign qualifications are more likely to be overeducated, suggesting that foreign qualifications are not as highly valued by employers as UK qualifications. Of the ethnic dummy variables only African-Asians have a significantly greater likelihood of being mismatched relative to the omitted category of Indians.

The estimates also include a number of interaction terms. From these, it is evident that African-Asians who whereborn in the UK and who have foreign qualifications are less likely to be overeducated. In contrast, Pakistani and Bangladeshi workers with foreign qualifications have a higher probability of overeducation. This difference in the effect of foreign qualifications across the two ethnic groups may reflect the higher quality of the African-Asian ethnic group's education.

A worker belonging to a ward with high ethnic concentration has a greater probability of being overeducated. The existence of poor matches in wards with

Table 11.5 Determinants of educational mismatch (multinomial logit): whites

	Overeducation		Undereducation	
	Coefficient	Marginal Effect	Coefficient	Marginal Effect
Age	−0.069 (1.31)	−0.012	−0.021 (0.39)	0.001
Age (squared)/100	0.048 (0.72)	0.006	0.052 (0.81)	0.007
Male	−0.004 (0.03)	−0.004	0.042 (0.27)	0.009
Married	0.038 (0.21)	−0.012	0.253 (1.37)	0.047
Ward unemployment 5–10%	−0.238 (1.21)	−0.037	−0.141 (0.76)	−0.009
Ward unemployment 10–15%	0.264 (1.07)	0.072	−0.207 (0.79)	−0.061
Ward unemployment 15–20%	0.266 (0.52)	0.052	0.052 (0.09)	−0.012
Ward unemployment > 20%	0.340 (0.62)	0.154	−1.264 (1.51)	−0.200
Ethnic ward density	−0.133 (2.11)**	−0.019	−0.095 (1.52)	−0.009
Shiftwork	0.226 (1.26)	0.097	−0.653 (3.16)***	−0.137
Workplace size 500 plus	−0.022 (0.10)	−0.003	−0.009 (0.05)	−0.000
Trade union at work	−0.205 (1.14)	−0.044	0.039 (0.23)	0.024
Public sector worker	−0.291 (1.64)	−0.040	−0.225 (1.30)	−0.023
Supervised	−0.690 (4.14)***	−0.151	0.210 (1.33)	0.097
Training	−0.097 (0.60)	−0.043	0.292 (1.75)*	0.066
No. of cars in household	0.025 (0.23)	0.003	0.021 (0.19)	0.002
Constant	2.230 (2.20)**		−0.372 (0.35)	
Observations	1,076		1,076	

Notes:
LR $\chi(32)$ = 143.60; Prob > χ^2 = 0.000; Pseudo R^2 = 0.0615; Log likelihood = −1096.5804; absolute value of z-statistics in parentheses.

* significant at 10% level; ** significant at 5% level; *** significant at 1% level.

1. Dependent variable: over 2 (1 = if overeducated, 2 = if adequately educated and 3 = if under-educated).
2. Excluded categories: single, ward unemployment less than 5% and working for firms with less than 500 employees.
3. The marginal effect for a continuous variable is calculated for a one-unit increase. For dummy variables it represents an average person with that particular characteristic relative to the base characteristic.

higher ethnic concentrations suggests that enclaves do not aid the matching process. This, however, is not evident for whites, since for them the probability of being overeducated actually falls with ethnic concentration (Table 11.5). Having a white employer may signal that non-white individuals have managed to break out of ethnic enclaves and are no longer employed by someone of their own community. Our data in Table 11.1 reveals that around 24 per cent of non-whites have a non-white boss. For non-whites, having a white boss increases the likelihood of overeducation, though this is only significant at the 10 per cent level. This is indicative not of hiring discrimination since workers are employed, but perhaps that white bosses are less likely to recognise foreign qualifications relative to non-white bosses.

Table 11.6   Determinants of educational mismatch (multinomial logit): non-whites

	Overeducation		Undereducation	
	Coefficient	Marginal Effect	Coefficient	Marginal Effect
Age	−0.209 (2.78)***	−0.044	−0.033 (0.36)	0.006
Age (sqared)/100	0.207 (2.24)**	0.044	0.025 (0.22)	−0.007
Male	0.165 (0.79)	0.023	0.263 (1.03)	0.025
Married	0.143 (0.57)	0.033	−0.056 (0.19)	−0.014
UK-born	0.958 (1.91)*	0.107	1.560 (2.76)***	0.175
Foreign qualifications	2.482 (6.18)***	0.523	0.597 (1.02)	−0.076
Caribbean	0.142 (0.32)	0.017	0.271 (0.56)	0.029
African-Asian	0.918 (2.50)**	0.153	0.902 (2.05)**	0.069
Pakistani/Bangladeshi	−0.594 (1.19)	−0.115	−0.110 (0.18)	0.012
UK-born: Caribbean	0.030 (0.05)	0.043	−0.903 (1.34)	−0.095
UK-born: African-Asian	−2.004 (1.99)**	−0.254	−1.562 (1.40)	−0.099
UK-born: Pakistani/Bangladeshi	−0.345 (0.45)	−0.034	−1.233 (1.33)	−1.000
Foreign qualifications: Caribbean	−1.003 (1.30)	−0.202	0.693 (0.81)	0.168
Foreign qualifications: African-Asian	−1.435 (2.39)**	−0.227	−0.198 (0.25)	0.022
Foreign qualifications: Pakistani/Bangladeshi	1.307 (1.85)*	0.261	0.752 (0.73)	0.008
Fluent	1.177 (4.01)***	0.188	1.130 (2.70)***	0.083
Ward unemployment 5–10%	−0.026 (0.05)	−0.065	1.023 (1.48)	0.159
Ward unemployment 10–15%	−0.114 (0.22)	−0.060	0.672 (0.93)	0.103
Ward unemployment 15–20%	−0.105 (0.19)	−0.061	0.687 (0.89)	0.110
Ward unemployment > 20%	−0.370 (0.66)	−0.118	0.774 (1.01)	0.137
Ethnic ward density	0.184 (2.90)***	0.038	0.041 (0.54)	−0.004
White boss	0.434 (1.74)*	0.079	0.282 (0.92)	0.016
Shiftwork	0.620 (2.71)***	0.157	−0.304 (1.04)	−0.066
Workplace size 500 plus	0.233 (0.87)	0.084	−0.724 (1.93)*	−0.087
Trade union at work	−0.142 (0.65)	−0.050	0.371 (1.42)	0.056
Public sector workers	−0.601 (2.76)***	−0.122	−0.141 (0.54)	0.011
Supervised	−0.420 (1.89)*	−0.086	−0.070 (0.28)	0.011
Training	−0.418 (2.03)**	−0.108	0.360 (1.48)	0.069
No. of cars in household	0.126 (0.88)	0.026	0.034 (0.20)	−0.001
Constant	1.622 (1.01)		−3.222 (1.58)	
Observations	734		734	

Notes:
LR $\chi(58)$ = 234.88; Prob > χ^2 = 0.0000; Pseudo R^2 = 0.1582; Log likelihood = −625.12902; absolute value of z-statistics in parentheses.

* significant at 10% level; ** significant at 5% level; *** significant at 1% level.

1. Dependent variable: over (1 = if overeducated, 2 = if adequately educated and 3 = if undereducated).
2. Excluded categories: single, Indian, ward unemployment less than 5% and working for firms with less than 500 employees.
3. The marginal effect for a continuous variable is calculated for a one-unit increase. For dummy variables it represents an average person with that particular characteristic relative to the base characteristic.

Being employed on shifts raises the likelihood of overeducation for non-whites and reduces the likelihood of undereducation for whites. This is consistent with responsibility for sharing capital equipment raising the requirement for appropriate levels of education. Public sector employment reduces the likelihood of overeducation for non-whites and whites. This is consistent with credentialism being more important in this sector. Likewise, having had responsibility for supervision reduces the likelihood of overeducation for both non-white and white workers. Having undergone training reduces the probability of being overeducated for non-whites only. There is no evidence that the number of vehicles in the household, widening the area of job search, has any significant effect on job matching for whites and non-whites.

The results for our earnings equation estimations are given in Table 11.7 for non-white immigrants, non-white natives and whites. Across all three samples there is an earnings premium associated with required education, with the largest premium being for whites. The premium associated with overeducation is positive for non-white immigrants (7.3%) and whites (13%), but smaller than that for required education. These estimates are in line with previous studies. For example, Groot and Maassen van den Brink (2000) in their meta-analysis covering the US and a number of European countries had estimated the rate of return to surplus education to be 2.6 per cent over the last 30 years. However, we need to bear in mind that our analysis covers all degrees of overeducation. In another study, Sloane, Battu and Seaman (1999) found a positive return of 2.8 per cent for each level of surplus education with the overall rate being 14 per cent (similar to our estimate for whites). With respect to undereducation we find that earnings are discounted; the negative return to undereducation ranges from around 12 to 31 per cent, with the penalty being higher for non-native non-whites. The consensus in the literature is that the returns to undereducation are negative and that the penalty for undereducation tends to be smaller than the returns to required education (Hartog, 2000). Although we can confirm the former we only find the latter for whites. For foreign-born non-whites the negative return to undereducation exceeds the positive return to required education. This perhaps indicates labour market discrimination against this group.

Throughout our results we find an earnings premium for males, though the gender gap in earnings is found to be greater for whites and smaller for non-white immigrants. With the addition of controls, three of the ethnic dummy variables coefficients are positive, but small and poorly determined. Only the Caribbean ethnic group has a positive and significant estimated coefficient, albeit with 10 per cent significance.

Spatial and assimilation effects are appraised through four sets of covariates. English language fluency is very important for non-white immigrants, with an earnings premium of around 10 per cent. This compares with 16 per cent in a study by Dustmann and Fabbri (2000) and 14 to 20 per cent for males across a

Table 11.7   Determinants of earnings (interval regression)

	Non-native non-whites		Native non-whites		Whites	
Age	0.039	(2.98)***	0.090	(2.10)**	0.036	(3.22)***
Age (squared)/100	−0.042	(2.64)***	−0.124	(1.74)*	−0.039	(2.77)***
Male	0.117	(3.10)***	0.157	(2.86)***	0.214	(6.01)***
Married	0.026	(0.53)	−0.093	(1.60)	−0.031	(0.78)
Years since migration	0.005	(0.59)				
Years since migration squared	−0.000	(0.07)				
Caribbean	0.094	(1.70)*	0.048	(0.68)		
Pakistani	0.029	(0.50)	0.006	(0.06)		
African-Asian	0.045	(0.96)	−0.080	(0.58)		
Bangladeshi	0.017	(0.24)	−0.044	(0.18)		
Overeducated	0.073	(1.75)*	0.049	(0.73)	0.129	(2.84)***
Undereducated	−0.313	(5.72)***	−0.119	(1.55)	−0.156	(3.59)***
Required education	0.178	(13.49)***	0.119	(5.98)***	0.207	(17.07)***
Fluent	0.102	(2.17)**	0.052	(0.32)		
Ward unemployment 5–10%	0.074	(0.89)	−0.008	(0.06)	−0.038	(0.91)
Ward unemployment 10–15%	0.085	(0.97)	0.045	(0.34)	−0.002	(0.04)
Ward unemployment 15–20%	0.019	(0.20)	0.028	(0.19)	−0.052	(0.44)
Ward unemployment > 20%	−0.018	(0.19)	−0.025	(0.16)	0.021	(0.16)
Ethnic ward density	0.004	(0.41)	0.011	(0.50)	0.010	(0.64)
Workplace size 500 plus	0.160	(3.45)***	0.045	(0.57)	0.107	(2.33)**
South-East	0.110	(2.90)***	0.204	(3.48)***	0.162	(3.89)***
No. of vehicles in household	0.073	(2.88)***	0.081	(2.11)**	0.025	(1.01)
Construction	0.009	(0.15)	−0.018	(0.13)	−0.456	(5.35)***
Minerals	0.331	(4.54)***	0.267	(1.70)*	−0.059	(0.66)
Engineer	0.323	(4.38)***	0.193	(1.12)	−0.086	(0.89)
Other mfg.	0.379	(2.78)***	0.332	(1.73)*	−0.136	(1.28)
Hotels	0.269	(3.54)***	0.329	(2.15)**	−0.017	(0.20)
Transport	0.058	(0.74)	0.225	(1.51)	−0.164	(1.96)*
Banking	−0.030	(0.43)	−0.041	(0.28)	−0.465	(5.67)***
Others	−0.074	(0.61)	0.284	(1.26)	−0.643	(6.21)***
Constant	3.541	(12.52)***	3.139	(4.80)***	4.233	(17.94)***
Observations	919		338		1,037	
	LR $\chi^2(30) = 519.02$		LR $\chi^2(28) = 164.46$		LR $\chi^2(23) = 599.35$	
	Prob > $\chi^2 = 0.000$		Prob > $\chi^2 = 0.000$		Prob > $\chi^2 = 0.000$	
	Log likelihood = −2019.3955		Log likelihood = −738.06889		Log likelihood = −2366.8589	

Notes:

Excluded categories: single, adequately educated, ward unemployment greater than 20%, working for firms with less than 500 employees, working in energy sector and having no qualifications.

Absolute value of z-statistics in parentheses.

* significant at 10% level; ** significant at 5% level; *** significant at 1% level.

range of specifications in a study by Lindley (2002). Years since migration have no significant effects on earnings for non-white immigrants. There is also no evidence of a positive enclave effect when we examine the ethnic concentration variable. This contrasts with other work suggesting that enclaves help immigrants to escape discrimination elsewhere in the labour market (Edin et al., 2003). Having access to private transport may be a mechanism for circumventing the constraints that arise from enclaves. A rise in the number of vehicles in the household, by raising the potential area of job search, is associated with higher earnings for both non-white samples. Though access to private vehicles may be endogenous the results do suggest that having access to a car is an important determinant of earnings for non-whites. No car-earnings effect is evident for whites. Alternative specifications of the earnings equations incorporated a dummy for foreign qualifications. This was found to be insignificant and the coefficients on the other variables remained largely unchanged (hence we do not report these results here).

We also find that weekly earnings rise with age and that both whites and non-white immigrant employees in large establishments enjoy an earnings premium. There is no suggestion of a wage curve effect at the ward level, since no relationship between living in a ward with higher unemployment and earnings was detected. Those resident in the South-East of England obtain an earnings premium in all three groups.[4]

11.5 CONCLUSIONS

Though there has been a burgeoning of research into overeducation across Europe and the US very little of this work focuses on ethnic minorities and the research that does exist tends to ignore the obvious heterogeneity within the ethnic population. This is especially important in the context of the UK where the ethnic population, many of whom were immigrants from Commonwealth countries, is very diverse.

This study acknowledges this diversity, using the FNSEM conducted in 1994. Our results indicate the following. Though overeducation is higher for non-whites relative to whites, this disguises various differences within the non-white sample. When we make an allowance for foreign qualifications in our measure of mismatch we find that all ethnic minority groups display levels of overeducation in excess of 30 per cent. Furthermore, undereducation is lower for all ethnic minority groups than for the white population. When we introduce controls into our analysis of the determinants of mismatch we find that the African-Asian group are more likely to be overeducated relative to Indians (the omitted category). In addition, foreign qualifications, being UK-born and language fluency all raise the likelihood of being overeducated and undereducated. This runs counter to the arguments of the assimilation theory and may be indicative of continued discrimination in the labour market.

The results from our earnings regressions support previous work in finding a positive return to surplus education, a positive and higher return to required education and a negative return to undereducation. The earnings penalty evident for being undereducated is higher for foreign-born non-whites. The results vis-à-vis our enclave variables are less clear-cut when it comes to earnings. On the one hand, the longer the stay in the UK and the greater the access to private transport the higher are ethnic earnings. On the other hand, increases in own ethnic concentration raise earnings. One explanation for this might be that employers in enclaves more readily recognise foreign qualifications, though we have no direct evidence of this. In our examination of supervision and training we find that overeducated non-whites are more likely to have received training and undereducated non-whites are less likely to have acted in a supervisory position, compared to those who are well-matched.

The positive return to overeducation also supports our basic premise that overeducation is driven by discrimination, rather than implying that too much education has been provided for ethnic minorities. Further work is clearly needed to quantify the importance of discrimination to overeducation. Additional research also needs to pay attention to the job finding methods utilised by different ethnic groups and to ascertain whether there is a relationship between different job search methods and match quality. The use of personal networks, especially for those that have recently arrived in a country, may be important.

NOTES

1 We would like to thank the Policy Studies Institute and the Data Archive at the University of Essex for giving us access to the Fourth National Survey of Ethnic Minorities (FNSEM) dataset.
2 The response rates were 61 per cent for Caribbeans, 74 per cent for Indians and African-Asians, 73 per cent for Pakistanis, 83 per cent for Bangladeshis, 66 per cent for Chinese and 71 per cent for whites.
3 For a discussion of the relative merits of these measures see Battu, Belfield and Sloane (2000).
4 The 1991 Census of Population shows that around 45 per cent of the ethnic minority population is located in London. In our dataset, the ethnic population is concentrated in two areas: London (South-East) and the West Midlands.

REFERENCES

Alba-Ramírez, A. (1993). Mismatch in the Spanish labour market: Over-education? *Journal of Human Resources, 28* (2), 259–278.
Alpin, C., Shackleton, J.R., and Walsh, S. (1998). Over and under-education in the UK graduate labour market. *Studies in Higher Education,* **3**, 17–34.
Arnott, R. (1998). Economic theory and the spatial mismatch hypothesis. *Urban Studies,* **35**, 1171–1185.
Battu, H., Belfield, C.R., and Sloane, P. (2000). Over-education: How sensitive are the measures? *National Institute Economic Review,* **171**, 82–93.
Battu, H., and Sloane, P. (2000). Overeducation and crowding out in Britain. In L. Borghans and A. de Grip, (Eds.), *The overeducated worker? The economics of skill utilization* (pp. 157–174). Cheltenham: Edward Elgar.

Blackaby, D., Leslie, D., Murphy, P., and O'Leary, N. (1998). The ethnic wage gap and employment differentials in the 1990s: Evidence from Britain. *Economics Letters*, **58**, 97–103.

Blackaby, D., Leslie, D., Murphy, P., and O'Leary, N. (1999). Unemployment among Britain's ethnic minorities. *The Manchester School*, **67** (1), 1–20.

Cabinet Office, Performance and Innovation Unit. (2002). *Ethnic minorities and the labour market: Interim analytical report.* London: Cabinet Office.

Chiswick, B.R., and Miller, P.W. (1995). The endogeneity between language and earnings: An international analyses. *Journal of Labor Economics*, **13** (2), 246–288.

Connor, H., la Valle, N.D., Tackey, N.D., and Perryman, S. (1996). *Differences by degrees: Ethnic minority graduates.* Brighton: Institute of Employment Studies.

Duncan, G.J., and Hoffman, S.D. (1981). The incidence and wage effects of over-education. *Economics of Education Review*, **1** (1), 75–86.

Dustmann, C., and Fabbri, F. (2000). *Language proficiency and labour market performance if immigrants in the UK, IZA.* Discussion Paper, No. 156.

Edin, P.-A., Fredriksson, P, and Åslund, O. (2003). Ethnic enclaves and the economic success of immigrants: Evidence from a natural experiment. *Quarterly Journal of Economics*, **118** (1), 329–357.

Groot, W., and Maassen van den Brink, H. (2000). Over-education in the labour market: A meta-analysis. In H. Oosterbeek (Ed.), The economics of over- and underschooling. *Special issue of Economics of Education Review*, **19** (2), 149–158.

Hartog, J. (2000). Over-education and earnings: Where are we, where should we go? *Economics of Education Review*, **19**, 131–147.

Kain, J. (1968). Housing segregation, negro employment and metropolitan decentralisation. *Quarterly Journal of Economics*, **82**, 175–197.

Kiker, B.F., Santos, M.C., and de Oliveira, M.M. (1997). Over-education and under-education: Evidence for Portugal. *Economics of Education Review*, **16** (2), 111–125.

Leslie, D. (Ed.). (1998). *An investigation of racial disadvantage.* Manchester: Manchester University Press.

Leslie, D., and Drinkwater, S. (1999). Staying on in full-time education: Reasons for higher participation among ethnic minority males and females. *Economica*, **66**, 63–77.

Lindley, J. (2002). The English language fluency and earnings of ethnic minorities in Britain. *Scottish Journal of Political Economy*, **49** (4), 467–487.

McCormick, B. (1986). Employment opportunities, earnings and the journey to work of minority workers in Great Britain. *Economic Journal*, **96** (382), 375–397.

Modood, T., Berthoud, R., Lakey, J. Nazroo, J. Smith, P., Virdee, S., and Beishon, S. (1997). *Ethnic minorities in Britain: Diversity and disadvantage.* London: Policy Studies Institute.

Owen, D., Green, A., Pitcher, J., and Maguire, M. (2000). *Minority ethnic participation and achievements in education, training and the labour market.* Department for Education and Employment (Research Brief No. 225).

Peach, C. (1996). Does Britain have ghettos? *Transactions of the Institute of British Geographers*, **21**, 216–235.

Raphael, S., and Stoll, M. (2000). *Can boosting minority car-ownership rates narrow inter-racial employment gaps?* Berkeley Program on Housing and Urban Policy (Working Paper W00–002).

Sattinger, M. (1993). Assignment models of the distribution of earnings. *Journal of Economic Literature,* **31** (2), 851–880.

Shields, M. A., and Wheatley Price, S. (2002). The English language fluency and occupational success of ethnic minority immigrant men living in English metropolitan areas. *Journal of Population Economics,* **15**, 137–160.

Sicherman, N. (1991). Over-education in the labor market. *Journal of Labor Economics,* **9** (2), 101–122.

Sloane, P, Battu, H., and Seaman, P. (1999). Over-education, under-education and the British labour market. *Applied Economics,* **31** (11), 1437–1454.

Stewart, M. (1983). On least squares estimation when the dependent variable is grouped. *Review of Economic Studies,* **50**, 737–753.

Tsang, M.C., Rumberger, R.W., and Levin, H.M. (1991). The impact of surplus schooling on workers' productivity. *Industrial Relations,* **30** (2), 209–228.

Weinberg, B.A. (2000). Black residential concentration and the spatial mismatch hypothesis. *Journal of Urban Economics,* **48**, 110–134.

Index

Index